THE PATH
TO
THE GURU

"I am delighted with Scott Teitsworth's *The Path to the Guru*. It is an exceptional approach to concentrate on just two chapters! Scott's interpretation is well suited for the modern day. I would highly recommend this book to spiritual seekers of all faiths."

BILL ROBINSON, PH.D., COMPOSER AND LECTURER
OF PHYSICS AT NORTH CAROLINA STATE UNIVERSITY

"The Bhagavad Gita is a multifaceted jewel shedding multicolored lights. The author has caught quite a few of these lights and thus has shed more light on this ancient classic that will prove to be of immense help to all lovers of the book."

VANAMALI MATAJI, FOUNDER AND PRESIDENT OF
VANAMALI GITA YOGA ASHRAM TRUST AND AUTHOR OF
SEVEN BOOKS INCLUDING *THE COMPLETE LIFE OF KRISHNA*

"Scott Teitsworth's relevant and in-depth analysis of its first two sections of the Bhagavad Gita skillfully balances a perspective that is both accessible and true to the heart of the original text."

JASON BOWMAN, VINYASA YOGA TEACHER

NOV   2014

THE PATH
TO GURU
THE

The Science of
Self-Realization according
to the Bhagavad Gita

SCOTT TEITSWORTH

Inner Traditions
Rochester, Vermont • Toronto, Canada

Inner Traditions
One Park Street
Rochester, Vermont 05767
www.InnerTraditions.com

Text stock is SFI certified

Library of Congress Cataloging-in-Publication Data
Teitsworth, Scott.
  The path to the guru : the science of self-realization according to the Bhagavad
Gita / Scott Teitsworth.
    pages cm
  Includes bibliographical references and index.
  ISBN 978-1-62055-321-3 (pbk.) — ISBN 978-1-62055-322-0 (e-book)
  1. Bhagavadgita—Criticism, interpretation, etc. 2. Spiritual life—Hinduism.
3. Yoga. I. Bhagavadgita. Visadayoga. English. II. Bhagavadgita. Sankhyayoga.
English. III. Title.
  BL1138.66.T395 2014
  294.5'924046—dc23

                    2013040263

Printed and bound in the United States at Lake Book Manufacturing, Inc.
The text stock is SFI certified. The Sustainable Forestry Initiative® program
promotes sustainable forest management.

10   9   8   7   6   5   4   3   2   1

Text design and layout by Virginia Scott Bowman
This book was typeset in Garamond Premier Pro with Trajan Pro used as the
display typeface

To send correspondence to the author of this book, mail a first-class letter to the
author c/o Inner Traditions • Bear & Company, One Park Street, Rochester, VT
05767, and we will forward the communication, or contact the author directly at
rsteitsworth@yahoo.com or **scottteitsworth.tripod.com**.

---•---

To the three gurus whose wisdom
inspires me every day:
Narayana Guru, Nataraja Guru,
and Guru Nitya Chaitanya Yati

The mission of the contemplative in this world of massive conflict and collective unreason is to seek the true way of unity and peace, without succumbing to the illusion of withdrawal into a realm of abstraction from which unpleasant realities are simply excluded by the force of will. In facing the world with a totally different viewpoint, he maintains alive in the world the presence of a spiritual and intelligent consciousness which is the root of true peace and true unity among men.

THOMAS MERTON,
FAITH AND VIOLENCE

CONTENTS

PROLOGUE

The Bhagavad Gita has just two protagonists, a flawed human named Arjuna and a wise elder named Krishna. Their conversation is an ideal way to describe problems and offer solutions. They hold their discussion in the midst of a great war, symbolic of the pressures of life we all encounter.

In the buildup to the war, powerful interests stripped Arjuna and his four brothers of their princely birthright, took their lands, and banished them to a wilderness, while promising to permit their return in the distant future. When the time came for them to reclaim their legitimate station, they were treated as outcasts. They had to slip back into the royal city in disguise. When they made their claim, it was denied, and war was declared, with threats to take from them the last shreds of their dignity.

This is a magnificent image of the human condition. From birth we begin to compromise with our environment. Other people and institutions are to be placated, so we suppress our own desires in hopes of achieving peace and amity. We assume a social mask to obscure our naked face. Before long we have given up all our personal predilections and entered a wilderness of dissociation from our true nature. Religious tracts assure us of restoration only after death, and we try to believe them. These ruses may work for a while, allowing us to fit in to a pitiless society, but there is a vital urge in us that never stops trying to be actualized. It often comes in conflict with what is expected of us. We are taught that our vital urge is an evil to be done away with, but it feels like our authentic self. It seeks a means of expression. Expressing it is the reason we were born. The more it is suppressed, the more the pressure builds, until it explodes or is medicated away.

Arjuna and his brothers, the Pandavas, symbolize our authentic nature. In the face of greed and selfishness, symbolized by the Kauravas, they continually gave ground. Like well-behaved children they went along with every requirement, even allowing themselves to be cheated. And now they find themselves with nothing, standing on a postage-stamp-sized plot of land that is about to be taken from them.

We, too, have surrendered our legitimacy to external forces, for the most part unwittingly. The Gita addresses the crucial moment when we must wake up to our abandoned inner truth or spiritually die. Ordinary responses are to throw ourselves back into the futility of battle or run away and hide. Neither of these options allows for the expression of our finest abilities. Krishna is standing by to teach Arjuna how to extricate himself from this universal predicament, thereby demonstrating how each of us can reclaim our authenticity. It will be a long and fascinating process.

We intuitively sense that we are divine, princesses and princes who have been deposed from our thrones and banished to the wilderness. Regaining our rightful place is a mystical, rather than a political, accomplishment. Escape won't do it, nor will fighting against the apparent usurpers. They suffer from the same malady that we do, so they couldn't restore us to our true nature if they wanted to. Petitioning or combating them is a waste of time. The Bhagavad Gita is a broad template of what really needs to happen to reacquaint us with our inner genius.

INTRODUCTION

THE GLOBAL GITA

Once upon a time, the world's longest and arguably its greatest epic, the Mahabharata, was written down. It contains a compendium of myriad types of human beings, from the sublime to the grotesque, the wise to the ridiculous, almost as if it were a summary of all life on Earth intended for the cosmic library at the center of the universe.

Nestled right on the verge of the titanic war that forms a major climax of the epic is a jewel of wisdom that puts the entire panoply in perspective. Lifted out of its context it has come to be known as the Bhagavad Gita, the Song of the Guru. A guru is that which removes the darkness of ignorance, and the dawning of the light of understanding is the sweetest song of all. The Bhagavad Gita—fondly referred to simply as the Gita—is nothing more or less than a textbook of enlightenment applicable to all humanity, bestowed by the great teachers of old, who were called *rishis*.

Nothing is known for certain about the origins of the Bhagavad Gita. Linguistic analysis points to the written version appearing somewhere around the first century CE, but it is obviously taken from a far older oral tradition. An astounding amount of philosophical ferment peaked around 500 BCE, with Buddha and Mahavira's Jainism, and the Gita speaks to it as a contemporary. After hundreds of years as spoken wisdom it was gathered together in written form by an anonymous

1

author, more or less as we know it today. The author is traditionally referred to as Vyasa, a word meaning simply compiler or editor.

While few scriptures have enjoyed—or suffered from—as many explications and commentaries as the Gita has, the work is perhaps more mysterious today than it was when it first appeared. This is partly due to the subject matter itself and not to any limitation of the minds that have lent themselves to the task. The meaning of life, epitomized in terms like God or the Absolute, is an eternal mystery, not a fact, and as such will defy description for all eternity. But the attempt to pin meaning down does throw light on it, light which can improve and illuminate our lives. At the same time, the wildly misleading ideas that have sprung up have obscured the intended meaning like a jungle engulfing an ancient temple. Periodically it is essential to hack away the undergrowth.

Most Gita commentaries pursue a religious tack or deal in abstruse and outdated philosophies. Some even assume that the Gita was originally written to present the very detritus of orthodox beliefs that have grown up around it. Not at all! The material itself rejects orthodoxy in no uncertain terms, defining itself clearly as an absolutist mystical text. Unearthing its buried wisdom is the goal of the present commentary. The intention is to present the work stripped of all excess, so that it can touch those who wish to benefit from the application of its very practical wisdom.

THE OVERALL PLOT OF THE GITA

The setting is meant to evoke our eternal dilemma as human beings, which is to be confronted with intense and often paradoxical challenges. The Gita begins on the brink of an all-out war between the forces of good and evil. Krishna is Prince Arjuna's chariot driver, and they are about to enter the fray, but as the battle cry is sounded, Arjuna is overcome with doubts. He is conflicted between his duty as a warrior and his kindly instincts as a human being, and he asks Krishna to help him sort them out. They turn to each other right in the middle of the chaos and begin to probe the meaning of life. After an in-depth study and self-analysis lasting for the entire eighteen chapters of the Gita, Arjuna's doubts are eradicated and his enthusiasm for life is restored. We know that later in the Mahabharata epic Arjuna reenters the war, but the Gita ends on the note of Krishna insisting that it is up to Arjuna what to do. He has become capable of making his own decisions wisely and well. It would spoil the case if those decisions were spelled out for him in any way.

There is a tendency to view a scripture like the Bhagavad Gita as a system of worship or practice and therefore exclusive and forbidding to outsiders, and many commentators play up this angle. In fact the work is a guided technique for paring away the misconceptions that are impediments to a fully realized and enjoyable life. It is supremely open, especially in the interpretation presented here. There are no requirements—only an invitation to learn and grow on your own terms and in your own way. No one is an outsider, although most of us feel like one, because we are separated from our authentic nature. There is no hierarchy here, only seekers of truth and joy making their way through the endless miracle of the universe.

The philosophy of yoga presented by the Gita invites us to extricate ourselves from a dysfunctional life in a dysfunctional society, in order to investigate how to live with a fresh and empowered attitude. It is to be read as a guidebook for personal transformation, where Arjuna is meant to stand for each and every one of us. Each verse is to be brought home in a practical fashion. It's not about other people's faults, or establishing a fixed cosmology. It does not tell us how to live but how to learn to live.

The Gita is the product of a loose confederation of intelligent and intense contemplatives informally pooling their best ideas, later gathered together by a mastermind and presented almost as a fable. It consists of 700 aphoristic verses in eighteen chapters, with nothing superfluous whatsoever. There is no vengeful God in it, only a benign and loving principle, called *brahman,* or the Absolute. It is replete with the finest spiritual advice tendered without compunction or guilt. As Krishna himself says, every person approaches truth from their own unique perspective, and that is just how it should be. Moreover, every being is equally precious. There are no chosen and cursed souls, only more or less damaged and confused ones. The game here is to rectify the damage and dispel the confusion with clear thinking and action. Doing so is its own reward, revealing our vast potential that has long been neglected. We imagine we are little men and women, but that is because we know almost nothing about ourselves.

The heroic element in the Gita is a hint that we have learned to be timid and deferential, but those attitudes, while adequate for social interactions, have cut us off from our own strength of character, which is capable of taking us to the highest expressions of excellence. Deference means being motivated by others; heroism means being self-motivated and resolute. In learning from the Gita we have to find and express our own inner motivation.

WHY THE GITA IS SET ON A BATTLEFIELD

Sometime in their lives, often in their forties and fifties, many people go through a crisis. Whether precipitated by a traumatic event or not, previously accepted notions of right conduct no longer provide them with a feeling of security. Trusted beliefs are revealed to be empty promises. In that moment they are unsure where they stand, broken free as they are from long-cherished supports. The abruption between their awareness and the social order can be extremely painful, and occasionally their anguish makes them brave enough to challenge the predominant paradigm, if only briefly. They flail about, trying to sweep back the cobwebs of outmoded habits. Decisions taken during this period of heightened intensity will have repercussions for the remainder of their lives. Arjuna represents anyone who stands at such a crossroads.

While such a crisis is a crucial first step in recovery for individuals who have bartered away their freedom to the surrounding social reality, many are convinced they are abnormal for simply having this experience. Despite being a critical stage of growth, there is little approbation for it in the workaday world. This usually leads to further self-doubt, followed by a sheepish return to the fold. Accommodation with an unsympathetic world can be eased by any number of compromises. Some indulge in wild behavior and partying. Others redouble their efforts in work, drowning their sorrows in activity. Still others become pious religious devotees and learn to tolerate misery as a prelude to a better life after death. Many are secretly and bitterly disillusioned and live out their lives as timid spectators rather than participants. There are all kinds of alternatives through which to suppress the self, with those rocking the boat least being the most acceptable to their fellows, caught as they are in the same existential conflict.

But there is a road less traveled, and it offers the healthiest alternative of all: intelligent contemplation of the self to break the chains of habit, allowing the individual to connect with and fulfill their optimum capabilities. Those who take this road are the revered souls who have exceptional impact on their world. They become wise teachers, effective transformers of society, revolutionary artists, inventive scientists, loving friends to all. Many are drawn to them by a sort of magnetic attraction that awakens their own dormant longing for liberation. Humanity's richness can be measured in such people. Without them our collective spiritual poverty would be immeasurable.

THE SUBJECT MATTER

The Bhagavad Gita is particularly beneficial for those who feel trapped in their lives. Spiritual liberation calls to those who feel a deep-seated urge to break the bonds of their humdrum daily existence and reawaken their lost sense of aliveness.

As Rousseau so eloquently put it, "Man is born free, and everywhere he is in chains." Inside each of us is the original free spirit that once was born into a loving and unfettered existence but rapidly was forced to compromise it away. Sooner or later troubles set in, sometimes as early as the womb. Whenever the struggles begin we are compelled to respond, so that sooner or later that gentle core is overlaid with layer upon layer of offenses and duties, held in place by fear. By the time we are adults, our original state of paradise has become almost entirely a vestigial, unconscious memory. Many of us feel utterly oppressed by our obligations to family, work, and society. This can grow into an unhealthy condition approaching desperation.

Such is the state we find Arjuna in as the Gita opens. Like most of us, his first thought is to run away to shelter. Some of us run to other places, most run to psychological hideouts, but ultimately there is no place to hide. We all develop some kind of mask to hide our true feelings. Arjuna wants to become the kind of person who doesn't have to deal with the situation in which he finds himself. But he is extremely lucky—if it is only luck—to have a guru already standing at his side, who can lead him to the most satisfying resolution of his predicament.

Krishna's first piece of advice is to stop being afraid and trying to escape, and to face the situation squarely. He then unfolds a wisdom teaching that reconnects Arjuna with his true inner nature, his forgotten core, on which basis a free and expert life again becomes possible.

Everywhere, children in adult bodies go about their lives, guarded and worried, desperately trying to follow vaguely grasped laws and internalized exhortations. All Krishna is really asking of Arjuna is that he grow up. The Gita is in a sense a rite of passage tale, in which an adult human being is born. Arjuna is an obedient boy who has outgrown his subservience and wants to discover what it means to be everything it is possible for him to be. Krishna deftly shows him who he is (and who he isn't), how he fits into the universal context, gives him some useful advice, and sets him free to follow his own star.

An adult should be able to act independently, with as much free will as possible. Independence and freedom overlap to a large extent. But the vast majority never grow out of the habit of doing other peoples' bidding, often without even realizing it. Or they reject outside interference and spend their energy acting contrary to what is expected of them. Both these ploys are bound to the status quo. Only someone who can stand above both attitudes at once is able to experiment in the area of unfettered activity.

The human race is capable of greatness but is hobbled by systems that prevent individuals from maturing beyond their early roles as submissive children. Religion often becomes the substitute parent after the child leaves home. No wonder so many long for the return of a messiah, worship a king, or vote for a leader who promises to take care of them. Who among us even wishes to be independent, let alone strives for it? It is all too rare.

Part of the thrill of studying the Bhagavad Gita is the reawakening of all the suppressed parts of us that are dying to have a chance to be expressed. It's the call of our inner being to be let out of its socially constructed cage. Our best contribution to the world and our own well-being is to extricate ourselves from our psychic prison. We can hardly imagine the heights humanity is capable of attaining if it were comprised of independent, sovereign, thoughtful adults.

WHY THIS BOOK IS NEEDED

The Gita is a textbook of liberation. Yet when asked about its central message, most people—including most commentators—would say it's all about duty: learning what your duty is and carrying it out. God is assigning you a specific role and your duty is to conform to it. Nothing could be more opposed to the Gita's intent. That kind of thinking undermines the value of everything Krishna teaches.

The work begins on a note of self-doubt, and its culmination is the restoration of full confidence based on self-knowledge. It is a false interpretation that the Gita recommends adherence to duty as the means to recover this confidence. That would be like a psychiatrist recommending a better-crafted social mask or persona in order to cope with the world, or prescribing a drug to suppress the symptoms. The Gita, like a responsible therapist, aims to restore the connection with our true inner identity, which necessitates extrication from all outside obligations and duties, at least theoretically. Only a thoroughgoing inner expertise based in freedom can induce the confidence to live without crutches.

Indian thought distinguishes between *shruti* and *smriti*, between wisdom received directly from a guru or other authentic source and a compendium of obligatory duties and moral instruction. The Gita was born as a shruti but has been downgraded into a smriti by generations of misguided enthusiasts. It is to rescue this sublime treasure of liberating wisdom from such degradation that this commentary has been undertaken.

The Gita was originally written in Sanskrit, an allusive language in which a vast amount of information is transmitted with poetic economy. By its very breadth, which opens the door for a wide range of possible interpretations, Sanskrit brings the reader in as a full partner in the learning process. My guru's teacher, Nataraja Guru, electrified the world of Gita commentary with his own scientifically-minded interpretation in 1961, and his book has been continuously in print in India ever since. In his translation, which is the one used in this book, he has done an admirable job of maintaining its allusions, and I have changed only a very few words of his version. My comments are examples of the kind of meditative expansion that any student of the Gita is expected to make as they study the work, fleshing out the bare bones with resonant insights.

YOGA

A special technique of the Gita is to unify all polarizations, inwardly and outwardly, in what is called *yoga*. The Gita is in fact a training manual of how to unite conflicting elements in yoga. When opposites are united, a transcendental understanding emerges. Throughout the Gita concepts are masterfully paired with their opposite, so that while each may be contemplated in isolation, uniting them comprehensibly is seen to be the essence of yogic practice.

The Western concept of simple dialectics is virtually identical to yoga. In it a proposition and its opposite, known as thesis and antithesis, are brought together to create a synthesis. The synthesis is greater than the sum of its parts, often *much* greater. Nataraja Guru taught that dialectics reveals the Absolute, or the essential core of every situation. The term *dialectics* is frequently used in this commentary to emphasize the reciprocal aspect of yoga and the importance of synthesizing contradictory elements.

The rational methodology is to scrutinize each particle of existence in isolation, which is fine as far as it goes. But in doing so the context is lost. Yoga restores the context, by discerning the relationship between the separate items. It is like the wave aspect of the particles: related items move in harmonious patterns and exhibit reciprocity. Science itself has begun moving in this direction also. The study of emergence parallels dialectical synthesis, where unanticipated behavior emerges from complex interactions of relatively simple component parts.

Reciprocity depends on an inner connection between apparently disparate elements, which has puzzled philosophers down through the ages. It is immediately clear to everyone that up has no meaning without down, bad has no meaning without good, and so on. These factors are therefore *relative* to each other, in that more up means less down, and so on. Reciprocity resembles a teeter-totter, which requires the ends being connected on a single pole and also an independently fixed— albeit hypothetical—fulcrum for the system to operate on.

Logically, then, some connection must be present between opposite poles, but where is it to be found? This inner coherence is provided by the supreme value of the Absolute as the fulcrum, which is more commonly called a universal ground or ground of being. This approach is rejected by rationalist philosophers because of a tendency to insist on visible proof of horizontal factors, while an absolute ground must necessarily be outside the limits of sensory experience. Historically, the great Indian gurus have had no such false modesty. They realized that if there is no inherent connection between polar factors, any assertion of their relative merit is arbitrary and thus false. But by postulating the Absolute as that which unites opposites in the equation, values immediately become not only possible but natural.

The quest of the yogi is to intelligently attain the state of perfect mental equipoise through acceptance of valid relations and rejection of false ones. A lot of turmoil is brought about when, for instance, good is taken for divine and bad is rejected as diabolical. It divides the psyche against itself in a highly corrosive manner, since what is good for one person may be bad for their neighbor. Much of the conflict of human life is directly traceable to being attracted to half of a polarity while rejecting the other half. It explains, among other things, why good intentions so often go wrong. The entire dynamic of every situation must be comprehended before expertise in action can be achieved.

GURU AND DISCIPLE

Being dissociated from our true nature and living beneath a social mask breeds a permanent state of negativity ranging from anxiety to profound depression. Our inner disquiet is often veiled by a compensation in which a part of us becomes our own caretaker, competent and seemingly well adjusted. Outwardly, we appear "in charge," but beneath the surface calm is an anxious soul, cut off from its connection with its own being. Thinking our way through life instead of allowing it to unfold naturally, we have a visceral sense that something profound has been lost but we don't know what it is. Such a compromised existence works adequately until a crisis reveals its limitations. Then the emptiness of our persona is shockingly revealed. Suddenly we desperately need to know what's missing in our life. If we are fortunate to find it—and it is always within us, waiting to be found—we will begin to fulfill our potential. Luckily, there are a few who have reconnected with themselves who are willing to help, and they are often right nearby just at the moment we are ready to turn to them. We call them gurus.

A guru is a representative spark of the Absolute itself, whose guidance restores the seeker to wholeness. In the Gita a sublime guru, Krishna, helps a baffled disciple, Arjuna, to restore the dynamism of his own nature from out of the desert of conditioning he has become trapped in. Reawakening life through reconnection with our authentic self is the Gita's dominant theme, and it offers some novel strategies to attain that state.

The spiritual dynamic of guru and disciple is a most excellent example of yoga dialectics, where as individuals they are a thesis and antithesis, and as they come together in an osmotic exchange they achieve a transcendent synthesis. The guru elicits the best capabilities of the disciple, and the disciple's questions prompt the guru to shed new light precisely where it is needed. Their coming together is called trust. The synthesis this produces is described in the eleventh chapter of the Gita, where Arjuna attains a direct vision of the nature of reality. His mind is so stretched by the experience that Krishna will spend the final seven chapters helping him to adjust to it.

Krishna is a human being, but in the reverential attitude of India, a guru is also a living incarnation of the Absolute, the supreme principle, that which leaves nothing out. In Vedanta—the philosophical system of the Gita and its close cousins, the Upanishads—everyone and all things are the Absolute in essence, and the seeker's path, such as it is, is to come to know this truth. It is a path that begins and ends right where we are.

The Gita maintains it is within everyone's reach to renew their life at the level of creativity, through ever-new, joyous participation in the torrent of viable expression welling up within them. You do not need to fall into abject misery before heeding Krishna's call to come awake once more. At whatever point you realize you are slipping out of communion with your true self, you just bring yourself back. As a regular exercise this restores life to its innate exuberance.

It is helpful to keep in mind that the true guru is a principle and not necessarily a person. A guru—literally a remover of darkness—is a teacher, but each of us is guided by the totality of our surroundings in this benign universe. Sometimes that takes the form of a human being, but the guru appears in whatever way the next stage of learning occurs. Often seekers will open a book chosen at random, start to read at random, and find the words speak directly to their current problem. Or they will sit by a stream and listen to the rush of water and suddenly have an insight into how to proceed with a difficult situation. Nowadays they might be stuck in traffic and have their revelation there. Whatever. The outer condition is eliciting our inner truth, our intuition, in a million ways, if we only allow ourselves to be open to it.

Where the original idea is to promote human unity with the cosmos, scriptures are often interpreted to exalt certain individuals and reinforce the widespread conviction that liberation is only for one single rare and exceptional person who lived in the distant past. That means there is no possibility of freedom for the rest of us without divine intervention on our behalf, or the miraculous return of that special person. The Gita is frequently cited to promulgate Krishna in such a role, and doing so totally undermines its most important tenet: that the Absolute is inherent in everyone and accessible to all who seek it.

THE ABSOLUTE

The Absolute is a philosophically rigorous term that has fallen on hard times due to linguistic confusion but is centrally important in Indian thought. It sums up the unitive position that all is one, and it is used in place of more limited terms like God or nature because it is impeccably neutral, whereas there is always a temptation to imagine some things are not God, for instance, or are abhorrent to nature.

Absolutism, which is another matter entirely, has given the Absolute a bad name. Absolutism is when a political belief is considered to be absolute and its acceptance is forced on everyone. Where the Absolute is all-inclusive, absolutism is harshly exclusive. A seeker of truth must clearly distinguish these two utterly different principles with similar names.

Despite the postulation of an Absolute, which keeps consciousness properly oriented and is common to all systems, whether philosophical, religious, or scientific, there is no such thing as absolute realization. Anything realized has to be relative, less than the whole, which means there is no absolute right or wrong, or any last word. Whenever the mind goes beyond its accustomed boundaries, it undergoes an expansion that feels like liberation or realization, but no one has yet ascertained any end to human potential. Greater expansion is a perennial possibility.

Because of this, there is always more to be discovered. Once we realize that our knowledge is inevitably partial, we will know that learning never ends and there is no ultimate panacea. Anyone claiming finalized answers is in fact seriously deluded and is most likely intending to manipulate others for their personal benefit. In any case the idea of finality brings growth to a halt.

If the Absolute is imagined to be a fixed item that can be disdained or rejected, it is not the Absolute. Nataraja Guru emphasized this frequently, asserting, "The notion of the Absolute has somehow to transcend all paradox, and even vestiges suggestive of it. This is an utterly necessary position, epistemologically speaking. Ultimate truth cannot be thought of as having a rival or be ranged against itself."[1]

Because of the widespread confusion, let's set forth a definition, from the *Encyclopedia of Philosophy*:

> The Absolute is a term used by philosophers to signify the ultimate reality regarded as one and yet as the source of variety; as complete, or perfect, and yet as not divorced from the finite, imperfect world. The term was introduced into the philosophical vocabulary at the very end of the eighteenth century by Schelling and Hegel. . . .
>
> In 1803 . . . Schelling argues that philosophy, as concerned with first principles, must be "an absolute science," that it is therefore concerned with what is absolute, and that, since all things are conditioned, philosophy must be concerned with the activity of knowing rather than things or objects.
>
> "Philosophy," he writes, "is the science of the Absolute," and the Absolute is the identity of the act of knowledge and what is known. Schelling gives the name "Absolute Idealism" to the philosophy in which this identity is recognized. The exponent of Absolute Idealism, he argues, seeks out the intelligence that is necessarily embodied in nature, and he achieves by means of "intellectual intuition" a grasp of the identity between knower and known.[2]

Indian philosophy predates these Western philosophers by at least two millennia, but the concept is identical.

The central claim of Vedantic philosophy, as presented in the Bhagavad Gita and the Upanishads, is that each and every person is a manifestation of the Absolute, and our challenge is to come to remember that truth in a world where objects and events constantly distract us from it, often even intentionally. This not only gives us unlimited hope, it empowers us to do our best. We are accorded the highest possible respect in advance. If everyone and everything is sacred, then there is no possibility of sacrilege. We have no need for divine intervention, because we are already miraculous. Life is a continuous "divine intervention," so what more could be needed?

For this reason, students of Indian wisdom are instructed to meditate that they are the Absolute and the Absolute is everything. Seekers start out imagining the goal is somewhere else. They are not realized, are not worthy, and so on. These are all fictions that evaporate under scrutiny.

Narayana Guru (1854–1928), South India's preeminent seer and revelator of ancient wisdom, once said that to know that the wave and ocean are not two is the goal of spiritual search. The starting point of our search is usually to see God or the Absolute as separate from the world. The truth of the matter is that they are one. Realizing this is all that matters, but it's far more than an intellectual exercise. It has to become a living reality at every moment. That takes a little digging for most of us.

Sadly, we are so brainwashed and have forgotten who we are so thoroughly that we shy away from even the prospect of seeking for our true nature. Instead of daring to be our cosmic selves, we have learned to reduce our expectations to just making the best of a bad situation. To restore our normal courage the rishis—the gurus of old—recommend meditating on the phrase *tat tvam asi,* "The Absolute is what I am."

Keeping in mind that anything that has an opposite is not the Absolute, it cannot be said that the Absolute is big or small. Obviously, if we define the Absolute as unknowable and indefinable, and we equate truth with it, then truth is going to come in as indefinite and unknowable. Curiously, the claim of Vedanta is that we CAN know the Absolute, via mystical intuition and by surrendering our partial vision for an overwhelming participation in the whole. Many spiritual traditions offer the assurance that such an experience is valid, not delusory. We are invited to judge for ourselves.

THE ARCH SHAPE

Visualizing the Gita as an arch is a helpful analogy. Placing the rounded arch of the Gita in the middle of a horizontal line representing the normal course of life produces a shape resembling the Greek omega: Ω. Transactional orientation comprises the horizontal aspect of life while timeless wisdom and ideals epitomize the vertical. Their intermixing in varying proportions produces the curvature of the arch.

Horizontal and vertical factors are implicitly demonstrated in the course of the Gita by the fact that at the beginning and the end the focus is primarily on Arjuna and his predicament, while in the middle Krishna is spoken of almost exclusively. As Arjuna moves toward the vertical in his thinking he is more and more drawn into the wonder of the Absolute and is less and less self-absorbed. After contemplating and finally experiencing the Absolute in the middle chapters, he then gradually returns to more concrete aspects of his life, where he can integrate what he has learned.

The first chapter of the Gita stands firmly on everyday actualities, where Arjuna finds himself in the midst of conflict, symbolic of all the challenges of life. Overwhelmed by the poverty of his options, he makes the exemplary decision to enlist the aid of a wise guru and describes his confusion to him. At the beginning of the second chapter, he states his position in philosophic terms, demonstrating that he is not merely panicking but has reached the limits of ordinary logic and cannot abide by them. He wants something better than the inferior options everyone else is fighting over. Krishna immediately begins to teach him, first correcting his flawed understanding of ordinary matters, then sketching out the broad outlines of a yoga of liberation. The Gita has begun its rise up from the muddy battlefield.

As the chapters progress toward the center, more abstract and metaphysical elements are introduced, as if an arrow of interest is moving away from the solid reality of the seeker to the ineffable essence of the goal. The middle two chapters are almost entirely about the mystical heights in the most general terms. Arjuna comes back into the narrative right after the descent has begun, with his stupendous vision—he finally sees the nature of what he has been pondering, and it is an overwhelming experience.

The descent is equally as gradual as the ascent. First Arjuna learns how to relate to the vision of wonder he has just had. Then Krishna lays out a schematic basis for integrating the numinous with the manifested world. How our concepts shape our experience leads us to the final chapter where Arjuna is set down on the good earth once again, fully prepared to live well and prosper. His fears and doubts about his world have been cured, and he knows how to make excellent decisions. He has been transformed from a seeker into a seer.

Everyone, just like Arjuna, pursues the horizontal course of their own life, until for some an extraordinary insight or stimulus suddenly elevates them into a rainbow arch of self-examination. In Arjuna's case, guided by Krishna he soars to sublime heights, at the critical moment transmuting his theoretical speculations into direct experience. He then returns to his ordinary transactional life and continues on his way, but he has been forever changed. The vertical core of life, previously taken for granted or ignored, is now known to him, and he will see it everywhere he looks. That makes all the difference between an ordinary life and one infused with wisdom.

CHAPTERS ONE AND TWO

The first two chapters of the Gita, the ones that are examined in this book, are of critical importance. Curiously, the first chapter was almost universally ignored until Nataraja Guru revealed its value in his revolutionary commentary. It is an exposition of Arjuna's doubt and confusion, which are the very things that impel him to seek instruction from a guru. The entire Gita is a kind of response to Arjuna's malady, leading him out of his troubles by the application of intelligence. There is no magic involved, only clear understanding. Arjuna's confusion, which the Gita calls a yoga (The Yoga of Arjuna's Despondency), teaches us the value of questioning and rejection of generally accepted beliefs.

The key factor is that Arjuna is expected to fight, but he wants to run away and escape his obligations. Desperate, he enunciates his problems in detail, then drops his bow, overwhelmed with sorrow. He will not pick it back up until the very end of the Gita's eighteenth chapter.

By the second chapter (Unitive Reason and Yoga), Arjuna has calmed down enough to state his case with philosophical exactitude and ask Krishna to teach him. Krishna launches right in, beginning one of the most sublime discourses in all of literature.

Krishna first sketches what might be called commonsense reasoning and uses it to challenge Arjuna's chaotic state of mind. This is the first step in creative discipleship: the guru opposes any lopsidedness, leading the disciple to a state of neutrality where learning can begin in earnest. The first half of the second chapter presents this initial balancing act.

In the second half, Krishna sketches the broad outlines of yoga theory and hints at its radical nature, in a sense giving the gist of the entire Bhagavad Gita. For this reason, the second chapter is often regarded as the epitome of yoga as conceived by the ancient rishis.

THE ROLE OF RELIGION

It is curious that the Gita is almost invariably spoken of as a religious scripture, whereas the Gita itself discredits religion in no uncertain terms. This runs parallel to the popular emphasis on social obligations in a work that enunciates them only so they can be recognized as impediments.

The long line of commentators who portray the Gita as a guide to duty and conformity have turned their backs on the Upanishadic wisdom and are peddling a sort of medieval Hindu-Christian mishmash, long on servility and short on realization and individual freedom. It can certainly be argued that the latter accurately represents the mainstream of most religions nowadays and so is "right" in that sense, but the present interpretation is offered for those who find such attitudes distasteful. My teachers made a convincing case that the original intent was much more radical and liberating, and well worth revisiting.

India's pride and joy, Vedanta, is a philosophy, not a religion. Its three pillars are the Upanishads, the Bhagavad Gita, and the Brahma Sutras. The Gita as a *yoga shastra,* a scientific textbook of yoga, deals with transcendental psychology, explaining how to overcome the conditioning of one's upbringing to become a whole and free individual. It recognizes that one of the deepest and most potentially insidious forms of conditioning is instilled by religious training. Treating this cosmic song as a religious work is a tip-off that the commentator has missed this crucial point and that much of its liberating advice will be watered down and washed away.

It's ironic that the great historical compilations of nonreligious or even antireligious wisdom have over time become the basis of religions themselves. Lao Tzu's incisive sayings expanded into Taoism, the Buddha's protestations that there is nothing anywhere laid the foundation of Buddhism, and the Bhagavad Gita, written in part to discredit the priesthood's stranglehold on the people of India and religion's stranglehold on the human spirit, is today worshipped as a religious scripture. One of the tasks of the sincere seeker is to circumvent the accretions clinging to the original text, separating the wheat from the chaff and penetrating to the heart of the matter. One must be highly skeptical of a religious cast to any commentary as being of at best a secondary level of understanding. Nataraja Guru puts this idea quite simply:

> In the Vedanta of India, with its textbooks such as the Bhagavad Gita and the large body of literature called the Upanishads, we have already stated that these books claim to be a Science of the Absolute called *brahma-vidya.* It is a mistake commonly made to treat this part of wisdom literature as belonging to Hindu religion. By its dynamic and open outlook such literature refuses to be fitted into any orthodox context of a closed and static religious setup.[3]

The present commentary is for those for whom a personal deity-concept is not appealing. For those who like it or need it, there are many, many versions already in existence. For the rest, a nontheistic interpretation is a welcome addition to the literature.

WHY THE BHAGAVAD GITA IS NOT THE SONG OF THE LORD

The word *gita* means "song." The Gita is a song in the sense that it is to be lived, not just read. Ideas, like words, are only symbols. We have to reanimate the ideas as living realities, and only then is their secret revealed. Great composers convert their cosmic music to lines and dots on paper. We can admire those books of sheet music, and see how the lines and dots make pretty patterns, and even collect stacks of them. But only when musicians play the music does it come back to life and the meaning stand revealed. This is the task of all students of religion or philosophy: to reanimate the ideas by bringing them to life in ourselves. It marks the difference between spiritual and academic attitudes.

Although most philosophic critiques of the Upanishads and the Bhagavad Gita tend to be rationally oriented, ecstasy is an important feature in them. The Gita is a song, and enlightenment lifts the heart like a song. A song differs from ordinary speech in the same way that ecstasy differs from ordinary life. The Gita's teaching is designed to convert the individual notes of knowledge we are composed of into an enchanting spiritual symphony.

The title *Bhagavad Gita* is commonly translated as the "Lord's Song." Krishna, the Bhagavad Gita's guru, is most commonly referred to in the text as Bhagavan, and it is he who gives his name to the Bhagavad Gita: "the Song of Bhagavan." The common translation of *bhagavan* as "Lord" is based on some highly dubious and dualistic conceptions that are out of synch with the unitive flavor of the work. Nataraja Guru detested what he called the "Lord-Lordism" that gushed from Gita commentaries, which basically converts the dignified wisdom of a philosophical treatise into a worshipful religious tract. In the process most of the psychological insights are lost.

The term *lord* is a feudal appellation for a ruler of serfs. Such a barbaric concept is precisely what the Gita intends to do away with. We are to become full-fledged human beings who can and do act independently, not groveling followers of orders from Above, or worse, supplicants of favors from a ruling elite. So while Bhagavan is primarily a respectful form of address, the translation "Lord" is completely incorrect. It debases both sides of a relationship that should transcend all master-slave dichotomies.

The temptation is great, when we think about attuning ourselves to the Absolute, to give all importance to That and none to our side of the equation. We may imagine that by debasing ourselves we impart greater glory to the Beyond, but that just throws the balance off more and more. The Beyond is right here. When the Upanishads tell us that we *are* the Absolute, they aren't speaking metaphorically. We glorify the Absolute by exemplifying it with increasing skill and insight. A self-deprecating attitude may seem politically correct, but it actually demeans the Absolute and creates a divisive schism, torpedoing the unitive state of mind.

Roberto Calasso, in *The Marriage of Cadmus and Harmony,* reveals a parallel degeneration of an ancient Greek term for God:

> By the time of the tragedians, *dîos* had come to mean nothing more than "divine," insofar as it is a "property of Zeus." But in the Homeric age *dîos* means first and foremost "clear," "brilliant," "glorious." To appear in Zeus is to glow with light against the background of the sky. Light on light. When Homer gives the epithet *dîos* to his characters, the word does not refer first of all to what they may have of "divine," but to the clarity, the splendor that is always with them and against which they stand out.[4]

The Monier-Williams Sanskrit Dictionary defines *bhagavan* as "possessing fortune, fortunate, prosperous, happy, glorious, illustrious, divine," before the more modern "adorable, venerable, holy," and so on. I have followed Nataraja Guru in translating it simply as "Krishna." What that name implies is revealed by a scrutiny of the entire Gita, especially X:20,*

---

*References in this format, that is, a Roman numeral followed by a number, are to the Bhagavad Gita as a whole, first the chapter (I through XVIII) and then the verse. This book incorporates chapter I, verses 1–47 and chapter II, verses 1–72.

where Krishna is "the soul seated in the heart of all beings," and "the beginning and the middle and even the end of beings." In other words he is a guru, an incarnation of the Absolute.

My aim is to restore the original vision in which bhagavan is not used as a term expressing abject devotion to a god but is indicative of respect and admiration toward an excellent teacher, which is the correct attitude to have toward a guru.

THE EPITHETS

Throughout the work, Krishna and Arjuna have many epithets substituted for their names, such as "Mighty armed," "Winner of wealth," and so on. Nataraja Guru suggests there is a world of implications contained in these monikers, but to avoid confusion, I have used merely the names Krishna and Arjuna. The epithets are really not all that significant. The adjectives almost certainly play a role by helping the text fit the exacting meter of four lines of eight syllables each for every verse. They do reveal a fascinating aspect of the Gita as an oral document, however.

Although the Gita itself is tightly structured, obviously the product of careful planning, the Mahabharata epic in which it is housed much more closely resembles the broad, rambling nature of the Iliad and Odyssey of Homer. Scholars of the ancient Homeric epics have concluded that the similar usage of epithets in them is evidence of their original composition as improvised oral performances. Any bard worth his salt has an arsenal of such handy phrases to fit every metrical demand. Moreover, the use of stock phrases is a gambit allowing time for the bard to simultaneously ponder the next thrust of improvisation.

Recognizing that these epics are an artistic compendium of oral archives accumulated over a long period of time makes it comprehensible that a single anonymous author or group eventually set them down. They are a precious historical record being preserved for posterity. Creating them purely from scratch would have required an unbelievably vast intellect, but collecting them is certainly possible for a mere genius.

For composers like Mozart, there is evidently a geyser of inspiration erupting within them, yet it is expressed in the musical language structure of the period. Invention and convention thus go hand in hand. The existing forms may be greatly enriched and expanded by the composer, but they also serve as the supporting ground from which the leaps of creativity are launched. None of us lives in a vacuum. We cannot help reflecting the mental structure we have imbibed from birth, even under the benign influence of overwhelming inspiration. The amalgam of structure and formless creative inspiration is the dialectical expression of life at its best.

In the case of the Gita, recording the mystical process of wisdom transmission offers the additional benefit of not merely providing instruction for disciples but gurus as well. We see many modern "gurus" who became enlightened by accident, in the bathtub or lying in bed, for example. They have a certain glowing cachet, but their appeal can be rather tepid and their teachings sparse until they assimilate some of the tried and true methods for conceiving and explaining what has happened to them. They have to learn how to express the ineluctable experience in comprehensible terms, for their fellow humans if not for themselves.

The Gita may thus be viewed as a course of instruction for gurus even more than for disciples. Many nuances of the bipolar dance of enlightenment are revealed or implied herein. The ancient secrets— ancient even at the time of their being set down in written form perhaps two thousand years ago—are codified to guide potential teachers for all eternity. In the present case the guidelines have held up very well indeed. Undoubtedly they have been tinkered with down through the ages, as have all the old scriptures, but in this instance at least, not to their detriment.

CASTE

According to the Gita, human types fall along a continuum of degrees of liberty, with those who crave a fixed template at one end and those who insist on full freedom at the other. This is the basis of caste distinctions, and it is meant as a tool for self-analysis, not as a rigid set of constraints. What caste became—essentially a variant of racism as a means of oppression—is a vast tragedy that should be eradicated. Krishna himself says he created caste and also abolishes it, in IV:13:

> The fourfold color grades were created by myself on the basis of innate disposition and vocation that accorded with each; know Me to be the maker of such as also to be its undoer, unexpended.

The key is the relation to "innate disposition": caste becomes bondage when it doesn't accord with a person's motivation.

Caste in the Gita has four main categories, based on the importance of freedom. Many people would rather have security than free choice, which carries with it a great deal of uncertainty. The type of human primarily concerned with duty and security is the *sudra* or laborer. When you work for someone else, you have to do what they want you to do. But the rest of humanity craves freedom in increasing admixture to necessity, in ascending order, merchants (*vaishyas*) with some freedom and a lot of duties; politicians and scientists (*kshatriyas*) who have a greater range of options; and priests and artists (*brahmins*) with the most. The Gita extols the relinquisher or the renunciate as the most excellent, meaning those who do not compromise their freedom with necessity at all, or very little. While all are dear from the cosmic perspective, the only "duty" Krishna recommends is to follow your own best assessment of every situation, in other words, to be true to yourself. If you are busy trying to accommodate yourself to an arbitrarily assigned niche, you won't be able to live up to your innate potentials, but when those potentials are given primacy, the inevitable limitations of life in a body are no longer seen as impediments; they become its practical means of expression.

Originality is a key element here. Most disciplines, whether scientific or religious, have strict parameters to define what they are. The Gita's philosophy, by contrast, is open-ended. In fact, it is open on all sides. The delight of the universe is in serendipity and originality, and the only constraints are what is possible: an exceedingly vast ambit we have only begun to explore as a species. A great part of the evolution of consciousness is investigating the seemingly endless possibilities afforded to us by nature.

Arbitrary, limiting parameters have been set up by the advocates of the various disciplines, usually in times long past. They are almost always based on a tightly constrained world view that is unnecessary for the seeker of truth to take into account. Scientific discoveries and spiritual insights well up whenever a thinker breaks the mold. Afterward there may be room for less original experimenters to explore some of the implications of what has already been discovered, but the Eureka! moments rely on breaking out of the known to embrace the unknown.

Knowing this, we should not take the Gita as a blueprint, full of explicit instructions on how to live. Instead it is a training course in how to break out of constraints to become who we truly are: creative geniuses that are the stupendous product of billions of years of successful evolution. As neuroscientist David Eagleman puts it, "If you ever feel lazy or dull, take heart: you're the busiest, brightest thing on the planet."[5] The Gita is a call to transcend our mundane duties and experience the joy of ever-new life.

THE PRESENT COMMENTATOR

My own lineage begins formally with Narayana Guru. His eminent disciple Nataraja Guru meticulously trained his disciple Nitya Chaitanya Yati, who in turn became an eloquent expounder of many aspects of wisdom. I was fortunate to take a number of full courses on the Gita with Nitya, beginning in 1970, and was his amanuensis during the preparation of his own commentary on it. Nitya's book was written during an extremely busy period, and it skips over many of the intriguing ideas he presented in his classes. Because of this there is a lot of latitude for a Gita exegesis based on his superlative vision.

Under my guru, Nitya, I underwent a similar kind of intensive training course to Arjuna's, so I am familiar with many of the subtleties implied in the text. This aspect is missing from most commentaries and translations, unfortunately. Working carefully once more through the entire Gita (a process lasting nearly a decade) has given me a fantastic opportunity to solidify my work with the guru and investigate many of the nuances we touched on together but didn't have time to fully appreciate at the time.

I offer what follows as a distillation of the wisdom of my immediate forebears, which to my knowledge has no equal. Aum.

PART ONE

THE UNADORNED TEXT OF CHAPTERS I AND II OF THE BHAGAVAD GITA

TRANSLATED BY NATARAJA GURU

CHAPTER I

THE YOGA OF ARJUNA'S DESPONDENCY

1 Dhritarashtra said:
   In the field of righteousness, the field of the Kurus,
   gathered together, intent on battle, what did my people
   and also the Sons of Pandu do, O Sanjaya?

2 Sanjaya said:
   On seeing the army of the Pandavas in battle array, Prince
   Duryodhana, having approached his teacher, then gave
   utterance to the following speech:

3 O Teacher, look at this grand army of the Sons of Pandu,
   marshaled by your talented pupil, the Son of Drupada.

4 Here are heroes, mighty archers, equal in battle to Bhima
   and Arjuna, Yuyudhana, Virata, and Drupada, of the great
   chariots.

5 Dhrishtaketu, Chekitana, and the valiant King of Kasi,
   Purujit and Kuntibhoja, and that bull among men, Saibya.

6 The heroic Yudhamanyu, and the brave Uttamaujas, the
   Son of Subhadra, and the Sons of Draupadi, all of great
   chariots.

7 But know who are the most distinguished among us, O
   Best of the Twice-born, the leaders of my army; these I tell
   you, for you to recognize by name:

8 You and Bhishma, and Karna, and also Kripa, the victor

in war, Asvatthama and Vikarna, and also the Son of
Somadatta,

9   and many other heroes who are willing to die for me, who
have various missiles and weapons, all skilled in warfare.

10 That army of ours which is under the care of Bhishma
is insufficient, but this army of theirs which is under the
care of Bhima is adequate.

11 And so let all of you, standing in your respective positions
at the entrance to every formation, keep guard on
Bhishma.

12 So as to cheer him, the mighty old Kuru patriarch roared
loudly like a lion and blew a conch.

13 Then conches and drums and gongs, (other) drums, and
horns, were played together suddenly, and that sound
made a confused clang.

14 Then standing in their great chariot, to which white
horses were yoked, Krishna and Arjuna together blew
their divine conches.

15 Krishna blew Panchajanya, and Arjuna blew Devadatta.
He of wolf-like appetite and deeds of enormity (Bhima)
blew his great conch, Paundra.

16 Prince Yudhishthira, Son of Kunti, blew Anantavijaya,
and Nakula and Sahadeva (blew together) the Sughosha
and Manipushpaka.

17 And the King of Kasi, excellent bowman, Sikhandin,
great charioteer, Dhrishtadyumna and Virata and the
unconquered Satyaki,

18 Drupada, and the Sons of Draupadi, O Lord of the Earth,
and the Son of Subhadra, of mighty arms—from all sides
each blew his conch separately.

19 That loud blast, filling earth and sky with sound, pierced
the hearts of Dhritarashtra's Sons.

20 Then, beholding the Sons of Dhritarashtra standing

marshaled in order, while the flight of arrows was
beginning, Arjuna, the Son of Pandu, of monkey ensign,
took up his bow;

21   and, O King, he spoke thus to Krishna: O Acyuta! Stop
my chariot right in the middle between the two armies,

22   so that I may behold these standing eager to fight by my
side in the present battle-undertaking,

23   and might observe those here gathered together who desire
to please in war the evil-minded Son of Dhritarashtra.

24   Sanjaya said:
Thus addressed by Arjuna, Krishna, having stationed that
excellent chariot right in the middle between the two armies,

25   facing Bhishma and Drona and all the rulers of the earth,
Krishna said: O Arjuna! Behold these Kurus gathered here.

26   Then Arjuna saw standing fathers as well as grandfathers,
teachers, maternal uncles, brothers, sons, grandsons, and
companions too.

27   And upon seeing these relatives, fathers-in-law, and
friends, all standing, in both armies,

28   filled with a supreme pity, in mental distress, said:
Beholding my own people, O Krishna, standing together,
wanting to fight,

29   my limbs fail and my mouth dries up, my body trembles
and my hair stands on end,

30   (the bow) Gandiva slips from my hand, my skin feels as
if burning all over, I am unable to stand, and my mind is
whirling round;

31   and I see conflicting portents, O Krishna, nor do I foresee
good from killing one's own people in battle.

32   I do not wish for victory, O Krishna, nor kingdom, nor
pleasures; what is kingdom to us, what enjoyment, or even
life?

33   They for whose sake kingdom, enjoyments, and pleasures

are desired by us, are standing here in battle, having
renounced their interests in life and wealth:

34 teachers, fathers, sons, and also grandfathers, maternal
uncles, fathers-in-law, grandsons, brothers-in-law, as well
as other kinsman.

35 These I do not want to kill, though they kill me, O
Krishna, not even for the sake of dominion over the three
worlds—how then for the sake of the earth?

36 Having killed the Sons of Dhritarashtra, what delight can
there be for us? Only sin would come to us after killing
this marauding rabble.

37 And so we ought not to kill the Sons of Dhritarashtra,
our relations; for how indeed can we be happy after killing
our own people, O Krishna?

38 Even if they, whose minds are overpowered by greed, see
no wrong in the destruction of family, and no crime in
treachery to friends,

39 yet why should we not learn to turn away from this
sin—we who do see wrong in the destruction of family?

40 In the destruction of family, the immemorial clan
traditions perish, and on the loss of tradition the whole
clan comes under the sway of lawlessness.

41 When wrong ways prevail, O Krishna, the women of the
family become corrupt, and when women become corrupt,
mixing of clans arises.

42 This mixing leads (both the) family and the destroyers of
the family to hell, for their ancestors fall when deprived of
their offering of rice balls and water rites.

43 By these misdeeds of the destroyers of families, causing
intermixture of clans, the immemorial traditions of clan
and family are destroyed.

44 Men of families whose clan traditions are destroyed are
destined to live in hell—thus we have heard.

45 Alas! A great sin are we engaged in committing in endeavoring to kill our own people through greed for the pleasures of kingdom!

46 It would be better for me if the Sons of Dhritarashtra, arms in hand, should kill me, unarmed and unresisting, in the battle.

47 Sanjaya said:

Thus having spoken in the midst of the battle, Arjuna sat down in his chariot seat, casting away his bow and arrow, his mind overwhelmed with sorrow.

CHAPTER II

UNITIVE REASON AND YOGA

1   Sanjaya said:

To him who was thus filled with tenderness, whose eyes were filled with tears, and agitated, and who was in distress, Krishna spoke these words:

2   Krishna said:

In the midst of this difficulty, whence comes to you this dejection typical of non-Aryans, heaven-barring and disreputable, O Arjuna?

3   Give yourself not to impotence, O Arjuna, it does not befit you. Cast off this base faint-heartedness. Arise, O Terror of Foes!

4   Arjuna said:

How could I encounter with arrows in battle Bhishma and Drona, who are worthy of worship, O Krishna?

5   Desisting from the killing of the Gurus, who are highly honorable, it would be more meritorious in this world even to have to eat of a beggar's pittance. Choosing, on the other hand, to kill these Gurus as fortune-seekers, I should be feasting even here on blood-stained benefits of life.

6   Neither is it clear which would be of greater advantage to us: that we win or that they win over us. Those

33

very persons are standing ranged before us, the Sons of
Dhritarashtra, killing whom we would no longer wish to live.

7   Struck down by the evil of a tender disposition, with a
mind confounded in regard to what is right to do, I ask
you: that which is definitely more meritorious do indicate
to me. I am your disciple; do discipline me coming thus
for refuge to you.

8   I cannot visualize what could rid me of this distress which
dries up the senses in this way—even should (it transpire
that) I obtain unrivalled dominion of the earth's plenty or
overlordship of the gods in heaven too.

9   Sanjaya said:

Having spoken thus to Krishna, Arjuna, the Terror of the
Foe, saying "I will not fight," lapsed finally into silence.

10   On this, Krishna, with a semblance of smiling, spoke
these words to him who was in grief between the two
armies:

11   Krishna said:

You are sorry for those for whom sorrow is unreasonable.
You speak in terms of reason too. Veritable philosophers
are not affected in regard to those whose breath has gone
and those whose breath has not gone.

12   Further, never was I nonexistent, nor you, nor these chiefs
of men; neither shall we, all of us, ever cease becoming
hereafter.

13   As there is here in the body, for the embodied, childhood,
youth, and old age, so also the passing on to another body
in the same manner; those firm in mind are not thereby
bewildered.

14   Momentary sense contacts, on the other hand, yielding
cold-warmth, joy-pain, alternately coming and going, are
transitory. Do you endure them, O Arjuna.

15   That human indeed of firm mind who is unaffected by

these, equal-minded in joy as well as pain—he is destined for immortality.

16 What is unreal cannot have being, and non-being cannot be real; the conclusion in regard to both these has been known to philosophers.

17 Know That to be indestructible by which all this is pervaded. None can bring about the destruction of This that knows no decrease.

18 These bodies (however) of the everlasting indestructible and undefinable embodied One are spoken of as having an end. Therefore go on with the battle, O Arjuna.

19 He who thinks of This as the killer, and he who thinks of This as killed—both these know not. This does not kill, is not killed.

20 This is neither born nor does This die, nor, having once come into being, cease to become any more: unborn, perpetual, eternal is This Ancient One. It is not killed on the killing of the body.

21 About him who knows This as the indestructible, the everlasting, the unborn, never-decreasing one—of such a person how could the questions arise "whose death he causes," "whom he kills," O Arjuna?

22 As a man casting off his worn-out garments assumes others that are new, likewise casting off bodies that are worn-out, the embodied One takes to others that are new.

23 Weapons do not cut This, fire does not burn This, and water does not wet This; wind does not dry This.

24 Indeed It is uncleavable; It is non-inflammable; It is unwettable and non-dryable also—everlasting, all-pervading, stable, immobile; It is eternal.

25 It is undefined, unthinkable is It, as non-subject to change is It spoken of: therefore, knowing It as such, there is no reason for you to feel sorry for It.

26 Or again if you should hold This to be constantly ever-born or as constantly ever-dying, even then you have no reason to regret it.

27 In respect of anyone born, death is certain, and certain is birth for anyone dead; therefore, regarding something inevitable, you have no reason to feel any regret.

28 Beings have an unmanifested origin and manifested middle states, and again unmanifested terminations. Where is room for plaint herein?

29 A certain person sees This as a wonder, likewise another speaks about This as a wonder. Another hears of It even as a wonder, but even hearing no one understands This at all.

30 This embodied One within the bodies of all is ever immune to killing, Arjuna. Therefore in respect of any being you have no reason for regretting.

31 Further, having regard also for the pattern of behavior natural to you there is no reason for vacillation, for there could be nothing more meritorious than a war that is right for a true fighter.

32 True warriors have reason to be happy, Arjuna, to have the chance of such a war presenting itself unsought before them as an open door to heaven.

33 If, on the other hand, you will not take to this battle which conforms to the requirements of righteousness, then thwarting what is consistent with your own nature and your good repute you will become involved in evil.

34 Living beings will also pronounce a never-ending verdict of calumny on you, and to one used to honor, dishonor is worse than death.

35 The great car-generals will look upon you as quitting the battle from fear, and having been honorably looked upon by them you will be held in derision.

36 Those against you will speak of you in unspeakable terms,
    scorning your ability; what pain could there be keener
    than this?

37 Dying you will attain heaven or winning you will have
    the enjoyment of the earth. Therefore arise, O Arjuna,
    making up your mind to fight.

38 Equalizing both pleasure and pain, both gain and loss,
    both victory and defeat, enter wholly into battle. Thus
    you will avoid sin.

39 What has just been taught is reasoning according to
    Samkhya, but hear now of the same according to Yoga,
    attaining to the unity of which reasoning you will be able
    to throw off the bondage of works.

40 Here there is no forfeiture of any merit, nor is there
    involved any demerit by transgression. Even a little of such
    a way of life saves one from great apprehension.

41 Here, O Arjuna, the well-founded reasoning is unitive,
    but many branched and endless are the reasonings of them
    in whom reason is ill-founded.

42–44 Such flowery speech as uttered by the foolish, adhering to
    the doctrine of the Veda, negating any other (transcendental)
    verity, the self of which is nothing but desire-made, holding
    heaven to be the highest goal, offering only birth as the result
    of works abounding in many special observances, which aim
    at enjoyment and domination; in the case of those whose
    minds are under the sway of such teachings, who are attached
    to enjoyment and domination, a well-founded reason does
    not come under the sway of the peace of contemplation.

45 The Vedas treat of matters related to the three *gunas;*
    you should be free from these three modalities, Arjuna,
    free from (relative) pairs of opposites, established ever in
    pure being, without alternately acquiring and enjoying,
    (unitively) Self-possessed.

46 There would be as much use for all the Vedas to a
    Brahmin of wisdom as there could be for a pool of water
    when a full flood prevails all over.

47 Your concern should be with action (as such) alone, not
    for any benefits ever. Do not become benefit motivated; be
    not attached to inaction either.

48 Engage in activity, Arjuna, taking your stand on the
    unitive way, discarding attachments, and capable of
    regarding both attainment and nonattainment as the
    same: in sameness consists the unitive way.

49 Far inferior is the way of action to the unitive way of
    reason, Arjuna; resort to reason for final refuge; pitiful
    indeed are they who are benefit motivated.

50 Affiliated to reason one leaves behind here both
    meritorious and unmeritorious deeds. Therefore affiliate
    yourself to the unitive way; yoga is reason in action.

51 By affiliation to unitive reason the wise, transcending
    birth bondage, renouncing benefit interest, go onward to a
    state beyond all pain.

52 When your reason has transcended the dross of vagueness,
    then you attain to that neutral attitude, both in respect of
    what is to be learnt and what has already been heard.

53 When, disillusioned respecting the (contradictory
    injunctions of the) scriptures, your reason stands unshaken
    and steady in *samadhi,* then you shall have reached yoga.

54 Arjuna said:
    What is the way of one whose reason is well founded, who is
    established in samadhi, O Krishna? How does he discourse,
    what is his state of being, how does he move about?

55 Krishna said:
    When one banishes all desires that enter the mind,
    Arjuna, satisfied in the Self by the Self alone, then he is
    said to be one of well-founded reason.

56 He whose mind is unaffected by mishaps, who on happy
    occasions too evinces no interest, rising above attachment,
    anxiety, or anger—such a sage-recluse is said to be of well-
    founded reason.

57 He who remains in all cases unattached on gaining such
    or such desirable-undesirable end, who neither welcomes
    anything nor rejects in anger—his reason is well founded.

58 Again, when, as a tortoise retracts its limbs from all sides,
    the senses are withdrawn from objects of sense interest—
    his reason is well founded.

59 Objective interests revert without the relish for them on
    starving the embodied of them. Even the residual relish
    reverts on the One Beyond being sighted.

60 Even with a man of wisdom, Arjuna, in spite of his
    effort, excited sense interests can forcibly distract the
    mind.

61 Restraining every one of them, he should rest unitively
    established, having Me for his Supreme ideal. He in whom
    sense interests are subdued—his reason is well founded.

62 Meditating on objects of sense-interest there is born in
    man an attachment for them; from attachment rises
    passion; in the face of passion (frustrated) arises rage.

63 From rage is produced distortion of values, from
    distortion of values memory-lapse, from memory-lapse
    comes loss of reason, and from loss of reason he perishes.

64 But he whose Self is subdued, whose attachment and
    aversion are both within the sway of the Self, although his
    senses still move amidst sense-interests, he wends toward a
    state of spiritual clarity.

65 By spiritual clarity there takes place the effacement for
    him of all sufferings, and for one whose spirit has
    become lucid, very soon reason becomes properly
    founded.

66 For one unbalanced there can be no reason, nor is there any creative intuition for the unbalanced, and for one incapable of creative intuition there could be no peace, and for the unpeaceful where could there be happiness?

67 Still moving amid sense interests, that item to which the mind submits draws away the reasoning as the wind does a ship on the waters.

68 Therefore, Arjuna, he whose senses have been in every way withdrawn from sense interests—his reason is well founded.

69 What is night for all creatures, the one of self-control keeps awake therein; wherein all creatures are wakeful, that is night for the sage-recluse who sees.

70 Still getting filled, while fixed firm in immobility, the ocean remains; so, too, he in whom all interests enter—he attains to peace, not the craver of desires.

71 That man who, giving up all attachments, moves about desirelessly, without owning anything, and without egoism—he goes to peace.

72 This is the state of being in the Absolute, Arjuna, on reaching which one suffers from delusion no more. Established in this at the very last moments of life, one reaches that final state of pure being in the Absolute.

PART TWO

COMMENTARY ON CHAPTER I

THE YOGA OF ARJUNA'S DESPONDENCY

VIRTUALLY EVERYONE GLOSSES over the first chapter of the Bhagavad Gita as being merely introductory. It was Nataraja Guru in his groundbreaking commentary of 1954 (published in 1961) who first stressed its profound significance. In his introduction he remarks:

> The first chapter is . . . the only one which contains the problems of the Gita stated correctly before the discussion by the Guru Krishna. This chapter therefore requires the closest attention. And yet oddly enough, commentators even including Sankara, have almost ignored it or even treated it as superfluous. Sankara's commentary begins only with verse 10 of chapter II, and he dismisses what precedes in a summary fashion not at all in proportion with the rest of his labours. The remaining seventeen chapters of the Gita make an attempt to dialectically revalue these same problems. It is, therefore, very important not to leave unnoticed even those minor peculiarities of this chapter in which the author hides here and there certain indications for the guidance of the intelligent reader.[1]

In fact, certain crucial elements of a transformative experience are introduced so artfully in the first chapter that for over two millennia almost no one noticed. Keeping in mind that the Gita is about reclaiming our authenticity, the key idea is that in order to find a cure, it is essential to first recognize the disease. Before entering a path of self-correction we must not only be dissatisfied with our current state but have some inkling why we're unhappy. To properly present ourself at the feet of a guru, someone who can throw light on our predicament, we must have already recognized our own limitations. The patient cannot expect the doctor to do all the work but must be committed as an enthusiastic participant.

At the moment the Gita begins, two factions of the Kuru clan are intent on battle. The Kauravas have deviously confiscated the rightful territory of the Pandavas, the family that includes the two protagonists of our story, Prince Arjuna and his friend and chariot driver Krishna. Conventional wisdom urges the Pandavas to go to war and redress the crime. Negotiations have been tried and abandoned, since the triumphant usurpers dare not allow the situation to be framed in moral terms. Warfare is their only hope of maintaining their dominance.

Arjuna's hurt feelings impel him to just give up and slink away, as he is certain that fighting is a lose-lose proposition. But the Gita wants him—and by proxy, us—to discover a third route, to stand up *as a neutral* for his rightful place in the world. For someone caught in a paradoxical dilemma, both fighting and escaping lead to endless complications. Only wisdom, which Arjuna will soon seek out from his seemingly ordinary companion Krishna, can bring about a felicitous outcome.

Arjuna thus stands for each one of us. His challenges symbolize ours, and in our journey through the Gita the parallels will be made clear. With this first chapter we are entering a path of enlightenment that bursts all the boundaries of orthodoxy and grants us the right to be utterly and spectacularly ourselves.

VERSE 1

DHRITARASHTRA SAID:
IN THE FIELD OF RIGHTEOUSNESS,
THE FIELD OF THE KURUS,
GATHERED TOGETHER, INTENT ON
BATTLE, WHAT DID MY PEOPLE AND
ALSO THE SONS OF PANDU DO,
O SANJAYA?

Dhritarashtra has only one line in the Gita, and this is it. He is the king of the Kauravas, the overwhelmingly powerful oppressors of their cousins the Pandavas. He is asking his aide Sanjaya to describe the action because he is blind but also to promote Sanjaya to the role of narrator. Besides Krishna and Arjuna, Sanjaya is the only other speaker in the entire Gita, except for this one verse.

Longstanding Sanskrit tradition demands that the parameters of a work be set out in the first verse. Here the king and his assistant are looking out over a field of battle that symbolizes the whole world and wondering what's going on in it. This means the Gita will address questions of action and conflict. Unlike many scriptures, it is not an escapist tome promoting an afterlife or invoking divine intervention. It is about taking control of our life and living it not only to the best of our ability but to a better ability than we are even aware we possess.

All actions are intended and performed to produce happiness. The opening verse is a view from afar, as from the clouds or an ivory tower, peering down on the panoply of the world and asking: What's going on? What is the meaning of all the chaos down below? One thing is certain: these humans are intent on fighting. The realm of humanity is the field of growth and the struggle for happiness through conflict.

The most important question each of us has to ask ourself as we mature is, What do I do to make my life a success? In other words, How should I act in this world that appears so like a battlefield wherever I look? In a sense each person's life is a long, drawn-out four-dimensional answer to this ongoing challenge.

Right at the outset, the author Vyasa tips us off that there is more here than meets the eye. The battlefield on which the impending war is going to take place is the field of righteousness, meaning the domain of proper conduct. The war of the Gita, then, is a metaphysical one addressing broad issues of right livelihood and is not about the actual physical war that surrounds Arjuna and Krishna in the context of the Mahabharata epic.

The field of *dharma,* often translated as "righteousness," refers to the ground of the Absolute, or the unitive principle; while the field of the Kurus—the participants on both sides of the battle—means happiness and refers to the realm of action. The dharma field is what we call the vertical aspect of eternal values, while the field of the Kurus represents the horizontal world of specific behaviors. In spiritual life we need to bring both aspects, the horizontal and the vertical, into balance, as well as into harmonious alignment with each other. The Gita's aim is to show us how to accomplish this and in the process to optimize our life.

The Gita takes an interesting slant here. Dhritarashtra is the blind king who leads the faction that has seized the rightful domain of the sons of Pandu, the Pandavas, who include Arjuna. When the leader of a nation is blind to moral values it invariably precipitates a crisis. The nation becomes divided into those who adhere to upright behavior and those who debase themselves for profit and position. This is a perennial problem, and it should not be hard for the reader to think of examples more recent than 500 BCE.

In our day the blind king might represent the entity that far exceeds the power of a president or king: the limited liability corporation. Intentionally morally blind, while wielding stupendous power, multinational corporations threaten to consume the entire world in their unbridled appetite for profits. The thrust of corporate intent is as problematic to parry as the vastly more powerful Kauravas are for Arjuna. There is no way to attack them head on, and fleeing from the confrontation just leaves the field open for more rapid exploitation. Since their charters outlaw moral considerations, they are immune to ethical appeals. A new solution is necessary.

Arjuna's dilemma may also be viewed as the battleground where we find ourselves on a daily basis. We can think of issues with our spouses, friends, or coworkers. Let's say the problem is that your coworker has got the boss's ear and convinced him that he alone is responsible for what the two of you have accomplished together. In fact, you did most of the work, and he is jockeying for the credit. Now he's in line for that promotion and they're thinking of firing you. If you lodge a protest, it will look like you are being selfish and manipulative. Put simply, your opponent is using aggressive tactics to have the argument framed on his terms and to cut you out. Such a self-seeking attitude is very dispiriting, and the immediate reaction is likely to be that you should just resign and concede everything the aggressor claims. You have to get a grip and calmly present your side, no matter how dire the circumstances, or you will lose everything. If you allow yourself to be drawn into quarreling and bickering, you are even more likely to be fired.

The actual problem may be very difficult to assess correctly. In the confusion of the battle, separating truth from fiction is essential and requires constant striving to maintain a clear perspective. A clever opponent can win through kicking up clouds of dust to heighten the confusion, as is often seen in political confrontations, for instance. All models of truth without exception have their limitations, which over time cause them to be supplanted by revised models. Therefore what is under consideration is a *process,* not a finalized viewpoint. This is a primary failing of the scientifically minded nearly as much as the religiously minded. Tenaciously holding on to a particular viewpoint may prove less successful in the long run than remaining flexible.

As far as spiritual technique goes, your attackers should not necessarily be taken at face value, though the wise person will consider it. Greedy people often use disinformation to blame their selfishness on you or confuse the issue so they can more easily get away with their scheme. The conflict needs only to be viewed as a field (*kshetra*) for the mining of deeper truths. The goal is always to have truth revealed despite the chaos.

Farther back in the epic, the blind king's wife, Gandhari, has done an interesting thing: she has wrapped her eyes in a blindfold in order to be on an equal footing with her husband. This is universally considered to be a magnanimous gesture on her part. Sri Chinmoy calls it "a sacrifice worthy to be remembered and admired by humanity." As Ram Das puts it in his generally very excellent commentary on the Gita, "Such devotion!" Such devotion indeed. One step above suttee, where the widow casts herself on the funeral pyre to join her husband in death. Comments like these merely reveal a sexist cast on the part of the interpreters.

The Gita does not necessarily approve of everything it portrays. Much of it is set down to demonstrate how what seems reasonable can go terribly wrong. Why is it so difficult to think that a revered scripture could be presenting the foibles of the ignorant along with exemplars of the wise? It says more about the reader than the book whether something is unquestioningly accepted as literal truth or whether skepticism is sustained until the meaning is truly understood. Such skepticism is not blasphemous, it is merely intelligent.

The penalty for taking symbolic instruction literally is blindness, or what we sometimes call spiritual death.

Here's what the story of Gandhari is really trying to tell us, as clarified later in the epic: the powerful demand for conformity makes us afraid to stand by our own vision. Anyone who is married to or otherwise serves a morally blind despot is generally required to close their eyes to truth in order to retain their post. Blindfolding themselves is the behavior of sycophants. If they notice something their leader is doing wrong, they'd better keep quiet about it.

The Bible offers a similar moral teaching in Genesis 9, where Noah is drunk and "uncovered" in his tent. This means that his ugliness is on display. His son Ham saw him and proclaimed it to his brothers, and so Noah cursed him for all eternity when he sobered up. His less honest brothers, keeping their eyes averted, backed into the tent and covered Noah, and so were blessed by him.

The organizational catchword is "you go along to get along." It permeates civic life from the lowest level right to the top and is a key cause of disasters great and small. Where a group of individuals freely examining matters in detail could steer the ship of state through rough seas, those fearing for their security must shut their mouths while watching the waves crash on the reefs dead ahead. To warn the captain would be to display a lack of faith and to very likely cost you your job. So let the chips fall where they may!

Once again it shouldn't be hard to recall recent examples and their horrifically tragic consequences.

One of the rarest of human types is the leader who recognizes the inevitability in themselves of degrees of blindness and welcomes contradictory points of view into the decision-making process. This is important to remember on the personal level as well. If we can keep in mind our own limitations, we will be more open to input from our friends that might be very helpful. They may well be seeing faults to which we ourselves are blind, so they should be encouraged to speak up without fear of losing our friendship.

Many of us were punished as children for our faults, and we learned to pretend we were blameless to avoid pain and humiliation. One of the hardest and most essential steps in spiritual life is to admit, even to ourselves, that we are flawed and imperfect, because in the back of our minds such admissions are unconsciously associated with painful outcomes. Until we face that simple fact, though, we can never make any real progress.

When a person is psychologically blind, it signifies they are unable to foresee the results of their actions. This is especially exaggerated in the rich and powerful, but it epitomizes a universal human condition. We all live to some degree in a fantasy world created by our ego and buttressed by our separation in time and space from the effects of what we do. The fact that our fantasies are a poor match with reality remains hidden from us. We are almost always forced to act on the basis of partial knowledge and have to fill in the blanks with our own hopes and fears. As new stimulation captures our attention, we turn away from previous involvements and comfort ourselves that all is well, whether or not that is the case. But the awakening impulse that throbs in the human spirit directs us to open our eyes to the actual effects of what we do, to enlarge our vision from the circumscribed here and now toward the everywhere and always. Thinking globally involves time as well as space. For most of us, if we knew the impact of our actions on others, we would positively modify our behavior. One key role of a teacher is to redirect our attention to that which we have been too blind to realize.

Kings, queens, princes, and princesses live in a guarded world where they are shielded from reality. This is pictorially communicated most famously by the story of Prince Siddhartha in his palace. He lived in ease and splendor, while his subjects suffered manifold privations, partly to support his lifestyle. Only when he sneaked out in the dead of night and began mingling with his subjects did the veil fall from his eyes. What he saw shocked him into a dedicated search for the meaning of life, and what he found eventually transformed him into the Buddha, the awakened one. He was the exception and therefore our inspiration. The blind king Dhritarashtra, on the other hand, never tried to escape from his predicament, as it was far too lucrative and comfortable. He personifies all the habitual character traits we need to overcome in order to see clearly. If there is an enemy in this story, he is it, and he is us.

VERSE 2

SANJAYA SAID:
ON SEEING THE ARMY OF THE
PANDAVAS IN BATTLE ARRAY,
PRINCE DURYODHANA, HAVING
APPROACHED HIS TEACHER,
THEN GAVE UTTERANCE TO THE
FOLLOWING SPEECH:

Although he appears in it only occasionally, Sanjaya is the third character in the Gita, dominated as it is by the dialogue between Guru Krishna and his disciple Arjuna. It is said that God has given him the boon of being able to see everything that transpires on the battlefield. This is nothing more than a poetic way of empowering him as the narrator by the author, Vyasa. A narrator must be able to describe events and conversations at a distance and hence must "see" much more than any ordinary person could.

Throughout the epic of the Mahabharata, the stories are related by a third party witness to someone else, and that narrative technique is followed here as well, with Sanjaya reporting the tale to Dhritarashtra. Whoever inserted the Gita within the epic expertly deployed its format to maintain continuity.

Religious-minded readers often think, "Oh, God is so great! He makes a man able to see everything everywhere!" Next comes the argument with a skeptical person who doesn't believe there ever has been such a fellow. As with most fundamentalist issues, it's completely irrelevant. The point is solely that Sanjaya is the narrator of this story. False arguments leading up blind alleys are to be dismissed whenever encountered, as one bedrock tactic of the spiritual search. We have much better places to put our energies.

Duryodhana is the son of King Dhritarashtra and is the leader of the Kaurava side. Prince Duryodhana's teacher referred to in this verse is Drona, who taught everyone present on both sides the art of war. Addressing this teacher of skill in conflict at the outset properly sets the stage for this archetypal drama, reenacted repeatedly throughout human history.

In our day, unfortunately, soldiers do not study peace, and therefore peace is no longer the goal of war. Perhaps it seldom was. If the resolution of actual military battles was its actual subject, the Gita would be obsolete. But the truth of the matter is that it deals with the individual's relationship to life, and the extended metaphor of the battlefield proves extremely apt as the vision of the work unfolds. As long as we have problems to solve, the Gita's insights will never be out of date.

In a sense we are all schooled in the art of warfare, having been taught to stay on guard, defend our turf, compete. We have learned an overarching orientation to conflict with our fellows. It should come as no surprise that we find ourselves time and again on a field of battle ready to let the arrows fly.

Modern psychology terms the girding of ourselves with mental armor as our defenses. Defenses not only offer protection, they also trap us inside them. They can easily become habitual features, taking away our freedom of movement. So we must be very clear about what we are walling in or walling out.

This is a good time to relate another symbolic event that took place the day before the battle. Over the course of the epic, the Kauravas have seized the entire kingdom. Caught up in their obsession with domination, they didn't want to leave the Pandavas even enough earth to stand on. The Pandavas had made concession after concession, but the usurpers' desire for more was never quelled. At last they found themselves with no choice but to stand their ground, because there was nowhere left to go.

Krishna had been trying to intercede to stop the war, but his every offer was rejected by the aggressors. Just as happens today, they were determined to fight no matter what, cocksure of victory, and peace talks were just part of the maneuvering for a more advantageous position.

Duryodhana, leader of the Kaurava army, decided to go see what help he could get from Krishna. When he arrived at his room, he found him resting on his bed, asleep. Being an arrogant king, he wasn't going to stand humbly by waiting on anybody, so he pulled a chair next to the head of the bed and sat down.

Arjuna also thought of going to his friend Krishna for a final consultation before the war. When he found Krishna asleep, he humbly made his way to the foot of the bed and stood there. Their relative positions emphasized the hauteur of the king and the respectful deference of Arjuna.

When Krishna awoke he was naturally looking at his feet and so saw Arjuna first. When he greeted him, Duryodhana became furious and demanded that he speak to him instead, since his rank was higher. Krishna determined that they both sought his help, so he made them an offer: they could either have all his troops and horses, chariots and weapons, or they could have him alone, unarmed and pledged to peace. In other words, they could choose either his material or spiritual aspect.

The Kaurava king thought that just having an unarmed man was useless. Focused on tangibles, he couldn't grasp that Krishna was the Absolute incarnate. Weapons and armies are what counted to him. He greedily took the hardware. Arjuna, by contrast, picked Krishna solely for his own sake.

The entire scene is a beautiful allegory for materialism versus spirituality. Krishna is a symbol of the fecund, all-embracing Absolute, generously supporting everyone in the way they find most suitable. Some choose wealth and solidity, sneering at those who find solace in poetry, music, love or any other immaterial substance. Others don't see much value in piling up their treasures where moths and rust can get at them. The companionship of the Absolute means more to them than all the opulence and power in the world. These are the two sides that are at odds on the battlefield of life, in an unending clash of values. One side takes whatever it can grab and the other gives ground, until some cosmic blast of fate turns the tables.

VERSE 3

O TEACHER, LOOK AT THIS GRAND
ARMY OF THE SONS OF PANDU,
MARSHALED BY YOUR TALENTED
PUPIL, THE SON OF DRUPADA.

As narrated by Sanjaya, Duryodhana will reel off the war's preeminent participants through the eighth verse and describe the setting for several more. While striking the modern reader as nothing more than a meaningless list of names, to those familiar with the Mahabharata epic it is the equivalent of an overture to a grand opera, building tension and expectations even before the curtain goes up.

It is important to keep in mind that we are entering a profound psychodrama here. The actual war scene is receding into the background, as the personal factor moves to center stage. We are going to explore humanity's—and our own—perennial quest for understanding from here on.

Arjuna's impending battle could be described in terms of limitation versus liberty. The Kauravas collectively represent the binding forces of conditioning, and the Pandavas the liberating forces of freedom. To be utterly honest, though, both sides have constricting and expanding elements in them. Each warrior mentioned in Duryodhana's list stands for one of these forces, and a lengthy study could be made of their symbolism. To avoid getting bogged down with this, it is sufficient to make a few general comments.

Most crucially, the realization propounded by the Gita is going to transcend the very categories of good and bad. Arjuna will be led to a neutral, balanced vision, where he "will be liberated from the bonds of action, whether its results are good or evil" (IX:28). Unlike many scriptures, the Gita's goal is not to accumulate good (or merit) and minimize the bad but to achieve a balanced state of mind that is superior to both. That's what yoga is, in fact: a dialectical synthesis of opposites. The inherent tragedy of fighting for good is that good and evil are actually two sides of the same coin, so if you amplify one you simultaneously energize the other. Well-intentioned people battle against evil, inwardly as well as outwardly, not realizing they are making it stronger by doing so. This paradox has confounded humans since the dawn of time, but its resolution will be revealed as we proceed. There is nothing simple about it, however. Arjuna has a lot to learn before he will properly grasp this.

The throng of warriors surrounding Arjuna reminds us we are bound in many different ways. We have physical limitations, psychological conditionings, social constraints, and the workings of fate, the "slings and arrows of outrageous fortune," all conspiring to knock us off course. Most of our limitations have their pluses and minuses, and sorting them out streamlines our existence, promoting expertise in our undertakings. Let's take a brief look at each of these four broad categories.

The way we are physically constructed necessarily limits our options. Humans can do many things very well with our bodies, but we can't fly or stay underwater for long. We have to breathe air and consume food and water. So our physical structure is both helpful and unhelpful, carrying us forward while also demanding a lot of care and attention.

The psychological unfolding of life, with its rewards, punishments, and traumas, causes certain possibilities to become available and others to be voided. Each time we make a decision we open up some potentials and close off others. To the extent we are caught in a flow of inevitability we are bound to make certain choices, which may or may not be in anyone's best interests. Since psychological factors are probably the most important shapers of our destiny, dedication to rectifying our decision-making process is central to a spiritual search. Our available options have many implications, so we need to be as aware of them as humanly possible to avoid becoming snarled in necessity.

The type of social setup we are born into forces us to either put up with numerous strictures or fight against them; either way we are helpless pawns in someone else's game. Curiously, those "someone elses" were themselves pawns in their predecessor's games, who were pawns of their predecessors in turn, regressing ad infinitum into the past. Who will dare to bring intelligence to bear on the age-old conventions that bind us, often reinforced as they are by being attributed to God?

Lastly, we live in a historical setting over which we have little or no influence, yet we ignore it at our peril. Modern people prefer the term "luck" over "fate," but it's the same thing. We tend to imagine that the way things are at the moment is normal and eternal, but with a small amount of contemplative distance it is easy to see that this is not the case. We are all swimming in a powerful tide, yet we are content to remain unaware of it most of the time. This can lead us into dangerous waters.

The Kauravas represent the rules and regulations of the social world, embodied in family members, teachers, and spiritual preceptors. On the more evil end of the spectrum they are people who manipulate others for their own benefit and who are greedy and selfish. On the positive side, they act with admirable, though narrow, aims.

The Pandavas are also family members, teachers, and preceptors. They bind with good intentions, and such bindings are often more difficult to extricate ourselves from than the obviously negative ones. They exhort us to do things "for our own good." We learn to behave socially because some recognized authority or parental figure promotes it. Schoolteachers help us to fit in to the current static image of society by citing lofty ideals. Someone we love may have their heart broken if we choose to deviate from their favored outlook, so to be considerate of them we comply. The bottom line is we are entangled in both good and evil obligations, divested of our individuality and freedom, and made to act helplessly in response to outside forces.

Arjuna, bound by all of these factors, is now caught in the ultimate trap to which they lead: full-scale war. Although there are fates worse than death, war is the vehement unleashing of extinction, threatening the ultimate eradication of our personal freedom. Soon Arjuna will be chafing at both his good and bad constraints, seeking to distance himself from them so he can become empowered as a free individual. We are invited to join him in his transformation from a hapless victim of circumstances into a liberated being empowered to forge his own way.

HERE ARE HEROES, MIGHTY ARCHERS, EQUAL IN BATTLE TO BHIMA AND ARJUNA, YUYUDHANA, VIRATA, AND DRUPADA, OF THE GREAT CHARIOTS.

Yes, those heroic binding forces are our "equals in battle" all right! Often they are our betters, able to defeat us handily. If we believe we can ignore them and they will just go away, they have won. That's because they don't surrender on their own: they lie hidden underground and grow even stronger.

Archers have always symbolized concentrated determination to achieve a goal, and an arrow of intention striking the target dead center is the ideal result. Curiously the word *sin* comes from the same imagery and means "missing the mark." The most essential prerequisite for a spiritual search is a burning desire to cast off our fetters so we can explore the unknown and discover its significance. A lukewarm attitude is likely to allow us to drift into trouble, possibly as an unwitting pawn of a charlatan or demagogue.

The first step to take in the thousand-mile journey of spiritual transformation, then, is to recognize the oppressive elements that have brought us to the moment when we can no longer bear to remain in their clutches. Surging through us are the urgent voices of all our caregivers and teachers, which, as unformed beings, we have relinquished our sovereignty to. At some point we realize we have vacated our true calling, our dharma, at their behest. We begin the process of self-renewal by deciding to reclaim our integrity as a legitimate participant in our world. We must seek out our authentic "still small voice" within the cacophony of competing shouts for our attention and help it to grow.

This is just what Arjuna will soon be doing. He will step into the no-man's-land between the armies to take stock of all the factors that are engulfing him: the dear friends, teachers, and family members that have brought him to his seemingly inescapable predicament. Just like Arjuna, at some point we must face up to the realization that the beliefs we once accepted without question have got to be carefully scrutinized and all that is false in them rejected. Otherwise we will never recover.

DHRISHTAKETU, CHEKITANA,
AND THE VALIANT KING OF KASI,
PURUJIT AND KUNTIBHOJA, AND
THAT BULL AMONG MEN, SAIBYA.

THE HEROIC YUDHAMANYU, AND
THE BRAVE UTTAMAUJAS, THE SON
OF SUBHADRA, AND THE SONS OF
DRAUPADI, ALL OF GREAT CHARIOTS.

Our blind spots are literally a "cast of thousands," as they used to say of old movies. The most oppressive to our psyche are the authority figures, the prominent men and women we cede our decision-making power to. We casually surrender our individuality to these outside entities, because everyone else does. But the Absolute has only one route into our psyche: from the inside, and it becomes ineffectual when we look to others for our cues to act. Another giant step toward maturity is to recognize that everyone is as ignorant as we are, and their authority is nothing more than a fragile construct held up by mutual consent, and not due to divine dispensation, as they might like you to believe.

Verses 4–6 list the warriors on Arjuna's side, which from Duryodhana's viewpoint are the enemy, and afterward he will list a few of his own. From a spiritual perspective, both friends and foes can be equally binding, or for that matter, liberating, if they goad us to a breakthrough. These forces are like a blindfold we wear throughout our life, ceding authority to others who also wear blindfolds. If we start to remove the blindfold, we will quickly learn just how complicated and clingy it is, and how much the "well adjusted" blindfold wearers resent us making the attempt.

BUT KNOW WHO ARE THE MOST DISTINGUISHED AMONG US, O BEST OF THE TWICE-BORN, THE LEADERS OF MY ARMY; THESE I TELL YOU, FOR YOU TO RECOGNIZE BY NAME:

Sanjaya the narrator is still describing the scene to the blind king Dhritarashtra, but remember that here he's telling him about what Duryodhana is saying to his teacher Drona. The previous list of names represented the "good guys," the Pandavas, and now he names the key "bad guys," but of course he's seeing it the other way round. As already noted, both sides create bondage. As will soon become apparent, Arjuna has been forced by his social role into such a lethal position of immobility that he is beginning to question his basic assumptions, which are symbolized by these people.

In most cases I have used the given name for the characters and omitted the descriptive terms that frequently occur in the Gita, such as Partha for Arjuna and Bhagavan for Krishna. Often these are mainly to keep the meter, which is eight syllables per line, with an occasional poetic outburst of eleven per line. But here we may get a whiff of ironic wit on the part of Vyasa, which has tempted me to leave "O Best of the Twice-born" alone. "Twice-born" describes a member of the brahmin caste, and it carries roughly the same implication as "Born-again"

Christian. A holier-than-thou attitude is typical of such types, and of course having degrees of holiness is an absurdity in the context of absolutist wisdom, in which all beings without exception are equally holy. Drona, a brahmin, is indeed an excellent teacher, but he basically stays within conventional bounds. At this juncture he has cast his lot with the Kauravas, the oppressors. As the Gita is aimed at having us throw off all oppressions, including caste and religious conformity, we may perhaps detect a derisive smile from Vyasa behind what would ordinarily be a merely polite form of address.

YOU AND BHISHMA, AND KARNA,
AND ALSO KRIPA, THE VICTOR IN
WAR, ASVATTHAMA AND VIKARNA,
AND ALSO THE SON OF SOMADATTA,

AND MANY OTHER HEROES WHO
ARE WILLING TO DIE FOR ME,
WHO HAVE VARIOUS MISSILES AND
WEAPONS, ALL SKILLED IN WARFARE.

The Kaurava side is caught in the egotistical myopia of gauging every-thing in terms of its own interests. All those heroes are prepared to die for a cause, and the cause is "what I want." Remember that back in the very first verse, Dhritarashtra asked about "my people." The Gita is going to direct us to transcend our petty interests and think in global or universal terms. The planarian perception that what immediately appeals to "me" is the sole criterion needed is about to give way to an appeal to higher reasoning. The law of the jungle is to be transformed by a seeker of truth into the kind of compassionate and thoughtful behavior often described as spiritual.

Children begin their conscious social development thinking in terms of "I," "me," and "mine," but after a growth struggle of many years some of them become adults who can think in terms of "we" and "ours." Unfortunately, very many stay stuck in selfishness, and true adulthood is rare. Being concerned with yourself doesn't seem too heinous at first blush, but it can be manipulated into dangerous states of mind all too easily. Arjuna finds himself being drawn in to just such a conundrum, in which the "blood-dimmed tide is loosed, and everywhere the ceremony of innocence is drowned" in the famous words of W. B. Yeats. Author Vyasa knows this well, as indicated by his telling us that the Kaurava strongmen are willing and even eager to die for their leader.

Possibly the most contrary state of mind to the nature of a human being, testifying to a lifetime of trauma, is a willingness to die for a cause. History is filled with churning hordes who believe their death in battle will bring about some utopian state but who are in actuality nothing more than tools of power-crazed leaders. If they learn their lesson in time and decide to live for a cause instead of dying for it, they are simply replaced by the next youthful hothead. Psychologist Alice Miller attributes this warping of normal intelligent sensibility to strict upbringing. If you are taught to obey your parents unquestioningly, it is easy to be made to obey your leaders, political or religious, in the same manner. Where your parents may well have your best interests in mind, few leaders do. The Gita is a powerful antidote to this mentality, passionately urging us to reclaim our integrity without abandoning our quest for justice.

Sadly, most of us learn early on to be "skilled in warfare," in our dealings with other people, first coming to conceive of them as enemies, then firing verbal missiles to destroy their positions, sniping at them, laying booby traps and mining pathways, taking pride in undermining the opposition in any way we can, most often with words but also with deeds when they are deemed necessary for conquest. It takes someone like a yogi to rise above the fray, converting it into a civilized discourse based on mutual concern and respect.

VERSE 10

THAT ARMY OF OURS WHICH IS UNDER THE CARE OF BHISHMA IS INSUFFICIENT, BUT THIS ARMY OF THEIRS WHICH IS UNDER THE CARE OF BHIMA IS ADEQUATE.

Here is the first strong indicator of the true profundity of the Gita's wisdom. For some reason, the much more powerful army is described as *insufficient*, while the weaker one is *adequate*. (The Sanskrit root is identical, even though Nataraja Guru has shaded the translation to heighten the contrast.) It echoes Arjuna's earlier choice of an unarmed Krishna over all his armaments.

One idea that has been grasped by some commentators is that the Kaurava army represents the relativist, partisan orientation, which is inadequate or "insufficient," while the Pandava army represents righteous, absolute values, which in the matter of justice are sufficient or "adequate." This is undoubtedly correct. The whole underpinning of justice is that it is based on universal norms rather than partisan whims. A mere selfish opinion or preference is not adequate, but a well-thought-out system embracing as many aspects of the situation as can be included does indeed measure up. The rule of kings and dictators is ever the former, while constitutional law attempts to fulfill the latter. But laws can never perfectly embody absolutist wisdom, which has to adapt itself to every circumstance. Arjuna, on his own, will soon be seeking—and finding—this elusive goal of humanity.

Some commentators have reversed the adjectives, because they couldn't fathom why a vastly stronger army would be less adequate. It's because the true field of battle here is the psyche, not the physical world of war. In spiritual life at least, might does not make right. A nonmaterial factor accounts for the difference. In this the Pandavas are far ahead.

A similar distinction of adequate/inadequate may be observed between verifiable scientific facts and wishful thinking. A corporation may hire mercenary scientists and mount an advertising blitz to support its contention that logging a forest is the best way to preserve it, but the facts cannot be denied that what replaces the forest is another entity entirely, namely a tree farm, or perhaps a desert. Or it may be claimed that unhealthy food is good for you, but the doctor's bill will have to be paid despite the claim. So the Gita's assertion that absolute wisdom trumps relativistic knowledge is of paramount importance. It is crucial that each of us distinguishes one from the other and steers our way by the light of truth rather than by closing our eyes tightly and going on faith in our acquired (or supplied) prejudices.

There is a second level here which is less obvious. Almost all of us start out as children who are subject to the dictates of an adult world. Over and over our impulses and ideas are squelched in favor of what our parents, teachers, and religious leaders tell us is "right," and we learn to doubt ourselves. We come to believe that what we think—what we *are*—is somehow flawed, but those who tell us what to do are so clearly full of confidence and certainty themselves, we are sure they must be in possession of superior knowledge. Children cannot distinguish that this is a charade. There are many strategies to cope with this frustrating and humiliating state of affairs, but most children adopt the attitude that they are wrong and the grown-up world is right, because it evades the issue rather neatly. The only problem is that it isn't true.

Thus we enter adulthood wearing a straitjacket: the belief that we are inadequate but all the seemingly well-adjusted people around us are adequate. Since these universal feelings are internalized and masked by bluster, we don't see that everyone has them. We become unsure of ourselves and readily grant those who pretend to be sure of themselves authority over us. By doing so we lose the full humanity that Arjuna is going to reclaim during the course of Krishna's upcoming instruction.

All you Arjunas, look around and know that everyone is in the same predicament as you. We are all in this together. The Gita sweetly sings this song throughout, and it will lift your hearts if you can but hear it.

VERSE 11

AND SO LET ALL OF YOU, STANDING IN YOUR RESPECTIVE POSITIONS AT THE ENTRANCE TO EVERY FORMATION, KEEP GUARD ON BHISHMA.

Bhishma is the old Kuru patriarch mentioned in the next verse. He is singled out as representing the highest achievement of the old order, the religious meritocracy featuring celibacy and purity. The Gita intends to dispense with all merit-based religious thinking, which is dualistic at its core. Here the oppressing forces are directed to protect the old order at all costs.

Because the army of relativity is inadequate, everyone must be on guard! Since its position is false, it may fail at any moment. This is the position of the fearful. You are inadequate. You don't know where you stand. If your leader is lost, you are nothing. Your psychic castle is built on sand, and the tide is coming in.

When your position has been gained by treachery, there is no guarantee that it won't be taken away by treachery. You must mistrust everyone, take nothing for granted. Your days are consumed in anxiety and the struggle to maintain your perch. What a miserable way to live!

The spiritual message is to look into our soul and see where we have posted guards and grant them a furlough. We will be moving toward an unguarded state of openness as we go forward.

SO AS TO CHEER HIM,
THE MIGHTY OLD KURU
PATRIARCH ROARED LOUDLY
LIKE A LION AND
BLEW A CONCH.

Bhishma is the patriarch referred to, leader of the Kauravas on the battlefield. There is a modern phrase for what he does: blowing your own horn, or simply, boasting. What's more, a lion has ever been the symbol of pride. In ordinary life, each participant in a conflict puts forth their own point of view, loudly and forcefully. According to the Gita, this is exactly the way to become mired in a disaster. Extrication can only come by embracing the whole picture through a yogic or dialectic synthesis, and humility is an essential ingredient of the open attitude that makes this possible.

When you are fearful and confused, it is a relief to join forces with a group or gang that promises a protective fraternity. Then the leader sounds the call to battle, and you rally to his side, ready to do his bidding. Nowadays we speak of things like waving the flag instead of sounding the conch, but the idea is the same. In this way, in place of allegiance to the unlimited Absolute we become partisans of nations, religions, tribes, towns, or families. Any limitation on the extent of our identification with the whole brings about a limitation of justice and is therefore a basis of conflict. The Gita is going to counsel the abandonment of all limitations, but in order to do this we have to know what they are first. Right now we stand with Arjuna in the midst of them, and the pressure is building fast.

VERSE 13

THEN CONCHES AND DRUMS AND GONGS, (OTHER) DRUMS, AND HORNS, WERE PLAYED TOGETHER SUDDENLY, AND THAT SOUND MADE A CONFUSED CLANG.

The blast of noise roars out to begin the battle. Its horrible, mind-numbing clang epitomizes the relativist side of the war, symbolized by the Kauravas, and their braying battle instruments are still metaphorically echoing down through the ages to our time. Everyone shouting in favor of their own selfish interests is a recipe for social chaos and collapse. After a few brief forays into civil communication as a species, we are back to living in yet another time when bellowing as loudly as possible from permanently entrenched positions is the mark of public discourse.

Common complaints about the Gita include that it takes place in the middle of a war, and therefore advocates fighting, and so is just about male problems. While historically actual war is mainly a "guy thing," conflict is the lot of everyone. The battle here is symbolic of the painful dilemmas and paradoxes we are doomed to confront no matter what our gender. For example, in divorces both men and women suffer. Girls are hurt by the pains of adolescence possibly even more than boys. Childbirth has even been used as a prime example of necessary, inevitable action. Most importantly, mental distress knows no boundaries based on gender. It is not helpful to imagine that women are nothing more than innocent victims of male derangement. While men tend to be more outwardly aggressive than women, all of us are confronted by both inner and outer challenges and need to learn how to cope with them. The noisy chaos presented here is an apt image for the spiritual struggles we all too often find ourselves in.

To be honest, conflict may be a necessary stimulus to our spiritual growth. Most of us enjoy routines and can easily become content with comfortable habits. Until we learn to make progress without the goading of uncertainties and threats, we will continue to experience them. The universe seems to want us to evolve and encourages it in whatever way works. But fighting is not the way to make progress, and Arjuna knows this. He desperately wants to find an alternative.

Although the literal setting is all male at this moment, if we can accept its archetypal symbolism as universal it will be supremely educational. Whoever we are and whatever our problems, the Gita provides a general template to assist us in meeting every challenge. Our job as astute readers is to tailor the teachings to our own conditions by transposing the terms.

VERSE 14

THEN STANDING IN THEIR GREAT CHARIOT, TO WHICH WHITE HORSES WERE YOKED, KRISHNA AND ARJUNA TOGETHER BLEW THEIR DIVINE CONCHES.

Yes, there is also a divine or spiritual point of view, which, while in outward appearance no different from any other, can lead us to freedom rather than bondage. Such is the Aum-like song of the divine conch, sounded in tune by the guru and disciple who are about to take center stage.

Touchingly, the two protagonists blow their horns together first, symbolizing the unity of their endeavor. Then in the next few verses they will be joined by a "roll-call" of the righteous, the Pandavas.

Arjuna is by no means the nonconformist hippie type we associate with spaced-out spirituality. In the Mahabharata epic he is a straight arrow, sincerely pious, and obedient to society's beliefs. He is thus a typical human being, albeit with well-developed skills in the art of warfare. By using him as the archetypal disciple, the Gita is demonstrating how ordinary attitudes, when carried to their logical extreme, lead to the very conflicts that require extraordinary solutions. They bring us to a dead end, from which the only escape is transcendence and the only help available comes in the form of a special teacher or guru. By singling out Arjuna, there is a clear implication that the path being presented is open to all. No one needs any special qualification to learn wisdom, only an attitude of dedication.

It is nearly impossible to not think of Arjuna as a soldier participating in a war taking place long ago and far away. But that should be kept in the background. There is no doubt that Arjuna is meant to represent you, the reader. If you do not identify with him or his problems, the profundity of the work will be vitiated to a significant extent. So ask yourself, what are the conflicts and paradoxes you face? Are you willing to meet them, or are you trying to ignore them? Do you know how to resolve them satisfactorily? You can always translate the Gita's terms to fit your own dilemmas.

KRISHNA BLEW PANCHAJANYA, AND ARJUNA BLEW DEVADATTA. HE OF WOLF-LIKE APPETITE AND DEEDS OF ENORMITY (BHIMA) BLEW HIS GREAT CONCH, PAUNDRA.

Notice that the forces of bondage all conspire together, blowing their horns in a blaring cacophony, but the forces of liberation weigh in independently. It's a sweet touch. Even right at the beginning of the Gita a subtle symbolism is apparent. The way the conches are blown implies that upright individuals are the ideal, while mob behavior— even "respectable" mob behavior, a.k.a. society—is degrading. Societal madness is a *collective* psychosis; the cure is individual enlightenment.

In *The Wisdom of Crowds*, James Surowiecki explains the quasi-mystical decision-making power of independent individuals, as opposed to groups that are swayed by peer pressure. The former routinely out-perform the latter in measurable ways:

> Diversity and independence are important because the best collective decisions are the product of disagreement and contest, not consensus and compromise. An intelligent group, especially when confronted with cognition problems, does not ask its members to modify their positions in order to let the group reach a decision everyone can be

happy with. Instead, it figures out how to use mechanisms—like market prices, or intelligent voting systems—to aggregate and produce collective judgments that represent not what any one person in the group thinks but rather, in some sense, what they all think. *Paradoxically, the best way for a group to be smart is for each person in it to think and act as independently as possible.*[2] (emphasis mine)

We should keep this in mind throughout our Gita study, which is a handbook of individual empowerment, with little or no concession to social demands. What the rishis realized, and scientists are coming to appreciate, is that agreement is overrated. Certitude must be found within, in our connection with the Absolute, while the false certitude we experience from going along with others is likely to usher us into a fool's paradise.

Independence is often characterized as pure selfishness by unreflective people, but they are not the same thing. A truly independent person is unselfish, always taking into account as much as possible of every reasonable perspective. Selfishness—raised to an incontrovertible virtue in the modern political miasma—is inimical to independent and dependent people alike, because it degrades everything. It blocks out way too much important information to form the basis of sound judgment. By contrast, generosity and unselfishness, intelligently exercised, are much more inclusive. By aiming for universal benefit they contribute to the betterment of everyone.

The Gita focuses almost exclusively on the development of independence through freedom from all conditionings, and so it appears to be highly antisocial. There is only the barest implication that the hard won independence of a disciple, product of an intense period of study under an uncompromising yet compassionate guru, is to be applied to the social realm. But that is precisely where it *is* exercised. No one is totally free of interactions with their fellow humans, and most of us are deeply dependent on the entire web of human commerce. And yet we must learn independence not only for our own happiness but, as Surowiecki so ably demonstrates, for the happiness and well-being of all.

VERSE 16

PRINCE YUDHISHTHIRA, SON OF KUNTI, BLEW ANANTAVIJAYA, AND NAKULA AND SAHADEVA (BLEW TOGETHER) THE SUGHOSHA AND MANIPUSHPAKA.

After Krishna and Arjuna, we meet Arjuna's four brothers: Bhima, Yudhishthira, and the twins Nakula and Sahadeva. Notice that each blows his horn in the order of his spiritual importance—Prince Yudhishthira is only fourth. Though as the eldest he is politically pre-eminent, the Gita ranks him after guru and disciple and second-eldest, Bhima, who was a truly extraordinary being, more like a force of nature. Graded series will be found throughout the Gita, usually with the most valuable quality first.

As far as we are concerned, there is no point in introducing all the characters mentioned in the first chapter, since they will all be quickly swept into the background, leaving only Arjuna and Krishna in their guru-disciple dialogue, along with Sanjaya the narrator. If you read the Mahabharata epic you can get to know all these interesting people at that time.

AND THE KING OF KASI, EXCELLENT
BOWMAN, SIKHANDIN, GREAT
CHARIOTEER, DHRISHTADYUMNA
AND VIRATA AND THE
UNCONQUERED SATYAKI,

DRUPADA, AND THE SONS OF
DRAUPADI, O LORD OF THE EARTH,
AND THE SON OF SUBHADRA, OF
MIGHTY ARMS—FROM ALL SIDES
EACH BLEW HIS CONCH SEPARATELY.

In case we haven't quite caught on yet, the Gita now makes it more explicit: the absolutist side is made up of free individuals, therefore each blows his conch separately, though harmoniously, like a symphony orchestra. Earlier the relativist gang of thugs expressed themselves in a confused blast of party loyalty, without coherence, but here we find personal dignity and integrity highlighted.

In the Gita we are in the presence of a sublime masterpiece, with nearly every word freighted with significance. The "Lord of the Earth" is Dhritarashtra and is an epithet that shows the limitations of Arjuna's assailants. Their interests are in worldly matters only, whereas he is about to begin a search for higher values. Material goals are no longer enough, as Arjuna will soon state quite definitely. Nor is Arjuna aiming to become a Lord of Heaven, in direct opposition to outright materialism. He will become a yogi, meaning he will treat earth and heaven as two poles of a dialectic, which he will unite in a synthesis that reveals the Absolute in all its transcendent grandeur. In plain words, humans require both physical and spiritual nourishment to thrive.

VERSE 19

THAT LOUD BLAST, FILLING EARTH AND SKY WITH SOUND, PIERCED THE HEARTS OF DHRITARASHTRA'S SONS.

We have more subtle hints of yoga here, with the Absolutist blast filling both earth and heaven, synthesizing the dialectic. The clarion call of freedom reaches far beyond the limited world of selfish interests and is the weapon by which the Pandava side launches their attack. It goes to the heart, uplifting instead of destroying. This type of warfare was echoed by the flower children of the mid-twentieth century, who placed flowers into the barrels of the rifles being brandished in their faces.

Psychotherapist Thomas Moore, in his excellent book *Care of the Soul,* writes, "It takes a broad vision to know that a piece of the sky and a chunk of the earth lie lodged in the heart of every human being, and if we are going to care for that heart we will have to know the sky and earth as well as human behavior."[3]

VERSE 20

THEN, BEHOLDING THE SONS
OF DHRITARASHTRA STANDING
MARSHALED IN ORDER, WHILE
THE FLIGHT OF ARROWS WAS
BEGINNING, ARJUNA, THE SON OF
PANDU, OF MONKEY ENSIGN, TOOK
UP HIS BOW;

The opening drum roll has built to its peak, and the curtain now rises on Act One, where Arjuna steps to the center of the action. He takes up his bow, symbolizing his intention, not so much to fight but to come to grips with the situation. Before long he will be overwhelmed with doubt and sorrow, causing him to lose his grip on the bow and drop it, and he will not take it up again until the very end of the final chapter of the Gita as a whole. He has an awful lot to learn in his transition from a disappointed socialized being to an enlightened and independent soul.

The arrows filling the air symbolize projections of particularized points of view. Everyone is putting in their opinion, offering advice, pressing for their side to prevail. This familiar and ordinary tumult has now escalated to a lethal degree. On the battlefield of life, arrows of selfishness are zinging around all the time, from every direction. When they strike home, they wound you, they draw blood.

Jungian psychologist Marion Woodman made some relevant comments about arrows in an interview by James Kullander, in *The Sun* magazine:

> WOODMAN: Personal growth and spiritual development are based on honesty and integrity, and it's only in intimate relationships that real honesty and integrity surface. Life with an intimate partner is no bowl of cherries, and you've got to be strictly honest with each other and recognize your unconscious projections onto each other and deal with them. If you don't, you drift apart.
>
> KULLANDER: What sort of "unconscious projections?"
>
> WOODMAN: Say, for example, something about the other person really annoys you. That annoying quality likely also exists in you, but you don't know it, so you attack the other person for it. The quality that you hate in the other person is also something that you hate about yourself. That's a negative projection. A positive projection can be something you admire in another person but unconsciously devalue in your own life. There are even qualities in others that we hate and admire at the same time. Whenever we refuse to accept something as a part of us, we project that something onto others. A projection is like an arrow that flies out of your unconscious and finds its mark in someone out there.[4]

AND, O KING, HE SPOKE THUS TO KRISHNA: O ACYUTA! STOP MY CHARIOT RIGHT IN THE MIDDLE BETWEEN THE TWO ARMIES,

Arjuna and Krishna are very old friends, but their relationship is about to grow into one of the deepest possible: that of guru and disciple. Discipleship involves an intense determination to release your conditioned mindset in order to discover your actual nature beneath its camouflage of borrowed behavioral clothing, and its course is filled with many ups and downs. Conditioning does not surrender without a fight.

Right here, Arjuna has done something amazing: he has found the correct place for a seeker of truth, right in the middle between the warring factions. The importance of this positioning cannot be overstressed. Contrast it with verse 2, where Duryodhana is looking strictly from his own side, which gives him a selfishly skewed viewpoint. Arjuna wants to be in the best place for a global perspective, where the most intelligent decisions can be made. He has overcome his natural affinity to his group so he can judge the conflict without prejudice.

If you want to have substantive, positive change, you have to pull your "chariot" (or whatever you're riding on) into the middle of the action and calmly study both (or all) points of view. If you're attached to one side or the other you won't be able to do this. In the search for truth you cannot be partisan. Similarly, looking on from a remote location as an "armchair philosopher" or "detached observer" is not helpful. Nataraja Guru used to say, "Armchair philosophy bakes no bread." Detachment usually fails in this respect. You have to be in the thick of the action, or your reactions become abstracted and distant, and consequently less transformative. Finding the neutral position in the center means you are still engaged, even though you are detached from partiality or prejudice.

Positioning the chariot in the middle is a pictogram of dialectics or yoga, which the Gita will present in detail throughout its course. One great secret it espouses is that the Absolute is revealed by the yogic or dialectic balancing of the poles in any and every situation. An honest yogic appraisal requires your side and your opponent's side to be treated neutrally, given equal weight. When we retain our affiliation with our side, even if we strive for evenhandedness, our view is inevitably tilted toward our own team. Importantly, our team includes "I" and its assessment of the "Other." Any emotional coloration prejudices the process even further. A wise referee or guru is invaluable at this point, because they can see what we are blind to. Only when a true picture emerges from the chaos can an effective act of yogic harmonization occur. The inwardly or outwardly guided seeker must find the position of neutrality equidistant from the extremes and harmonize all the elements. Accomplishing this extricates them from their conditioning to reveal the optimal perspective of a judicious overview.

A good example of yoga dialectics as it relates to public affairs is in terms of the degree of independence in our lives. We begin our sojourn on Earth as totally dependent beings, and our early adjustments are mainly to incorporate the directives of others—parents, teachers, and government officials like police officers—into our programs. When Arjuna steps into the no-man's-land between the contending armies, these are who he sees all around him. What is taught to children is usually done with the best of intentions, but the result is a person who has had to abandon their free will in deference to very rigid social norms.

At some stage of a healthy life, usually around the mid-teens, the developing person feels a powerful need to be more independent, to find out who they really are, and to become more "themselves." They feel strong desires to do things that are not permitted or not polite. Quite properly and logically, the first steps in the direction of independence are to reject the innumerable dependencies that they have relied on up till then. Rebellion is a kind of visceral rejection of the bondage experienced by awareness of our prior conditioning. But it is still based on, and therefore controlled by, the rules and regulations of society. Rebellion produces a false sense of freedom that comes from the relief we feel from throwing off the chains of ordered existence, but it is still dependent on those chains for its impetus.

Advertisers and entertainment corporations play to this imaginary freedom and sense of relief, finding it incredibly lucrative to fuel antisocial fantasies. As a side benefit, the rebellious become tamed by watching televised images of rebellion as a polite substitute for actual rebellion. That way you don't rock the boat!

Most of society is made up of these two types, those who advocate a "return to traditional values" or "the good old days," who insist that "being good and behaving yourself" is the key to heaven, and those who scorn such childish attitudes, who experience the thrill of being "bad" once in awhile, sneer at others' conformity, and so on.

Philosophic types find that both these attitudes have their limitations. A yogic thinker steps back and embraces both, thus being able to see the pluses and minuses of each, as well as to experience a state of neutrality that is the true ground of freedom. From this contemplative state unbounded action can arise in a natural and unforced way. All that rebellious or conformist energy can be put to much better use in a dedicated search for our lost authenticity.

As already noted, the lion's share of the Gita is aimed at achieving this state of neutrality or balance between contending factors. Don't despair if you are somewhat confused about these ideas here at the outset, because we still have a lot of ground to cover. Best of all, "Even a little of such a way of life saves one from great apprehension," as II:40 puts it. That means we will benefit very quickly from the efforts we make, as long as they are well directed. It's just that the Gita's philosophy can't be compressed into a few slogans. We have to really think about it.

VERSE 22

SO THAT I MAY BEHOLD THESE STANDING EAGER TO FIGHT BY MY SIDE IN THE PRESENT BATTLE-UNDERTAKING,

Arjuna stands out in the open, sizing up his side in this verse and his antagonists in the next. This is not a wise strategy for an actual battle-field. It's easy to imagine that Arjuna and Krishna would be instantly annihilated if this was about real warfare. The Gita can only be speaking of a metaphorical or metaphysical conflict. As the sage Ramakrishna advised, loving everyone and everything doesn't mean we should kiss the hissing cobra. Appropriate, intelligently directed action is called for at all times in the external world.

But while not realistic in the literal sense, figuratively this is exactly what has to happen. We have to surrender our fortified outpost and move to a place where we can take in the entire field. We have to shed our defenses and permit ourselves to be vulnerable.

In particular this movement to the center is essential for a proper relationship with a guru, or for that matter in any kind of intimacy. Even as we recognize their superiority, if we treat the teacher or friend as being "other" than us, it sets up a disruptive state where we remain somewhat guarded and closed off to their influence. The process of gaining and giving trust allows for a closeness in which the inculcation of wisdom (or affection) can successfully take place.

The hard-earned trust between Krishna and Arjuna is a prerequisite of Arjuna's transcendental vision of the Absolute that is depicted in chapter XI.

Yoga is also applicable to very practical matters. Take the case of relationship problems with a spouse or other close friend, for instance. Your friend has become the "enemy" side, at least temporarily. You are obviously identified with "your" side. The fight will only escalate when one side is pitted against the other, even if both are trying to move toward an armistice. If you can step into the middle of the field, you have a vantage point between your positions, from where you can scrutinize both sides with an air of detachment. You concede that the other person's position has value, even though you still may not agree with it. By being acknowledged, your dear friend feels invited to be less defensive and make their own positive gesture, and healing may begin. Within the pain of ruptured friendship, simply moving to neutral ground is a heroic accomplishment, and a lot of the preliminary work in yoga is to learn how to get there, as it is the only place where a balanced perspective can be obtained.

It may be that your significant other is still in the wrong, but in any case you will see their side in a new light. And it is virtually certain that you share part of the blame for the blowup, skirmish, or battle between you. When we defend our side we automatically make ourselves blind to our own faults and exaggerate the other person's. From a neutral post we can honestly begin to admit our own faults. And it goes without saying that you can only lay out an intelligent course of action if you have an accurate idea of everyone's feelings and vested interests.

It's not that this technique is "only" about relational psychology, and spirituality is something different and more spectacular. The Gita's vision of spirituality is to work with intelligent expertise right within the transactional frame of reference. It is very practical and not pie-in-the-sky, intangible hocus-pocus. Wisdom is not to be divorced from action; it only counts when it is applied to something significant. The relationship between wisdom and action will be explored in depth, particularly in the third and fourth chapters of the Gita, but for now we can see that Arjuna, representing all of us, is embroiled in a dilemma so real that his very life is at stake.

AND MIGHT OBSERVE THOSE HERE GATHERED TOGETHER WHO DESIRE TO PLEASE IN WAR THE EVIL-MINDED SON OF DHRITARASHTRA.

Down through the ages Arjuna has been reviled by commentators as a cowardly loser, a warrior who has lost his nerve, primarily a hapless foil for Krishna's teachings. This completely misses one of the most important themes of the Gita: that he is a model seeker who epitomizes what the role of a disciple requires. These commentators have missed the boat because they are intent on having Arjuna return to his prescribed duties as a social being. It reveals their own veiled attachment to the status quo that undermines their appreciation of the Gita's message.

Guru and disciple mark the two ends of a continuum, a dialectical polarity defining the highest arc of evolution humans are capable of. Both poles are equally necessary for wisdom transmission to take place. The role of a worthy disciple is to be skeptical and ask probing questions, to which the wise guru provides original answers to clarify issues and allay doubts. Guru and disciple are thus equal partners in the learning process, the former striving to express truth in ever more suitable terms, while the latter works equally diligently to bring the words to life in their own being. A mutual transformation takes place in the process wherein the disciple becomes conjoined with the guru in a bond of perfect rapport that is the ideal learning situation.

Arjuna's willingness to go straight to the middle and examine both sides of the conflict reveals his extraordinary degree of preparation for the upcoming evolutionary leap. He is in fact the best possible candidate for wisdom in the entire field. Everyone else remains attached to their allotted role, but he no longer believes in his prescribed duty. The time is ripe for Arjuna to leave his expectations behind. Again, it is not a weakness but a strength that there is no happy path for him in this field of conflict. The utter dead end he will soon see on all sides leaves him no other option than to mentally prostrate at the feet of a liberated being. Such an act not only produces a true disciple, in a sense it creates the guru as well. In this celestial dance the disciple must take the initiative and make the first move, which Arjuna routinely does throughout the Gita. The gesture is always mirrored by a response from the universe at large, in the form of a compassionate teacher.

Guru Nitya Chaitanya Yati describes the initiation of a disciple (*diksha* in Sanskrit) in his commentary on Patanjali's Yoga Sutras:

> The discipline called *diksha* is essentially to keep all four aspects of the individuated consciousness free from blemishes. The Sanskrit term *diksha* is very important because it suggests absolute bipolarity and continuing attention being given whole-heartedly to the persons, things, and events with which you are involved in the situation of your search. Only the most attentive can find his or her path inspiring. In such a discipline, you do not excuse yourself. Actually, initiation is from the side of the initiated rather than from the side of one who is initiating. The person who is seen to be ritualistically giving an initiation is at best only a witness. Absolute dedication has to come from the initiate.[5]

So the guru does not exactly initiate the disciple. The disciple is initiated by their own burning interest, their enthusiasm, after which the guru may acknowledge the fact with a ceremony of initiation.

Dejected apologists lament that Arjuna is abandoning his social duty, and they bend the meaning of the text so it appears that Krishna intends to restore him to that tightly circumscribed role. But the Gita is presenting the story of the rarest and most meaningful event in human life: the moment when a great soul begins to turn away from the bondage of ordinary duties and discover true freedom. In almost every case it is the reciprocal pair of guru and disciple that potentiates the quantum leap. For his part, Krishna is ecstatic that someone is at last willing to take the leap and will coax Arjuna though his learning curve with unmatched astuteness.

This is the Gita's primary teaching, inexplicably glossed over in virtually every commentary. When one has grown as far as one can in the ordinary course of life, it becomes necessary to expand one's consciousness to another level. The Gita is a training manual for how to effect the transformation. Whether the seeker thereafter returns to a mundane social role or not is a private decision between the indwelling Absolute and the transformed one, and this must not be determined by the demands of bystanders, lest the whole process turn out to be a snare and a delusion.

VERSE 24

SANJAYA SAID:

THUS ADDRESSED BY ARJUNA,
KRISHNA, HAVING STATIONED THAT
EXCELLENT CHARIOT RIGHT IN THE
MIDDLE BETWEEN THE TWO ARMIES,

Sanjaya has been speaking all along, but he is reintroduced here because we may have gotten mixed up by all the complex layers of the narrative. It's easy to do!

The "excellent chariot" of Arjuna underlines that he is a great seeker of truth, not some befuddled nincompoop. The guru moves with him to the middle of the scene, just as Arjuna requested, reminding us that it is the disciple who has to ask for aid and not the guru's role to offer it. Theirs are expert maneuvers, exactly right for the intricate interplay about to unfold between them.

Structurally speaking, the Kurukshetra or field of battle stands for the horizontal world of actuality, with the Pandavas ranged on the positive side and the Kauravas on the negative. We can be helped to understand the relationships involved here by envisioning two axes that bisect one another (like the x- and y-axes of the Cartesian coordinates). The horizontal axis can be seen as plus at its right hand end and minus at its left hand end. The lower end of the vertical axis is the alpha and the upper the omega. Arjuna detaches himself from his assigned place in the actual world and together with Krishna moves to the exact center, the point of symmetry and balance where horizontal and vertical meet. In a moment he will ask Krishna to become his guru. This deeply heartfelt action is symbolized by Arjuna making a symbolic ninety-degree turn from the horizontal to the vertical, bringing him to face Krishna. Then by recognizing Krishna's guruhood and requesting instruction, Arjuna moves himself to the vertical negative or alpha pole, while Krishna rises to the positive, omega pole. Within this perfect bipolar relationship, Arjuna reaches up as a seeker and Krishna showers down the grace of enlightenment, in the mystic marriage of guru and disciple.

FACING BHISHMA AND DRONA AND ALL THE RULERS OF THE EARTH, KRISHNA SAID: O ARJUNA! BEHOLD THESE KURUS GATHERED HERE.

Both sides taken together are the Kurus. Note that earlier Arjuna looked from one side to the other, but here Krishna indicates them together, as forming a single group. These are the before and after versions of the yogic vision. We start by assessing each separate element and striving to unite them, and we finish when we attain the cosmic view of universal oneness.

It is perfectly appropriate that at the outset the guru directs the disciple's attention to the whole panoply of existence, the entire field in all directions, preparatory to beginning the quest for independence from its undue influence. The Gita's way is inclusive and in no way escapist. If you are not willing to look at the total context, you are not ready to accept the complete honesty required for liberation. What you leave out of your philosophy will inevitably trip you up.

THEN ARJUNA SAW STANDING
FATHERS AS WELL AS
GRANDFATHERS, TEACHERS,
MATERNAL UNCLES, BROTHERS,
SONS, GRANDSONS, AND
COMPANIONS TOO.

Arjuna immediately does what Krishna asks of him, demonstrating his openness to the man whom he will soon ask to be his guru. Everywhere he looks he sees friends and relatives, which is the vision of an insightful person. Those caught in the web of actual events see the world as filled with hostile enemies and masses of indifferent souls, along with a handful of friends and allies. Only a philosopher with a neutral and unselfish outlook can perceive the unity beneath the chaos that makes the human race one huge family.

Arjuna is beginning to use dialectic thinking. As we've noted, our normal way of intellectualizing about situations is to identify with our own side and treat the other as separate. Linear thinking can embrace the dichotomy, but it doesn't truly resolve anything. That's because we're still visualizing it in terms of "I" and "You," or whatever the polarity is. The transformation comes when we realize we're already in the happy median, where "I" and the "Other" are aspects of the universal Self, albeit modestly delusional aspects from an absolutist perspective. The act of withdrawing from identification with the polarities and centering in the Self or Absolute is the essence of the yoga of the Gita. That's why Arjuna and Krishna actually go to the middle of the fray, rather than standing on their own side, safely behind a barrier, and trying to imagine the other side as equal in status. That would be the rational way. In yoga, you visualize all the aspects as being within yourself and draw them together, still within yourself. If this sounds confusing—and I'm sure it does—a lot more clarification lies ahead. Krishna is going to make sure we really get it.

It's relatively easy to accept the idea of unity, but it is very challenging to feel it as an undeniable truth of the heart. Even though he sees his connection to everyone on the battlefield with him, Arjuna remains confused. He still has to learn how to make the theory convincingly real, and that will take a lot of work, plus perhaps a touch of mystical good fortune.

For now, here are a couple of examples of yoga made practical. There is a continuum between the apparent opposites of light and dark. In pure darkness you can't see anything. Pure light is likewise so bright you can't distinguish anything. Only when there's a mixture of the two do objects become distinguishable. In one sense it's the dark (evil!) that makes us able to apprehend light. So we shouldn't lean one way or the other; what's called for is balance. This is true in physical as well as metaphysical situations. Consider also the binary computer. All information of one type of bit is no information at all. There has to be an alternation of on and off or yes and no to produce a meaningful stream of data.

AND UPON SEEING THESE RELATIVES, FATHERS-IN-LAW, AND FRIENDS, ALL STANDING, IN BOTH ARMIES,

Every person is born unlimited and a genius, barring physical damage during gestation, but over a lifetime we usually learn to think of ourselves in less than ideal terms. We begin to identify with an "I" that's limited with an endless string of conceptions. Negative identities include "I am stupid, incapable, ugly, frivolous, irrelevant." Positive identifications are limiting in the same way, although they do provide a broader canvas for expression: "I am desirable, clever, talented, friendly, better than others." Then we have family and tribal identities, "I am from the Smith-Jones-Teitsworth clan," "I am a white-black-red-yellow shade," "I am Spanish-Indian-Arab-Jewish"; and religious identities, "I am Zoroastrian-Sikh-Pantheist-Atheist"; and we identify with our gender and species: "I am female-male-transgendered," even "I am human." While there is a powerful attraction to these identifications, none of them is as unlimited as the Absolute, because they each have contrary positions such as "I am not a Sikh." So without denigrating any of these categories, when we seek our common ground in the Absolute we need to treat them as useful within the transactional world but inhibiting of the natural absolute freedom that is our birthright and philosophical lodestar.

We really *are* in this together. Somehow we are all cells in an ever-developing organism that mysteriously unites us for superconscious purposes. This is a yogically balanced view that includes everyone. And, contrary to the teachings of some exclusive religions, this Being grows through each and every individual expressing their uniqueness in new ways. The envelope of growth possibilities is especially stretched by those who dare to plunge into unknown territory. The Gita is extolling a creative approach to life, not self-extinction in the tried-and-true, in stepping in someone else's footprints. How boring to have everyone behaving the same way, following necrotic rules! What a dull world that would make for.

The *noosphere* is Teilhard de Chardin's word for the planet's zone of interconnected consciousness. It is light and flexible at its outer perimeter, propelled and enlarged by artists and lovers, thinkers and poets, but becomes denser and more static toward the center. Those who are afraid to do anything but what they're told form the stony core of this planetary being. Those filled with hate are crushed in the most lifeless places of all.

We move to the delightful periphery of the noosphere by embracing more and more of the light within everything around us, in other words, responding to the call of the spirit. But before doing that himself, Arjuna spends some time being overwhelmed by the tragic side of life. It's a legitimate place to start, and probably the most impelling.

One of the key distinguishing marks of a spiritually inclined person is that they care about their world and the people in it. The Gita makes this point by depicting Arjuna as supremely depressed by surveying the scene and seeing how everyone is out to rob, kill, and otherwise abuse each other. All those innately divine beings have so lost their self-awareness as to sink to the level of what he will soon describe as a marauding rabble. Given that kind of milieu, people either decide to become enthusiastic competitors in the melee, or they ponder how to break out of it and foster a change for the better. Sadly, by the Gita's reckoning not more than one in a thousand takes the latter vow and acts on it. Out of all the extraordinary people gathered on the Kurukshetra battlefield, Arjuna is the only soul courageous and insightful enough to turn away from the chaos and seek wisdom.

FILLED WITH A SUPREME PITY, IN
MENTAL DISTRESS, SAID:
BEHOLDING MY OWN PEOPLE, O
KRISHNA, STANDING TOGETHER,
WANTING TO FIGHT,

MY LIMBS FAIL AND MY MOUTH
DRIES UP, MY BODY TREMBLES AND
MY HAIR STANDS ON END,

(THE BOW) GANDIVA SLIPS FROM
MY HAND, MY SKIN FEELS AS IF
BURNING ALL OVER, I AM UNABLE
TO STAND, AND MY MIND IS
WHIRLING ROUND;

AND I SEE CONFLICTING PORTENTS,
O KRISHNA, NOR DO I FORESEE
GOOD FROM KILLING ONE'S OWN
PEOPLE IN BATTLE.

Up to this point in his life Arjuna has had full confidence in the beliefs instilled by his upbringing. Now that he is thrust into a real-life conflict, the paradoxes and inconsistencies of social dogmas are thrown into stark relief, and they no longer placate him. Make-believe arguments—even if they are wildly popular and form pillars of the society—don't hold up under close examination.

It is a familiar theme in spiritual life that we will adhere to our habits of thought as long as we can. Only when they really make us uncomfortable will we be motivated to change our lives. Shankara famously compared setting out on the spiritual path to the feelings of a fish in a pond that is drying up, or a deer caught in a forest fire. All you know is that you have to get the hell out of there!

Arjuna's distress is intensified by the illusions of his customary attitudes being stripped away, not only by the stark reality of his situation but by his willingness to look closely at it. This is the first prerequisite for spiritual growth. As Arjuna has just done, every seeker must abandon all their guarded positions, move to a neutral vantage point, and scrutinize the entire picture. From there they are free to go beyond what is visible to its invisible inner support system. Failure to take this step means we will stay bound to limited beliefs and chained to imaginary benefits such as merit, which lead to imaginary goals such as heaven. Krishna will disabuse Arjuna of those concepts very early in his training.

Again, we can think of everyday examples, such as when your dear spouse suddenly reveals that they no longer love you and are leaving for good or the job you excel at and count on for your daily bread is suddenly stripped away by a heartless decision in a distant boardroom. Arjuna's emotions are what any of us would naturally feel when the core assumptions of our very being are suddenly dissolved. It is a deeply shocking and painful confrontation, and like Arjuna in the coming verses, we naturally cast around for any interpretation that might offer us consolation. It is easy to take refuge in strange mental configurations when you are grasping at straws. Arjuna is fortunate to have a wise counselor by his side, to prevent him from jumping to tempting but false conclusions.

In the early stages of life, humans are taught by their caretakers to defer to various authorities. Parents and relatives initially dominate the decision-making process, but over time they relinquish the task of inculcating social beliefs more and more to church and school. Most of them do not even realize that that is what they're doing. They think they are simply helping us to fit in, which will make us safe and happy.

Because of our childhood reliance on all-powerful caretakers still lurking in the back of our mind, what we want more than anything is for a knight on a white charger to ride up and take command. Most religions satisfy the puerile desire to have someone else handle our decision making, and it can be a very profitable occupation. Governments tend to vie for this same power slot, which is why even dictators pay lip service to being caring and democratic. Separation of church and state was intended to dismantle the awesome power of their conjunction, since otherwise they would make *all* our decisions. (Oddly enough, religious zealots were the first to call for the divorce of politics and religion, which were historically wedded, whereas they now work tirelessly for a closer marriage.)

Once you begin to look for it, the "savior syndrome" can be seen everywhere, in westernized countries especially. It makes it seem that the only way out of the impossible predicaments we perennially find ourselves in is for some god or his chosen emissary to come down and set things to rights. The impact of such beliefs is to divest us of our faith in ourselves, in our own ability to accomplish difficult things. To put it plainly, it makes us impotent.

The Gita does not support this crippling power of external authority in any form, and it maintains we are the only legitimate upholders of our own lives. It was composed during one of the many periods of history when religious insiders were stifling and bleeding the populace. The Gita's thrust is always toward personal freedom and liberation and away from blind trust in fixed forms. Although in classic Indian fashion it posits a wise teacher to deliver its message, Krishna's prescription is to pull yourself together and make up your own mind, not simply do what you are told. Students are not expected to surrender their personal integrity to any outside agency.

The curious claim that schools train the young to think independently is understandable if we realize this actually means that they are being trained to correctly regurgitate preselected choices of "right" and "wrong." In a complicated world this is a huge project, since every possible contingency must have a memorized option available. Only after a person is thoroughly brainwashed can they be considered to properly "think for themselves." The process of successfully defeating and socializing an independently minded spark of the divine now takes twenty-five years or more.

Derrick Jensen has written eloquently about this. Here's a sample from *A Language Older Than Words:*

> I've since come to understand the reason school lasts thirteen years. It takes that long to sufficiently break a child's will. It is not easy to disconnect children's wills, to disconnect them from their own experiences of the world in preparation for the lives of painful employment they will have to endure. Less time wouldn't do it, and in fact, those who are especially slow go to college. For the exceedingly obstinate child there is graduate school.
>
> I have nothing against education; it's just that education . . . is not the primary function of schooling. . . .
>
> A primary purpose of school . . . is to lead us away from our own experience. The process of schooling does not give birth to human beings—as education should but never will so long as it springs from the collective consciousness of our culture—but instead it teaches us to value abstract rewards at the expense of our autonomy, curiosity, interior lives, and time. . . .
>
> Schooling as it presently exists, like science before it and religion before that, is necessary to the continuation of our culture and to

the spawning of a new species of human, ever more submissive to authority, ever more pliant, prepared . . . for the rest of their lives to toil, to propagate, to never make waves, and to live each day with never an original thought nor even a shred of hope.[6]

Jensen has endured shocks as intense as the one currently energizing Arjuna. Alternatively, human beings could operate much more openly with a small handful of commonsense principles, if society didn't fear unpredictability and joy quite so much. Free choice threatens the profitable immobility of the establishment.

This is why law books and rule books are ever-expanding, as a substitute for commonsense justice. In my own career as a firefighter, I observed this process first hand. The Standard Operating Procedures (SOPs) in use when I first hired on in the early 1970s were highly stretched to barely fill eighty pages in one small book. We were expected to grasp the basic principles and then use them in combination with our own intelligence to handle the welter of emergencies we would encounter during our careers. But soon managerial committees were formed to specify our actions in every possible type of incident. The human brain being what it is, each quantum leap in the SOP manual merely opened new cans of worms to be addressed by future committees. By the time I retired our operations manuals ran to thousands of densely packed pages, and even the authors were unsure about the contents. Of course, any failure to comply with any of it incurred a range of penalties as well. So this is the "blessing of education": to turn the free and happy planet into a nightmare world of misery filled with threats of punishment.

Thinking is pure pleasure when allowed free rein, and it is tormenting when constrained with anxiety-producing restrictions. It is no wonder, after a lifetime of stressful "education," laden with tests of the degree of its assimilation, that the confused and miserable result of the process finds great relief in abdicating their responsibility to others who are willing to "take the burden" on themselves. Religions have even been known to use this exact terminology.

A select few assimilate their own abdication of personal integrity so obediently that they become well adjusted to it. These are "the leaders of tomorrow" who will happily guide the next flock of lambs to the slaughter. Often these burden-takers manage to stay outside the rules they have foisted on others, as with sexually abusive celibate priests and law-breaking legislators. The drug police are often the very sources of contraband. And so it goes.

Despite its quiescent exterior, the modern world has become a vast sea of disconnected individuals either begging for help from those who appear confident or else seeking solace in whatever guise it most luridly presents itself. Unscrupulous people are waiting in the wings to offer false nostrums and simplistic solutions to whoever will buy them. The world economy is practically based on this, it is so widespread.

The difficult and isolating struggle to extricate ourselves from this miasma is what the Gita teaches: how to make our way back to ourselves as fully functioning, free individuals.

That "civilization" suffers war after war is just one of the disasters that emerges from our loss of integrity. We end up feeling that we are trying vainly to breathe life into the empty shell of an imaginary persona we have constructed to satisfy the demands of society. The gap between our true feelings and our learned "right" ones is the measure of modern humanity's schizophrenia. It is filled with empty pleasures, depression, and mental derangement. Vast quantities of drugs are required to stifle our innate passion for freedom and to breed compliance. Conversely, realigning ourself with our core nature resolves these problems in the same way that focusing the lens eliminates a blurred image in a camera or telescope.

The Gita is vividly depicting the gap between the unitive state and duality, which stops Arjuna in his tracks. His distress is by no means overstated. And like him, finding our way back to unity is the only struggle worthy of our efforts.

VERSE 32

I DO NOT WISH FOR VICTORY,
O KRISHNA, NOR KINGDOM,
NOR PLEASURES;
WHAT IS KINGDOM TO US,
WHAT ENJOYMENT,
OR EVEN LIFE?

As we've been noting, most people are more comfortable with guidance from without than freedom from within. Real independence requires constant scrutiny and open-minded consideration of circumstances. What passes for freedom is most often an ease and fluidity in accepting (or evading) dictated behaviors. Only when the "tried and true" leads us to a dead end do we begin to question it and seek alternatives. Until then we take the path of least resistance. Some "good citizens" would rather follow orders to bomb children than buck their early training in obedience and risk their position in the social order. Pyramidal management structures where all orders come from the top and are to be obeyed unquestioningly—characteristic of the military but also essential to many business models—reinforce the strictures, making independence virtually a vow of poverty and a guarantee of social ostracism.

Arjuna is intelligently renouncing the dog-eat-dog world of the rat race, demonstrating he is ready to learn higher spiritual values in place of struggling endlessly for material gains, which so often come at the expense of less well-connected rivals.

In the interpersonal context, defeating our enemy means driving away a friend with whom we are in conflict. Victory in the traditional sense is thus a total loss in the spiritual sense. Arjuna does not want to gain the whole world and in the process lose his own soul.

THEY FOR WHOSE SAKE KINGDOM,
ENJOYMENTS, AND PLEASURES
ARE DESIRED BY US, ARE
STANDING HERE IN BATTLE,
HAVING RENOUNCED THEIR
INTERESTS IN LIFE AND WEALTH:

TEACHERS, FATHERS, SONS, AND
ALSO GRANDFATHERS, MATERNAL
UNCLES, FATHERS-IN-LAW,
GRANDSONS, BROTHERS-IN-LAW,
AS WELL AS OTHER KINSMAN,

These verses voice a paradox from ancient times, when the actual interested parties did their own fighting. Nowadays war is more often fought by proxies with even less to gain and a lot more to lose from the outcome. Here Arjuna realizes that he is fighting for the benefit of the very people who have joined in the conflict and thus abandoned themselves to possible destruction. They seek constructive ends but use destructive means. Logically this is absurd, but such illogic continues to plague the human race to this day.

What Arjuna sees is ordinary people who have lost their decorum and been transformed by anger and greed into demons of destruction. The world of polite social nicety has changed into a steaming hotbed of hate. What is it about humans that we can so easily lose our heads? Arjuna is dismayed by the viciousness that has burst through the masks of propriety usually worn by everyone. We struggle to maintain a veneer of respectability, but underneath we are seething with paranoia and neediness. It doesn't take much stress to bring it out into the open.

Only if we step back and survey the whole scene, as Arjuna is doing at the moment, can we learn the lessons of the battles we fight in the course of our lives. Frequently we find that our own weaknesses and faults have led us directly into the crisis in which we find ourselves. Usually in the midst of routine we can readily ignore our shortcomings. Only when we are challenged by some seemingly hostile force, when we're "under fire," do they come to the fore. If we are prepared to stand our ground and not surrender to them, these are the moments we can consciously deal with them. The intensity of the conflict is instrumental in pressing us to overcome our ego defenses.

As Arjuna notices here, it's his own beloved friends and family that embody those apparently hostile forces. That means we should not simply dismiss them as alien to us, somebody else's problem. Very often the lessons we need to learn are played out with friends and associates in everyday interactions rather than with some obvious "enemy." They could well be treated positively as spiritual growth opportunities rather than as undeserved adversity.

At first, when our friends reveal our faults to us, we may try to bluff our way through with some aggressive bluster, not unlike the clangor of conches echoing over the Gita's field of battle. We are sure *we* don't have any faults; *they* do. Some of us never stop pretending we're blameless, and most of the rest succumb to the urge to withdraw. Once our ego is thwarted we initially feel an impulse to simply give up—abandon the field—and let the other side have its way. But it's a surreptitious ego tactic to preserve its pride, not the honorable retreat we prefer to imagine. Arjuna is voicing the same desire to abdicate the struggle in this section of verses. Yet ultimately, with Krishna's support, he will do the right thing and stand his ground. He will turn to his wise counselor and begin to work honestly and fearlessly on his impossible dilemma instead of retreating into ordinariness.

The Gita here underscores a crucial truth: when the course of our life leads us to a spiritual crisis, it is the greatest blessing disguised as opposition. Don't fight and don't run, but stand firmly on truth and learn. Face yourself honestly. Benign help is invariably nearby, ready to serve you. Its form may be hard to recognize, but it will be there.

THESE I DO NOT WANT TO KILL, THOUGH THEY KILL ME, O KRISHNA, NOT EVEN FOR THE SAKE OF DOMINION OVER THE THREE WORLDS—HOW THEN FOR THE SAKE OF THE EARTH?

The "three worlds" are earth, heaven, and in between, where humans live. This is Arjuna's cosmology, and it is a widely held belief even today. Now we might call them the physical, metaphysical, and intermediate realms, or life, death, and pleasure. Arjuna pleads that the war is only about earthy, material issues, which are of little import to him, certainly not worth killing over. He doesn't want dominion, or domination, over anyone or anything. Such an attitude represents an early but substantial stage of progress on the spiritual path, of beginning to dissociate oneself from the context of suffering. There is a real core of sanity and compassion in Arjuna's complaint.

Spiritual quickening notwithstanding, we can distinctly hear the note of despair here. Arjuna is in a lot of pain. He is willing to admit defeat and surrender without a fight. Slinking away may seem like an honorable way out, but our troubles follow us wherever we slink off to. We can let our spouse or friend go and insist we don't care any more, but the hole in our heart is not healed. Even if we take the enemy here as corporate greed, we must not compromise our principles in confronting it. If we combat evil with evil, we have already lost. History is replete with high-minded revolutions that were rapidly co-opted in this way to become the next wave of oppression.

At this early stage, Arjuna is struggling with renunciation, which is admirable, but his take on it is negative, which is not. Renunciation will be treated in depth toward the end of the Gita, where it is shown that it has to be exquisitely balanced. A positive or negative slant will contaminate the result, making it egotistical instead of pure. When we tell our dear friend "Okay, just go!" we don't really mean it, we really mean "Please stay!" Quitting is the ego's response and not the heart's. Over the course of the Gita, Arjuna will learn how to take Krishna's impending advice (in II:3) to "cast off this base faint-heartedness."

It's important to notice that in all of Arjuna's confusion, there is no reference to a controlling god who might take offense, and Krishna doesn't postulate one either. Their dialogue is grounded in practical matters free of theistic taint, something that is difficult for many people to appreciate. We are so immersed in cultures based on doing God's bidding we can scarcely conceive of what life would be like without a permeating sense of dread. "Remote control" is a primary idea that distorts the human thinking process, and it is undoubtedly this bias that most influences interpretations of the Gita.

HAVING KILLED THE SONS OF DHRITARASHTRA, WHAT DELIGHT CAN THERE BE FOR US? ONLY SIN WOULD COME TO US AFTER KILLING THIS MARAUDING RABBLE.

While apparently straightforward, there is a lot of subtle confusion evidenced in this verse. Arjuna is ostensibly renouncing his personal delight, and yet he justifies his attitude here based on that very value, since he is hoping that the mere avoidance of sin will lift him out of his miserable condition. He is beginning to suspect that his prescribed duty is not designed to produce delight but exists merely for others to use him as a tool for their benefit. Yet his inner urge is for happiness, spiritual satisfaction. If duty doesn't bring happiness, what does? He needs help in resolving this conflict. Furthermore, he has been inculcated with the unjustified belief that his actions accrue either future merit or demerit, the latter popularly known as sin. While actions definitely do have consequences, there is no celestial scorecard being logged toward a looming Day of Judgment. Krishna will disillusion him of this and many other erroneous beliefs early in his instruction.

Humans routinely make plausible excuses so that their personal feelings appear to be carefully reasoned out. Arjuna viscerally shrinks from the gruesome prospect of the battle but protests that he is simply avoiding sin. Who can argue with him? After all, isn't killing the worst of sins? When pared to its essential features, this is exactly the kind of excuse humans are always making to defend their egos. Sin is an incontestable idea to legitimize Arjuna's otherwise inexplicable behavior. The only problem is, from the standpoint of yoga it's a fictitious concept. Krishna will soon point this out.

As a proper guru, Krishna addresses sin in the Gita because his disciple specifically brings it up here. Since it is widely misunderstood, sin is an obsession for many people, and Arjuna is presenting it on everyone's behalf for correction. Gurus have to dispel all the darkness brought to their attention, and we will see how diligently Krishna answers every question Arjuna puts to him.

The Gita is dealing here with a key factor in the oppression of the human race. Arjuna has been taught to respect all the social strictures and rules of decorum and that it would be sinful to do away with them, since they have come from something like "God" and are divinely ordained. Societies have often enforced their more or less arbitrary systems with exhortations about hell worlds and sin, casting disobedience as an outrage against everything sacred and a guarantee of doom. The Gita, by contrast, considers socioreligious systems themselves to be stumbling blocks to wisdom and spiritual freedom, repeatedly advocating their ouster from the seeker's orientation. A wise person acts freely without any need for threats, and conversely, anyone who is driven to behave by threats is not wise.

Most commentators side with Arjuna's confusion in this matter and advocate proper path-following and rule-following behavior, revealing their lack of understanding of the Gita's radical outlook and furthering the very systematic imprisonment of the spirit the Gita aims to do away with.

AND SO WE OUGHT NOT TO KILL THE SONS OF DHRITARASHTRA, OUR RELATIONS; FOR HOW INDEED CAN WE BE HAPPY AFTER KILLING OUR OWN PEOPLE, O KRISHNA?

Arjuna has been taught that the way to happiness lies in venerating the social order, not abandoning it. He believes that salvation comes through following a well-defined pathway, that of orthodoxy, and he is still identified with it. But confronted as he is by stark reality, his fantasies no longer seem adequate. He needs to discard them and replace them with a more solid framework. It is doubts, much more than convictions, that lead intrepid souls to a search for truth.

In the literal story line we've been observing, Arjuna does not want to defeat his friends. He realizes that "beating" them means losing their love and possibly their very existence. The paradox clutches at his heart, because he is sure the path of happiness does not lie here. But where is it to be found?

In any case, Arjuna is clear that killing is not going to make him happy. This is a logical enough inference, but we will see over the next few verses how he goes from this point of universal agreement to some wildly bizarre assumptions. This is typical of humans. We start with reasonable ideas and don't notice when we move away from them into untenable waters, even when we drift far out to sea. The Gita will teach us how to recover our solid ground through diligent contemplation.

Nataraja Guru attributes Arjuna's exaggerated speculation to his relativistic stance, indicated by the phrase "our own people" here and in verse 28. Separating people into *his* and *not-his* is an illegitimate division. Absolutism holds to universal truth, while relativism or dualism can lead us far afield. Therefore yogis do not allow themselves to indulge in relativism. Nataraja Guru insists that:

> Contemplation is not different from commonsense in its keenness of the sense of the actual. Lazy indifference to actuality is not the kind of mysticism upheld in the Gita. [It] underlines the need for seeing things as they actually are before the contemplative life is recommended, so that no escapism may be implied in the teaching.[7]

Unlike Arjuna here, a yogi is not thrown off balance by circumstances, or is at least able to minimize their disturbance. If our happiness isn't dependent on external events, our sadness shouldn't be, either. A yogi remains the same, grounded in truth, no matter what happens. Even while laughing or crying about it, the yogi's core is not disturbed. This will be addressed in depth later in Arjuna's training.

For now we have to move away from the literal interpretation and penetrate to the symbolic meaning. In order to fully appreciate the Gita's teachings, we have to sense that there is an internalizing transition going on here. The focus is fading away from the actual battlefield and moving into the psychological realm. The menacing warriors become symbols of conscious limitations. Most importantly, killing them as people is changing over to killing them as elements of the psyche that inhibit full awareness. The semi-literal cover story becomes a figurative passion play. Nataraja Guru speaks of several curtains or filters that are progressively raised to reveal more and more subtle considerations. Only at the very end of the Gita will we return to the actual battlefield, where we can apply our newfound wisdom to every practical aspect of our life.

The "Sons of Dhritarashtra," then, represent the various conditionings and mental blocks creating mayhem in Arjuna's psyche, epitomized as *desire* in chapter III of the Gita. Knowing this, his question in this verse becomes, "How does happiness arise from wiping out the attractions and motivations I have been taught to yearn for and work toward?" In other words, if we turn away from the transactional realm we know so well, what will we find, and will it make us happy? Without a satisfactory answer to this initiating perplexity, a person has no incentive to enter a spiritual path.

The double entendre here about "killing our own people" is usually missed. Arjuna is having recourse to a guru who will most definitely tell him how happiness does come from "killing" the conditioning laid down in him by his own people. He will show him how it oppresses him and estranges him from his dharma, his authentic self. Arjuna is confused; Krishna is not.

Commentators who believe the killing advocated is of real people are also confused, and they have seriously damaged the Gita's reputation, converting a paean to peace, justice, and living with expertise into a call to slaughter. We will examine this fallacy in detail in a number of places. For now, suffice it to say the Gita advocates kindness to all beings, compassion and nonhurting, among other "wisdom virtues." It is really a shame that such an unparalleled masterpiece has been shunted to the sidelines by those who insist on a literal interpretation of its symbolic imagery.

VERSE 38

EVEN IF THEY, WHOSE MINDS ARE OVERPOWERED BY GREED, SEE NO WRONG IN THE DESTRUCTION OF FAMILY, AND NO CRIME IN TREACHERY TO FRIENDS,

Arjuna's complaint over the next seven verses is often taken as part of the Gita's gospel, but it is in fact his previously accepted unexamined position that will soon be subject to radical revision by the guru Krishna. We can see that Arjuna is cast as being subject to the representative prevailing beliefs of his time. Author Vyasa is basically saying "Here is an ordinary human, and here is what an ordinary human typically believes." Modern attitudes aren't much different than this: ancestor worship and divinity worship are the two main strands of religious beliefs of all times. Modern religions cherish their sacred history and immanent mysticism, while science bows to evolution and nature. We all take cognizance of the past and try to make sense of the present based on what we believe about it. It works adequately, until it bumps up against something that reveals its falsehood. Then we either change or struggle to accommodate the outdated explanation.

According to Vedanta, Arjuna's position is the anterior skeptic, that is, the doubter, the starting point of the investigation. The anterior skeptic asks why, and the preceptor offers clarification. Krishna will revise and reevaluate all of Arjuna's assumptions in several ways, with the intention of converting his disciple to a much more liberated viewpoint.

There is so much evidence in our present day of the destructive power of greed that it seems almost ludicrous to discuss it. The political cabals and giant corporate entities that dominate the Earth's power structures are currently rapt in a paroxysm of looting. They see no evil in what they do, because not only are corporations morally blind by law, the psychopaths who gravitate to power positions are neurologically incapable of distinguishing right from wrong. It appears that the entire world economy may well be shattered by unmitigated greed, which will truly be destructive of families and friends in the long run, just as Arjuna foresaw in his time, though on a more local scale.

Martial law and electronic surveillance of the populace is the logical outcome of the belief in social systems being more important than individual freedom. Human beings have a strong inclination toward repression and setting their power positions in stone, but unchecked power opens a Pandora's box of unintended consequences. Who will watch the watchers is a reasonable question.

Real freedom, certainly, is less about bodily movement than about freedom of thought. Free speech is merely a subset of freedom of thought. While paying lip service to freedom, political and religious leaders preach subservience to restrictive laws. Contrary to popular misconception, freedom produces artistic beauty in thought and deed; it is the conditioned and constrained soul that has to seek its outlets in crime. Unhappy people sometimes cast about for happiness through unhealthy and even execrable means.

All this we will delve into in due course. The important thing to keep in mind here is that Arjuna has gotten to the point in his development where commonly accepted beliefs are seen to be contradictory and even hypocritical. They can no longer satisfy him. He wonders where to turn, and miraculously there is a guru close at hand. The invisible hand of Providence is always ready to assist in the next stage of spiritual growth.

YET WHY SHOULD WE NOT LEARN TO TURN AWAY FROM THIS SIN— WE WHO DO SEE WRONG IN THE DESTRUCTION OF FAMILY?

A very subtle psychology is revealed by close examination of Arjuna's confusion. When we enter a crisis, we cling tenaciously to our models of truth regardless of their relevance. Since we're grasping at straws to ameliorate the danger, when the first straw breaks we flail around for another, and another, and another. As this section unfolds, Arjuna becomes increasingly desperate and melodramatic. He begins with the reasonable premise that the war will quite literally destroy his family, at least a significant part of it. Then step by step he uses ever more ridiculous arguments to prop up his house of cards.

Over the course of our lives we have become supported and cushioned by the myths of the society in which we live. Unable to stand up to rational examination, these are often enforced by threatening concepts like sin. As a child, when I asked my father why some arbitrary rule forbade my doing something, his answer was always "Because I said so!" If I didn't accept it, I would be smacked. The use of force precludes the need to understand, allowing unexamined beliefs to persist. The well-behaved child learns to self-censor its natural urge to question and grows up to be a supporter of the prevailing social climate.

Marital relations are likewise often based on mythical assumptions, and a delusional couple does not dare to probe too far into their beliefs, lest they discover they don't actually agree. They live in hope of the apple cart of mutual fantasy never being upset, and when it is they scramble to put it back together and reload it with all the old apples. Only the brave of heart can rejoice that their cart was bound to overturn, and now a new way is open to them. They leave their rotten apples for compost and look around for fresh produce.

On the literal level, there is a devilish paradox here. The enemy has been busily destroying Arjuna's family for a very long time, and his role is to defend it. Yet the prescribed way to defend it, war, will destroy even more of it. Obviously he needs to seek a new way to remedy matters. As do we.

IN THE DESTRUCTION OF FAMILY, THE IMMEMORIAL CLAN TRADITIONS PERISH, AND ON THE LOSS OF TRADITION THE WHOLE CLAN COMES UNDER THE SWAY OF LAWLESSNESS.

Here we encounter Arjuna's conservative streak. There is a widespread assumption even today that current social standards are rooted in traditions dating from the beginning of time. Even a casual perusal of history explodes this myth. The world and everyone in it experience continuous change and fluctuating circumstances. Fads come and go. The elders of the tribe aren't upholding immemorial tradition, only their preferred interpretation of it. The "good old days" never were what they claim. Nostalgia for an imaginary past is a sure sign, not that the past was so great, but that we are discontent with the present. And that's perfectly understandable, but there are far better things to do about it than try to reconstruct a vanished and imaginary historical period. We need to resurrect the present, not the past.

Anyone who has lived through an important moment of history knows how impossible it is to describe that moment accurately. Each person has a unique perspective on it, and the whole is vastly more than any fragmentary sum of parts. The victors write history, it is said. Whoever prevails in a conflict or is merely promoted by the communication media has their own description of events ratified by default. Admittedly, myths enshrining a particular interpretation of history have some value in maintaining social coherence, but they mainly serve to keep the weak subservient to the mythmakers. A spiritual seeker has to call all of them into question.

Behind these conservative attitudes is a lack of faith in the unitive principle of the Absolute as a source of inspiration and a guide for life's unfoldment. Creativity springs from the removal of inhibitions and restraints, which allows our inner resources to emerge from the depths. Ordinary conditioned responses to life's challenges act to close off these wellsprings. It's another frustrating paradox that the devout actively block out the divine impulse while piously praising it, substituting stereotyped imagery for living reality. Fledgling philosophers crave laws set in stone and learn to mistrust the dictates of the heart. The only article of faith necessary at the outset of a spiritual quest is that there is a guiding light within us that we are going to open our eyes to. It starts as a hypothesis, but one that is soon confirmed by experience. Or else a lucky accident like a near death encounter or a psychedelic trip reveals the living light right at the start.

Since humans value stability and dread change, tyrants have ever invoked "law and order" to rally the populace to their cause. Their egregious behavior is propped up by a widespread fear of lawlessness. We can either have a deranged leader, a blind king perhaps, or be hurled screaming into the void. "You're either with us or against us." Black-and-white belief systems leave no healthy option. It appears Arjuna has been conned by this sophistry, still flourishing in the modern world, but now he's beginning to wonder if its claims are valid or not. His reeling off the prevailing beliefs of his milieu will help the scales fall from his eyes as they prove untenable.

Contrary to Arjuna's fears, the aftermath of war appears to be the time when sanity is most likely to prevail in public affairs. International pacts—related to the Latin pax, or peace—succeed every bloodbath. The League of Nations was formed after World War I, the United Nations in the wake of World War II. Immediately after the Vietnam War, the last attempt to reign in the United States' secretive military-industrial complex brought legal restrictions that held up for a decade or two. Unfortunately, these cautious steps in the right direction seldom have a lasting impact. As long as citizens willingly surrender their independence to their leaders, this dismal state of affairs, where it takes a disaster to produce a faltering step in the right direction, will persist.

This pattern can be discerned in many places. Regarding marital relations, for instance, in the midst of a disadoption or breakup, everything appears to collapse. It can be painful in the extreme, but it is also liberating. When static forms fall apart it is a golden opportunity to permit regeneration, either with the old partner or a new one. Whatever the eventual outcome, this is the time for serious personal reassessment, perhaps along the lines of Krishna's yoga instruction, which will soon make its appearance.

WHEN WRONG WAYS PREVAIL,
O KRISHNA, THE WOMEN OF THE
FAMILY BECOME CORRUPT, AND
WHEN WOMEN BECOME CORRUPT,
MIXING OF CLANS ARISES.

Now Arjuna abandons all good sense. First he assumes that if his traditions are wiped away, their replacement will inevitably be terrible. This is a pure presumption, springing from his fear of the unknown. As noted above, traditions are created to support a static view of the present, usually benefiting the dominant interests, so they are often more a curse than a blessing. Breaking out of them allows more individual freedom, which leads to a healthier community.

Arjuna continues to struggle with his beliefs here, like a snake slowly shedding a skin that's too tight. He imagines that if women dare to marry out of their tribe, it is a form of corruption, even if there are no men from their own tribe left alive. He has been taught that the mixing of tribes is evil. The genetic facts that species are strengthened by diversity and weakened by inbreeding hasn't percolated into Arjuna's awareness yet. Worst of all, he blames women for all the corruption, even though the need for it was brought about by men in the first place.

Implicit as well is the outdated assumption that war is solely the domain of males. At the time of the battle of Kurukshetra, the tactic of civilians being legitimate targets in warfare was still two thousand years in the future. Women were thus left over after a war. They would either have to marry the victors or die, as they couldn't be permitted to live alone.

As a corrective, the Gita will proclaim a transcendent vision of the unity of the human species that has been echoed by generations of sages and recently become scientifically confirmed by the human genome project. The Gita definitively states (IX:32) that women and members of all levels of society, including the most humble, can attain realization of the highest truth, which acknowledges their equal status as infinitely capable beings.

We now know that humanity is a single "clan" or family descended from a common ancestor about fifty thousand years ago, though with plenty of superficial diversity due to local variations. Every war is thus a civil war. Nor is there necessarily any "corruption" of women possible, so long as they are given free choice in the matter. Mating across the entire spectrum is not only perfectly normal but healthy for many reasons. Provincial attitudes like the ones Arjuna is repeating have consigned women to second-class status for millennia, despite the Gita's sincere effort to end the problem.

We live in a time of a great "mixing of clans," where the branches of the human race are sharing their DNA far and wide. This can only benefit genetic diversity, producing new forms of genius along with fewer excuses for making out an enemy.

In this section, Vyasa is not presenting timeless truths to be upheld, but the foundation of sexism and provincialism prevailing in Arjuna's day. That most societies still suffer from these ills is partly due to inertia, but it must also be blamed on generations of commentators who used Arjuna's pleading to reinforce their delusory attitudes instead of following the Gita's advice and discarding them. Little wonder that "pundit" has become a derisive term, though it was not so originally.

VERSE 42

THIS MIXING LEADS (BOTH THE)
FAMILY AND THE DESTROYERS OF
THE FAMILY TO HELL, FOR THEIR
ANCESTORS FALL WHEN DEPRIVED
OF THEIR OFFERING OF RICE BALLS
AND WATER RITES.

Arjuna's religious training is increasingly shown to be absurd. We should be able to hear Vyasa laughing uproariously in the background. Oceans of ink have been spilled to justify such religious references, but the point is to make fun of these outmoded (even by 500 BCE) practices, not to support them. That modern humans cling to such absurdities is tragic and humorous at the same time. There is humor in the illusory fulfillment to be gotten from arbitrary beliefs, and the tragedy comes when such beliefs inevitably lead generation after generation into abject misery, by fostering misguided pursuits up to and including warfare.

The Gita does not support the idea of hell, beyond the negative effects of a person's actions. Its three worlds are heaven (or the beyond), earth, and in between. Heaven and hell are psychological states of existence in the present, not the future.

BY THESE MISDEEDS OF THE DESTROYERS OF FAMILIES, CAUSING INTERMIXTURE OF CLANS, THE IMMEMORIAL TRADITIONS OF CLAN AND FAMILY ARE DESTROYED.

Arjuna's desperation is reaching a peak, as he spirals down to the negative limit of psychic despair. He lashes out with ridiculous imaginings, which are—not coincidentally—the bedrock beliefs of his very conservative society. Author Vyasa is not just making fun of these notions, he is setting them up to be reassessed and revalued over the course of the Gita.

A prime example of the failure to understand that these verses express the uninstructed, confused attitude of upholders of caste and other destructive beliefs is found in Eric J. Sharpe's *A Universal Gita:*

> There are passages in the Gita which speak as clearly as one can imagine of the necessity of observing one's own specific caste duty. It is better to perform the duty of one's own caste badly than another's duty well. To confuse castes leads to the most horrendous consequences, even to the extent of women being debauched and the ancestors toppling out of heaven, deprived of their offerings of food and drink. . . . There can be no two opinions: the

Gita does indeed advocate caste and uphold the notion of caste law.[8]

Well, there *are* at least two opinions. With the exception of the second sentence in the above quote, which refers obliquely to two verses that appear in later chapters of the Gita (III:5 and XVIII:47), all these points are stated by Arjuna right here as a seeker who has come up against the limitations of the beliefs he was taught by his society. He is turning to Krishna to resolve these issues, and Krishna is going to—by sweeping them all away as relativistic drivel.

One can readily understand that at first blush these verses do appear to support Sharpe's opinion, which is very widely held. However, it is unconscionable that a commentator should fail to bring enough insight to the task as to see that the Gita clearly and unequivocally treats such beliefs as ignoble stumbling blocks to a proper philosophical orientation.

MEN OF FAMILIES WHOSE CLAN TRADITIONS ARE DESTROYED ARE DESTINED TO LIVE IN HELL—THUS WE HAVE HEARD.

By saying "thus we have heard," Arjuna makes it clear that the ideas he has been reeling off are all things he has been taught. He is questioning the value of his religious beliefs, as anyone should who is caught in a dire emergency. From here on he will couch his despair in more philosophic terms, which is a prerequisite for asking for the aid of a guru. First a seeker must realize that they are caught, which occasions a substantial degree of despair. Then they must assess their own limitations and the limits of what they have been taught. Only then are they fit to approach a guru for instruction.

Those whose lives have collapsed through divorce, bankruptcy, criminal activity, and the like are in a hellish condition, no doubt about it. The misery of their state is directly proportional to how hard they cling to the familiarity of the past. Life is forever opening up new venues, if we can but see them, but we perversely want to promulgate the old, even when it proves disastrous. If we cannot adapt to and even promote new circumstances, we will be consigned to live in the hell world of those whose hopes don't match their actualities. And no amount of wishful thinking is going to restore what has already passed away.

The key quality for excellence in a disciple is the ability to ask probing questions. In the Indian model, at least, the *sishya* or student is required to ask well-considered questions of the teacher. The teacher or guru is merged in contemplation of the Absolute and so only responds when a disciple draws them out. The image often invoked is of a milk-maid milking the great divine Cow that supplies all nourishment. You must pull on the udder to get the nourishing milk of wisdom. If you don't pull, the milk stays where it is, out of reach. Pondering deeply in order to come up with a germane question is the sacred duty of the sishya. Guru and sishya are therefore entwined in a dialectical, recipro-cal dance, and one is not superior to the other. Both are equally nour-ished in the process of question and answer. Arjuna is moving rapidly toward the moment when he will offer himself to Krishna as just such a seeker of truth. The "thus we have heard" also shows he is separat-ing himself from what he has been taught and is becoming prepared to learn intensely through alert questioning of his teacher.

ALAS! A GREAT SIN ARE WE ENGAGED IN COMMITTING IN ENDEAVORING TO KILL OUR OWN PEOPLE THROUGH GREED FOR THE PLEASURES OF KINGDOM!

Because Arjuna speaks of sin in his pained outburst, pundits through the ages have taught that the Gita treats sin as a great evil and something to be avoided. Later on, in chapter V, verse 15, Krishna says, "The all-pervading One takes cognizance neither of the sinful nor the meritorious actions of anyone," which should be taken as the Gita's final say in the matter. Of course, Arjuna is still correct that killing is evil, within the horizontal, social milieu in which he is presently bound, but Krishna is going to draw him out of the limited context to one that is infinitely vast and unlimited. Moral codes are only appropriate for social interactions. Arjuna's greatness has led him to need to incorporate the transcendental—here represented by the person of Krishna— into his world. As of yet he does not know how to infuse his present circumstances with a cosmic perspective. But with Krishna's help he will. For now, he is truly caught in the toils of necessity.

VERSE 46

IT WOULD BE BETTER FOR ME IF THE SONS OF DHRITARASHTRA, ARMS IN HAND, SHOULD KILL ME, UNARMED AND UNRESISTING, IN THE BATTLE.

The section bringing chapter I to a close presents a wonderful example of how rational, linear thinking can take the seeker far afield. Arjuna is now so confused he would rather die than act normally, even to defend his own life. It is crucial to remember that he began his train of reasoning from a shaky premise, which has now led him to all sorts of unwarranted conclusions. He based his ideas on unquestioned attitudes passed on to him by society, along with his direct perception of objects and actions. Such logical but futile thought patterns are plentiful in our day as well. They actually serve well enough in everyday, material matters but fall short in the domain of the mind and spirit, such as in contemplation, where we seek to rise above mundane considerations. The Gita will counter this ordinary and unexamined process with dialectical reasoning, which it sometimes calls yoga or else merely implies by the juxtaposition of opposites in the text. Where linear thinking can lead one astray, dialectics converges on a central truth value. Because Arjuna is evolving from an ordinary bumbling mortal into a contemplative seeker of truth, he is ready to incorporate this higher form of reasoning into his arsenal of mind-weapons. A full appreciation of yoga dialectics will emerge gradually from a study of the Gita as a whole.

SANJAYA SAID:
THUS HAVING SPOKEN IN THE
MIDST OF THE BATTLE, ARJUNA
SAT DOWN IN HIS CHARIOT SEAT,
CASTING AWAY HIS BOW AND
ARROW, HIS MIND OVERWHELMED
WITH SORROW.

Being moderately upset just won't launch you properly onto the spiritual path. Arjuna is now seriously miserable, which gives him the energy to break out of his dilemma. Symbolically he drops his weaponry, the tools of his trade, which he will equally symbolically pick back up at the end of the Gita, when he is ready to carry on with his life as a fully instructed disciple. A seeker must take a break from their routine—no matter what it is—in order to plumb the depths. The Bhagavad Gita is an eighteen-chapter lacuna in the epic Mahabharata, a break which transforms Arjuna from a seeker into a seer.

In summation, most people lose themselves in their allotted role in life. When asked "Who are you?" they answer "I'm a student," or a housewife or a middle executive or a bricklayer. They become intimately identified with their role. Only when the chips are down and the situation becomes charged with tension and unhappiness will they question this identification. It is important for us to discover that we are much more than what we do, what we enjoy, and even what we know.

Our first response to excessive stress is generally to want to get away from it. Arjuna contemplates a noble escape, desiring to become a religious renunciate. In our day the more usual options are to throw ourselves into work, be entertained, or use stress-relieving drugs. None of these is sufficient by itself to reveal the Absolute, the core truth of our inner being.

Whatever the chosen escape, Krishna will point out that it is dishonorable. It doesn't make the grade. The only valid option is to stand and face the music. While he appears to be exhorting Arjuna to literally fight in the next chapter, this is only because Arjuna is indeed a warrior in an actual war. It is not meant as an exhortation to fight per se, but only to do what is appropriate. Krishna first counsels action in tune with one's role in life. If that is not satisfactory—and for a sincere seeker it seldom is—then one should go beyond to become what the Gita sees as the optimal choice. It is unequivocally recommended at the end of chapter VI that Arjuna should become a yogi.

PART THREE

COMMENTARY ON
CHAPTER II

UNITIVE REASON
AND YOGA

CHAPTER I DEPICTED the epic context, a sea of humans caught in a fateful doom of their own making, with Arjuna and Krishna stepping to the exact center to search for a better outcome. Arjuna then described all the obligations and beliefs that repeatedly bring humanity to this terrible condition, but he could see no way out of it, and all he wanted was to get away. So far he has only treated Krishna as his friend and chariot driver, but soon he will ask him to teach him, to be his guru. Krishna is about to speak for the first time, testing Arjuna to see if he has what it takes to become a worthy disciple. With their mutual acceptance, the Gita begins its instruction in earnest.

Needless to say, the firm resolve Arjuna must take is meant to be ours too. The Gita is not intended for casual perusal. It is a full-fledged science of the Absolute, a textbook of the most practical wisdom, designed to lift seekers of truth out of their self-sabotaging morass of ordinary mentality. Of course, anyone can read it, but to gain the most benefit from it we need to really think about the ideas it teaches and then make them a part of our life. The commentary provided is not exclusive: it is one example of the kind of dedicated thinking that can be brought to bear, in what the Gita calls a wisdom sacrifice. It's actually fun and very rewarding.

Chapter II is split in half, with the first part covering the high points of Samkhyan philosophy and the second half introducing yoga. Samkhya refers to rationalism and linear thought, related to the transactional world. Yoga in the Gita is dialectic, multidimensional thought—what it calls well-founded reason—where all aspects of a situation are treated with equanimity. Rationalism is appropriate to ordinary activities; yoga dialectics is the path of spiritual penetration beyond the surface. That being said, a verse later in the Gita (V:4) conjoins both halves, claiming "That rationalism and yogic self-discipline are distinct, only children say, not the well informed; one well established in either one of them obtains the result of both." Notice they're not the same, only mutually complementary. The second chapter as a whole can thus be seen as a subtle exercise in dialectics.

SANJAYA SAID:

TO HIM WHO WAS THUS FILLED
WITH TENDERNESS, WHOSE EYES
WERE FILLED WITH TEARS, AND
AGITATED, AND WHO WAS IN
DISTRESS, KRISHNA SPOKE THESE
WORDS:

The narrator Sanjaya puts in a brief appearance here to tell us what would be unseemly for the participants themselves to mention. Arjuna is agitated and upset. Sanjaya lets us know that this is an outgrowth of his extreme tenderness. Arjuna is a kindly soul, and his heart is breaking for the tragic situation everyone around has become mired in, through failure to honor their natural state of divinity. In modern terms, they have become conditioned. Seeing how far humans fall below their full potential is very sad, and the humiliation and suffering it engenders is sadder still. Precisely because Arjuna cares so much and is willing to put his whole life on the line, Krishna will teach him how to regain his openness, his native intelligence. But first he has to sound him out as to whether his dedication goes beyond mere confusion to a real desire to discover the antidote.

VERSE 2

KRISHNA SAID:
IN THE MIDST OF THIS DIFFICULTY,
WHENCE COMES TO YOU THIS
DEJECTION TYPICAL OF NON-
ARYANS, HEAVEN-BARRING AND
DISREPUTABLE, O ARJUNA?

Almost every commentator misses the boat on this one, revealing their proreligious prejudice. Vedanta, the philosophy of the Gita, does not subscribe to the notion of heaven, nor does it give any importance to reputation. (Heaven is disdained as early as II:42, as we shall see, and often thereafter. An indifferent attitude to honor and disgrace is mentioned specifically in VI:7; XII:18–19; and XIV:25.) Notions of heaven and social repute are external values referring to religious and social stature and not part of *brahmavidya,* the science of the Absolute. This tells us that Krishna is not castigating Arjuna here; he is *teasing* him. It's as if he's saying "What's the matter Arjuna? Aren't your unquestioned beliefs supporting you now? Don't they hold up in the midst of conflict? No? Does that mean delusion isn't good enough for you any more?" Krishna is in fact *proud* of him and is preparing to pay him the ultimate homage by teaching him.

In order to be properly prepared to learn from a guru, the seeker must work free of the death-dealing arrows of religious and social conventions that fill the air around them.

Krishna's teasing has a methodological component as well. When a distraught seeker comes to a teacher, the first thing the teacher needs to ascertain is whether the student is only seeking solace, or is sincerely looking for intelligent liberation. The teacher may make some gentle, diversionary, possibly lightly mocking comments to assist in the determination. In response to such a test, Arjuna will state his case with philosophical exactitude, proving he is after more than a consoling pat on the back. Only then will Krishna see fit to instruct him.

There is another important clue that is often overlooked in this verse. The philosophy of the Gita harks back to the pre-Vedic wisdom of the ancient Indians, who were dark skinned. When the light-skinned Aryan immigrants entered India from the northwest, they pushed the Dravidian people into the far south and instigated the Vedic religion, which not surprisingly lodged them at the top of the hierarchy that replaced the more democratic spirituality of the ancients. Where the older style was directly experiential and unitive, the newer version was more contractual and dualistic: you do something and the gods (via their intermediaries on Earth) give you something in return. The history of religion is a cyclic rise and fall of powerful insiders intent on persecuting and marginalizing the mystics, those who insist on going beyond strictures and ideas to know truth directly. Needless to say, the Gita is a how-to manual for direct mystical experience, though over time orthodox thinkers have more or less successfully neutered its message.

Krishna happens to be black himself, which makes him a non-Aryan. The word *krishna* literally means "black." So Krishna calling Arjuna a non-Aryan is not a slight but a high compliment. He recognizes that Arjuna has transcended his Aryan genetics enough to long for trans-Aryan or universal wisdom.

VERSE 3

GIVE YOURSELF NOT TO IMPOTENCE, O ARJUNA, IT DOES NOT BEFIT YOU. CAST OFF THIS BASE FAINT-HEARTEDNESS. ARISE, O TERROR OF FOES!

Krishna lays it on a little thicker, exhorting Arjuna to be his old self, a brave, potent warrior. When Arjuna does not take the bait, it proves he is ready for instruction.

Commentators who take every utterance of the guru Krishna at face value are invariably led astray by these lines, straining to fit these orthodox Vedic (religious) values into the Gita's anti-Vedic philosophy. Krishna is essentially saying, "Don't you want to go back to being ordinary, by giving up your passing urge for wisdom instruction? That's the path of worldly glory." Arjuna will assure him there is no going back, once he has seen through the tawdriness of flimsy allures such as heaven and wealth.

Despite this, over the next few chapters there are echoes of this call to stand up and fight, letting us know that there is a significant issue at stake here. Very often we are paralyzed by an awareness of our own failings and limitations. By self-analysis we have to bravely face our faults and acknowledge the need to correct them. At first they can be so horrifying that they seem to disqualify us for any kind of spiritual stature, and they might even make us seem utterly unworthy as human beings. Such paralysis must be thrown off before we can go forward. We must proceed with awareness of our need for improvement, yet conscious as well that no one is perfect. Our limitations make us just like everyone else. All those saints we deify in our minds had to come to grips with similar faults before they could become great.

VERSE 4

ARJUNA SAID:
HOW COULD I ENCOUNTER WITH ARROWS IN BATTLE BHISHMA AND DRONA, WHO ARE WORTHY OF WORSHIP, O KRISHNA?

Bhishma and Drona are great teachers of both the Pandavas and Kauravas, now allied with the Kauravas in opposition to the Pandavas. They represent the highest aspects of worldly achievement. From another angle, Bhishma and Drona symbolize *vasanas* and *samskaras*. Bhishma represents the ancestors, in other words, the past. Vasanas are the seeds of the past, whether genetic or karmic. Drona stands for our mental conditioning, our samskaras. He is the teacher of the arts of war. In ordinary life, we learn tactics and strategies to wage conflicts to our advantage, which erects a thick barricade between our ego and everything outside of it. Samskaras and vasanas are the twin categories of oppression, factors that limit our freedom. They cannot be defeated head on in battle but must be transcended by the kind of yogic effort taught in the Gita as a whole. Arjuna quite rightly realizes that he cannot fight fire with fire, that he cannot sweep away his "enemies" by substituting new conditioning for the old, so he implores Krishna to help him out of his impossible conundrum. Krishna is happy to oblige. More on vasanas and samskaras is found throughout the Gita.

Arjuna is asking, How can I oppose these admirable values that everyone else respects? And not just how but why should I? He is feeling a last twinge of doubt about entering the very path he has chosen. It isn't unusual to shrink from our destiny at the very moment it beckons to us, like a bird who pauses before flying out of the open door of its cage. But "he who hesitates is lost." We have to take the plunge and without undue delay. Seen in this light, the repartee between guru and neophyte here is a masterful sketch of the subtle psychological interplay taking place.

Have you ever seen a dog on a leash being dragged along with all its feet anchored, whining and rolling its eyes in terror? Not likely. Most often, they strain forward with every atom of their being, blissfully investigating every nuance of their environment, wagging their tails in delight. Such is the proper attitude of a seeker of truth. Unfortunate conditioning may make us afraid to participate in this wondrous world in which we have taken up temporary abode, but when everything extraneous is subtracted through insightful contemplation, our innate eagerness is effortlessly restored. This is the conversion that Arjuna is requesting of his guru, and Krishna will be delighted to show him how to bring it about. Arjuna's dutiful role as decreed by the world has pinched him painfully, and now the only clothes that will fit comfortably are those perfectly tailored for him, his true dharma.

Arjuna also expresses a basic realization of the seeker here, that the world is worthy of worship. It is astoundingly beautiful and endlessly, artistically complex. He no longer has the slightest urge to damage it or disrupt its flow out of selfishness. Still, he has to resist its superficial allures to pave the way for deeper understanding.

VERSE 5

DESISTING FROM THE KILLING OF
THE GURUS, WHO ARE HIGHLY
HONORABLE, IT WOULD BE MORE
MERITORIOUS IN THIS WORLD EVEN
TO HAVE TO EAT OF A BEGGAR'S
PITTANCE. CHOOSING, ON THE
OTHER HAND, TO KILL THESE GURUS
AS FORTUNE-SEEKERS, I SHOULD BE
FEASTING EVEN HERE ON BLOOD-
STAINED BENEFITS OF LIFE.

Paraphrase: I can shirk my duty and accomplish nothing, or I can do my duty and commit a terrible crime. Neither option is acceptable.

In our inner reading of the meaning here, taking the fortune-seeking gurus as representing conditioning in the form of samskaras and vasanas, if Arjuna doesn't fight them but goes along with them, whatever he accomplishes is merely a mechanical product of his conditioning. Acting solely as a conditioned person is a living death. On the other hand, if he actively fights his conditioning, it is like ripping out the foundation of his external life. He will then have to substitute his conditioning with rational intentions, which is likewise fraught with peril, because rationality by itself leaves out many factors. Meekly following one's prescribed course of life or charting a course with too little information are the two paths available to almost everyone. These are inadequate to seekers of truth, and the Gita is going to show us a third way of transcendental liberation, one that charts its own course after accessing a holistic source of inner inspiration.

Arjuna is now expressing his difficulty accurately, without exaggeration, and he is demonstrating a dialectical or yogic balance in what he says. He is experiencing the dilemma of a philosopher/seeker, not a coward. Yet his dialectics are flawed, as shown by the negative results he foresees. Krishna will counterbalance this negativity with positivity in equal measure in verse 37 of this chapter.

Evidence that this section is of special value is found in the meter. Almost all of the Gita is phrased in four lines of eight syllables each (or two of sixteen). On rare occasions the meter expands to eleven beats per line. There are nineteen of these verses scattered around, plus thirty-six describing Arjuna's vision of the Cosmic Form in chapter XI, and they invariably highlight concepts of special note. The first four instances are verses 5–8 here, where Arjuna states his case clearly and requests discipleship of Krishna. Nataraja Guru calls the extended lines the exalted or rhapsodic meter, describing them in his introduction in this manner:

> The interludes interspersed here and there in the Gita in a metre and verse form more ample and elaborate than the rest, have a tone of exaltation and ecstasy which gives to the Gita that pure and time-honoured touch which reflects credit to the highest of hopes of which the human spirit is capable. Such interludes attain to the heights of a spiritual rhapsody which is rare in any literature.[1]

NEITHER IS IT CLEAR WHICH
WOULD BE OF GREATER ADVANTAGE
TO US: THAT WE WIN OR THAT THEY
WIN OVER US. THOSE VERY PERSONS
ARE STANDING RANGED BEFORE
US, THE SONS OF DHRITARASHTRA,
KILLING WHOM WE WOULD NO
LONGER WISH TO LIVE.

Arjuna demonstrates more dialectic insight here: he has examined the current dilemma from both horns, or both poles, and seen that it is not advantageous that either one prevail. He does not yet know how to attain a dynamic synthesis through yogic contemplation, but he knows he needs something more than ordinary logic affords.

Before approaching Krishna, Arjuna has carefully subtracted his personal feelings from the equation. This is necessary for a proper dialectic as well as philosophical basis from which to address the guru. The simplistic argument of many commentators that Arjuna should be taught to return to a positive state of combativeness undermines the Gita's elegant insight.

The Gita's response to aggression is not to fight back and not to give up and sneak away either. We are to stand grounded in our very nature, which is the Absolute, discard selfish motives and desired outcomes, and play the game expertly as it unfolds around us. To paraphrase the I Ching, "He who acts from these deep levels makes no mistakes."[2] Or as Nataraja Guru often put it, "Achieving the state of yogic balance reveals the Absolute."

VERSE 7

STRUCK DOWN BY THE EVIL OF
A TENDER DISPOSITION, WITH A
MIND CONFOUNDED IN REGARD TO
WHAT IS RIGHT TO DO, I ASK YOU:
THAT WHICH IS DEFINITELY MORE
MERITORIOUS DO INDICATE TO ME.
I AM YOUR DISCIPLE; DO DISCIPLINE
ME COMING THUS FOR REFUGE
TO YOU.

It is easy to get caught up in what Arjuna should actively do in this situation and believe that Krishna will show him unequivocally what he is called to perform. Few realize that Arjuna does do the correct thing at this juncture: he turns to a guru. This is precisely the right act at the moment when doubts overwhelm you, when social dictates no longer have meaning. Where the ordinary person would blindly stumble ahead or look for a hiding place, Arjuna has the wisdom to admit his limitations and ask for help. In defiance of our expectations, however, in the final analysis Krishna does not prescribe any activity for him, he teaches his disciple how to make his own wise decisions.

Suggestions to turn to a beacon of light when in distress are common to many religions, whose exemplars may be considered gurus—removers of darkness—in their own contexts. All agree that acting impetuously when in a confused state is a recipe for trouble.

We encounter here true surrender. Arjuna has determined that he is incapable of resolving his dilemma on his own, and he submits to one who he trusts implicitly and honors as a worthy teacher. He casts off the typical attitude of mediocre seekers, that they are superior to any teacher and are just sounding them out, merely testing their abilities. The ego tends to be convinced of its rightness no matter how much suffering it is undergoing and defends its position with skepticism and judgmentalism, imagining that these qualities will bring it solidity. Casting off all defensive maneuvers to open oneself to the teacher is the healthy version of surrender. At the same time, no groveling or exaggerated self-deprecation are involved, as they are simply the flip side of excessive pride. Imagining that God or guru is made larger by you becoming smaller is absurd, and it makes absorbing the teaching impossible. Arjuna must both surrender and still pay attention with every fiber of his being. Attaining such a neutral state is a significant achievement.

It seems a bit odd to classify tenderness or a tenderhearted disposition as evil. We usually think of it as merely soft and sentimental, and many commentators note how unwarriorlike those attitudes are. For those of us who are not warriors, however, soft heartedness and sentimentality, with their overtones of compassion and gentleness, are far from evil.

The word translated as "tender" here is *upahata,* which according to the Monier-Williams dictionary means "hit, hurt, damaged, injured, afflicted, pained, or infected"—not at all what we usually think of as tenderheartedness. This type of tenderness comes from sensitivity occasioned by previous psychological wounds. In modern terms we would call them "sore spots." Everyone accumulates sore spots in the course of their life, yet few are able to stand apart from their influence. We bend and warp the course of our life in order to avoid them and more particularly to protect them so others cannot touch or even see them.

This type of tenderness evokes past injuries and overlays their coloration on the present. It may be called evil to the extent that it interferes with a straightforward response to current circumstances. Too much sensitivity is therefore just as bad as too little. Guarding oneself makes it impossible to act impeccably. Once again, the fact that Arjuna recognizes this weakness in himself sets him apart as a most superior candidate for wisdom instruction. The vast majority of humans are unaware that they are guarding their tender places both from others and from themselves.

All of Arjuna's contacts with his family and friends that wounded him in the past have made him tender, too tender to know what to do in the present. His confusion arising from his wounded psyche and the impossible paradox before him brings him to the ultimate act of an individual, when he can at last intentionally and properly surrender to a guru. He suspects what the Gita holds to be true: that the full flood of absolutist wisdom alone can wash away such stains of the past, allowing proper attunement with the present.

It is absolutely essential for the disciple to request teaching from a guru. A teacher never wants to impose anything on anyone but stands always ready to respond appropriately. It may always be the case that the requester gets more than they bargained for, but the request is nevertheless necessary to initiate the process.

VERSE 8

I CANNOT VISUALIZE WHAT COULD
RID ME OF THIS DISTRESS WHICH
DRIES UP THE SENSES IN THIS
WAY—EVEN SHOULD (IT TRANSPIRE
THAT) I OBTAIN UNRIVALLED
DOMINION OF THE EARTH'S PLENTY
OR OVERLORDSHIP OF THE GODS IN
HEAVEN TOO.

It's absolutely true that piling up stuff is not a cure for mental confusion, but that is a prime fantasy that has become even more acute in the present day. "He who dies with the most toys, wins," is a familiar American motto. Arjuna clearly sees that distractions of any kind are simply sources of frustration, and he utterly rejects them. When a baby cries we can sometimes coax it to calmness with a glittering bauble or some bouncing, but that doesn't work with a battered adult psyche. Generations of humans have struggled to divert themselves with ever more complex toys, but their underlying malaise is not assuaged by them, only driven underground where it breeds inexplicable longings and depression.

Arjuna has exhausted every avenue he can conceive of. It would be unfair and selfish to ask a guru to teach the preliminary ideas any-one should find self-evident with a little contemplation or a trip to the library. At this point he has eliminated the beliefs of his social and religious upbringing and found that even his own intelligence still falls short when observing the matter clearly. He is caught in an inevitable, insoluble situation. Only now can he properly surrender to Krishna, without holding out for some measure of consolation for his ego. This is extremely important. A disciple who has not taken these steps will con-tinue to judge the guru on his own limited terms and won't be able to reach the level of trust necessary to effect the transmission of wisdom.

Certainly we must start by questioning everything—teacher, soci-ety, and our assumptions—but we have to move beyond doubting to establish a trusting rapport that will allow us to assimilate what the guru has to offer. In the modern world this is an extremely alien atti-tude. It is very hard to conceive of surrendering the ego to someone else, because trust exists nowhere outside of the immediate family, if even there. Large-scale societies are based on mistrust. Everyone is taught to cling to their personal interests no matter what. In many cases this is healthy and prevents them from being taken advantage of. But in wis-dom transmission, as in an ideal marriage, trust builds up to the point that a person truly can open their heart to the partner or preceptor. In marriage this is called true love. In discipleship this is where wisdom transmission takes place.

VERSE 9

SANJAYA SAID:
HAVING SPOKEN THUS TO KRISHNA,
ARJUNA, THE TERROR OF THE FOE,
SAYING "I WILL NOT FIGHT," LAPSED
FINALLY INTO SILENCE.

The wording of this verse leaves some with the impression that Arjuna is sulky and sullen, and his silence is a negative state of withdrawal. Hardly. He has just finished stating his case perfectly and asked Krishna to accept him as a disciple. His silence is wholly proper. He must now listen with all his heart. Anything more he might say would be carping.

The ability to listen is actually a rare and exceptional accomplishment. The usual way for humans is to mediate everything coming into the ear with a stream of commentary inside their head. We are busy interpreting all input in terms of what we already know. This inner voice must be brought to a standstill before anything new can get past the filter. It would be tragic if the flow of grace from the Absolute were to be changed into a sterile image stuck in a pigeonhole in a person's memory banks, but unless the interpretive process is interrupted, that's exactly what will happen. Listening with an open mind is thus the ultimate prerequisite for learning from a guru.

Religious warnings against idolatry refer to this same problem. Instead of admitting the light of the divine—or for that matter, the light of whatever is coming to us—into ourselves, we make a "graven image" of interpretive words as a substitute. The substitute is only a poor caricature of the original, but it satisfies us enough to turn to it instead of the light. In this way our world becomes solipsistic, shrinking to exclude anything new.

Arjuna's silence means he has disconnected his graven image-making apparatus, opening himself to whatever ineffable grace Krishna, representing the Absolute, will offer.

Many seekers approach a guru eager to obtain some benefit—wealth or power or occult abilities, for instance. Desire-based seeking lies wholly outside the wisdom context, however. While there are many purported benefits to spiritual life, telepathy or clairvoyance for instance, they are to be treated as incidental side effects of a proper focus on the undifferentiated Absolute. In a sense, having a personal desire means you haven't yet become quiet in the way Arjuna has. You are still packing baggage. The Gita makes it clear that all such desires are to be relinquished as a prerequisite to instruction. Decommissioning all possible alternatives to arrive at a state of psychic balance is the Upanishadic method Arjuna has just demonstrated.

An extraordinary example of dialectic occurs in this verse, where Arjuna is described as the Terror of the Foe and simultaneously avers that he will not fight. These contrary movements cancel each other out to bring him to the expectant neutrality from which his discipleship will grow and flourish. Lastly, we should keep in mind throughout our study that Arjuna has made this assertion that he will not fight. Future exhortations by Krishna for him to fight, which are mitigated and refined over the course of the Gita, are the counterbalancing force of the guru being employed to neutralize the imbalance in the disciple. This is one of many subtle indications of what bipolarity means and how it effects the transformation of the disciple. Commentators who baldly assert that this means the Gita is in favor of warfare are absolutely wrong.

ON THIS, KRISHNA, WITH A SEMBLANCE OF SMILING, SPOKE THESE WORDS TO HIM WHO WAS IN GRIEF BETWEEN THE TWO ARMIES:

The Absolute is thoroughly neutral, and so it only wears the semblance of a smile. On top of its neutrality is the slightest positive pressure, which is enough to bring about the entire panoply of creation. If individual organisms had to create their worlds from scratch, it would be incredibly tedious and chaotic. Yet creation is self-evidently harmonious, filled with perfectly functioning and even artistic beings and interrelationships that can be seen wherever one looks. This benign force, gentle and powerful at once, is symbolized by Krishna's minimalist smile.

Krishna's beaming countenance is also a dialectical counterpoint to Arjuna's despair. It contains a message of hope. If we are permitted to read a little into it, it demonstrates satisfaction with Arjuna's eminently excellent approach to discipleship and proffers welcome to a soul ready to learn wisdom.

When our feelings are hurt it is helpful to have a smiling friend to lift us out of our negativity. Lacking that we must do it on our own, which is much harder. That initial effort brings us only to the starting point of the spiritual adventure. Then to take a stand on an energetic neutrality requires, in this case, the entire instruction of the Gita's remaining seventeen chapters. Normalizing our state of mind is not simply an improved posture; it requires a profound grasp of the "big picture." Only through a synthetic understanding that approaches absolute beingness can a free and optimal response to the specific situation be generated.

It is relatively easy for Arjuna to see the uselessness of combat and desist from such an obvious and obviously flawed response, albeit one that continues to enthrall superficial intellects even as late as the twenty-first century. It is more difficult for him to foreswear negative withdrawal, as it has an emotional appeal that goes along with the intellectual assessment of it as the easy way out. In the long run neither positive aggression nor negative withdrawal are satisfactory. The Gita teaches the dialectical synthesis of both options through yogic or unifying wisdom.

A dependent person expects that following the rules will bring happiness, and an anarchic person expects that breaking the rules will bring happiness. Neither can understand why this doesn't thoroughly satisfy them, but they tend to be reasonably content because they've met their own expectations. As both these attitudes are based on rules, modern society is experiencing an explosion of laws covering every detail of life. Rules and laws are worshiped. It appears to be almost impossible to extricate ourselves from the tangled web we've woven. No wonder Arjuna gives up in confusion and despair! Luckily, he turns to the guru, who smilingly reassures him that his predicament is less dire than he imagines. There is a way out.

Nataraja Guru notes that here and in X:1 and XI:1 the Gita employs the singular Word as opposed to words. The Word or logos is Aum, the absolute sound at the heart of all sounds and all words. Many words will be spoken, but they are all united within the eternal Aum, the hum of the machinery of creation at work.

KRISHNA SAID:
YOU ARE SORRY FOR THOSE FOR
WHOM SORROW IS UNREASONABLE.
YOU SPEAK IN TERMS OF REASON
TOO. VERITABLE PHILOSOPHERS
ARE NOT AFFECTED IN REGARD TO
THOSE WHOSE BREATH HAS GONE
AND THOSE WHOSE BREATH HAS
NOT GONE.

A guru may not even acknowledge a request for discipleship, launching into teaching without preamble. It helps keep the disciple on their toes, wondering if they are being taught or simply chastised. Krishna starts right in correcting the shortcomings in Arjuna's mental state. Arjuna will have to earn his appreciation through his performance, and he will.

The symmetrical presentation of the science of the Absolute by Krishna begins with his first utterance. Reason is complemented with unreason, and the dead with the living. For true philosophers to be unaffected by pairs of opposites they must take them together rather than selecting one or the other. This yoga is so fundamental to the Gita that it is woven into the very language in which it is expressed.

When the unmanifest initially comes into manifestation it is in perfect balance. After manifestation, chaos and imbalance can occur, though even they also contain a kind of symmetry. That Krishna's words appear as a spoken mandala in balance is one of the secret keys to the Gita's teaching. Yoga must ever unite opposing elements harmoniously in order to approach the Absolute. Conversely, opting for one side over the other, for instance choosing "good" over "bad," throws the seeker off the track, into an endless confusion of conflicting interests. As Krishna puts it, they become *affected* by their partisan attitude, whereas a true philosopher does not.

The last line is usually translated as the living *or* the dead, but the Gita specifically says the living *and* the dead. The dialectics of yoga means treating both sides as the same. In this case, and many others, there is a world of difference between *and* and *or*, because it is one state under consideration, not two. Nataraja Guru writes eloquently of this in his own inimitable commentary (especially on this verse and II:16), and most everyone else misses the mark.

As to Krishna's main message about sorrow being unreasonable, the idea is that if we have a meaningful picture of life then there is no cause for lament anywhere. We are sad because, like a frustrated child, we don't have what we want, not realizing how much we still have and how we could be content at every moment. Existence is a magnificent opportunity that we should enjoy to the dregs and relinquish when required, with gratitude. Reason that doesn't go as far as this is mediocre, half-baked.

Philosophers of ancient Greece and India, in particular, used their reason to banish sorrow. In fact, coping with problems is one of the main purposes of philosophy. For example, here's what Alain de Botton says about Stoic philosopher Seneca, from around the time of Christ, in *The Consolations of Philosophy*:

There is a dangerous innocence in the expectation of a future formed on the basis of probability. Any accident to which a human has been subject, however rare, however distant in time, is a possibility we

must ready ourselves for. . . . Because Fortune's long benevolent periods risk seducing us into somnolence, Seneca entreated us to spare
a little time each day to think of her. We do not know what will
happen next: we must expect something. In the early morning, we
should undertake what Seneca termed a praemeditatio, a meditation
in advance, on all the sorrows of mind and body to which the god-
dess may subsequently subject us.[3]

Part of Seneca's recommended meditation was the line "We live in
the middle of things which have all been destined to die." The point
of what he's saying is that unexpected events throw us out of balance
emotionally, while those that are anticipated may cause us pain but will
not wipe us out. Perhaps his local library held a copy of the Gita, or else
he was a veritable philosopher himself.

FURTHER, NEVER WAS I NONEXISTENT, NOR YOU, NOR THESE CHIEFS OF MEN; NEITHER SHALL WE, ALL OF US, EVER CEASE BECOMING HEREAFTER.

The central tenet of Vedanta philosophy is that everything is the Absolute in essence, and so we are all one. This is also true on the atomic and subatomic levels. We are temporary expressions of a more or less eternal condition called the universe. The word *universe* literally means everything turned into one. Truly knowing who we are means realizing we are part of a vast unity that permeates all things. Everyone exists equally into the infinite past as well as the infinite future. This is the Absolute's assertion here. Those who disagree are accorded a hearing throughout the chapter, however.

Normally we identify with the temporary part of the equation, the visible entities that are constantly being born and dying, but the wisdom of the Gita directs us to turn to the eternal aspect and identify with that (often distinguished as That). There are a number of benefits to this: greater acceptance and less fear of the unknown, reduced stress, enhanced spirit of inquiry, increased self-confidence, and many more. Identifying with the part that will soon pass away is the norm, and it leads to dissatisfaction with present circumstances and a consequent craving for salvation, padded with turmoil and harshness of spirit. We are intolerant of others to the degree we are unsure of our own status, even if it is masked by a pretension of certitude.

From the human perspective, isolated as we are from memories of prebirth or postdeath, an assertion either way is unprovable. Whether we are eternal or temporary is strictly a matter of belief. As Albert Einstein said, there are two ways to view the universe: either nothing is a miracle or everything is a miracle. Shades of belief lying between these two poles are based on a promiscuous mixing of parts of each, which is readily seen to be absurd as soon as it is analyzed. This is a clear dichotomy: either we are eternal beings or we are mortal and expire with the body. The transcendental view, however, is that we are both together. From a synthetic perspective, parts of us are constantly dying, yet there is eternity every instant, within all the changes. Immortality is a state of mind, not a bodily condition.

If you stop to think about it, the unavoidable fact that something has arisen from nothing is the greatest possible miracle; all else is gravy, icing on the cake. Some unhappy philosophers insist that this something is really nothing, and therefore there is only nothing no matter what everybody thinks, but too bad for them. The Gita's philosophy is aimed at making us more alive, not less.

The Gita takes from the older Samkhyan philosophy that the immortal aspect in us uses the mortal body as a vehicle, a beast of burden to carry it around in manifestation. Those who identify with the body think of themselves as doomed, whereas those who identify with the spirit think of themselves as eternal. This is the basic dichotomy addressed in this chapter, otherwise known as the difference between matter and spirit, or in Sanskrit *prakriti* and *purusha*. At its height, the Gita aims to unify this duality in a comprehensive vision akin to a unified field theory.

Keeping in mind the archlike shape of the Gita as a whole, the second chapter is just one notch above the horizontal toward the vertical.

The full-fledged duality of the battle of life in chapter I is being resolved into its basic components of the physical and the metaphysical, or the actual world and the world of thought. Eventually this duality will be banished altogether, but for the time being it needs to be addressed. We are only beginning the ascent.

AS THERE IS HERE IN THE BODY,
FOR THE EMBODIED, CHILDHOOD,
YOUTH, AND OLD AGE, SO ALSO THE
PASSING ON TO ANOTHER BODY
IN THE SAME MANNER; THOSE
FIRM IN MIND ARE NOT THEREBY
BEWILDERED.

It's important to keep in mind that Krishna is presenting the philosophy of rationalism here, as he points out in II:39. Several versions of reincarnation appear in the Gita, culminating in a final revision in chapter XV. At this point we have a fairly standard picture of how reincarnation is popularly viewed, where an individual lives in a body and when it dies moves into a new one. Death is thus a stage of growth like any other. While not entirely discredited, this will be refined later on and presented from an absolute as opposed to a relative position, in which it is the Absolute that reincarnates as individuals, while individuals have only a transient existence.

Indian rationalism is much broader in scope than what is called rationalism by modern academia. The latter discipline is more appropriately called materialism, although modern materialism is vitiated by so many unexamined assumptions as to be a mockery of itself. By contrast, Samkhyan rationalism is an all-embracing and fearless assessment of reality, brave enough to critically examine its assumptions.

Belief in reincarnation doesn't really do much for anyone. Mostly it introduces a fantasy level of wishful thinking that can only detract from contemplation. Our destiny, whatever it is, will happen regardless of what we imagine in advance. Krishna brings it in here to counteract Arjuna's limited perspective, not as a foundational belief of some religion he is propounding. The idea is for us to become grounded in a steady yet optimistic state; to cast off the "base faintheartedness" that keeps our mind churning in unhelpful patterns.

Bewilderment comes, as always, from fixating on the temporal flux and forgetting the eternal aspect. Once that is brought in—as a realized reality and not simply as a form of lip service—it is much easier to remain "firm in mind."

MOMENTARY SENSE CONTACTS, ON
THE OTHER HAND, YIELDING COLD-
WARMTH, JOY-PAIN, ALTERNATELY
COMING AND GOING, ARE
TRANSITORY. DO YOU ENDURE
THEM, O ARJUNA.

As we grow up and as our consciousness becomes more sophisticated, we begin to distinguish separate items from out of the original uniform substance. This is actually a very useful thing to do, allowing us to participate in the world around us. It's by no means a sinful act, but it does produce an ego, which is nothing more than the locus of sensations and ideations experienced by the individual. The problems arise when we forget the unity underlying all the separate entities. We are trained to be expert in addressing all the manifold happenings—again, a great thing—but we get caught up in the game and forget the field it is being played on. Because we project our inner sense of bliss onto all those separate items, we imbue them with a meaningfulness that is not intrinsic to them. Then when those items fade away, they leave us feeling bereft. And they always do fade away, eventually, despite our valiant attempts to hold on to them. Since we've imagined they supplied our happiness, we fear our happiness is going away with them.

The Gita intends to help us reestablish our connection to the unity that is our true source of happiness. It's always there, in and through everything, but we don't see it because, well, for one thing it's invisible. Only separate items are visible. When people say "we believe what we see," they are unwittingly limiting their purview to omit the ground of the Absolute. Plus, seeing has been demonstrated to be much more subjective than we realize. To begin to know reality, we must develop a new way of seeing that isn't dependent on subjective sense data induced by the world of manifold items. We should be able to say "we believe what we know," or "we believe what we understand," instead of "we believe what we see."

Vedantins call the state of being focused on separateness "ignorance." Once we identify ourselves with a separate self and its items of knowledge, we automatically divide the universe into the known and the unknown. While most of us are comfortable with the known part of ourselves, somehow a profound and primal inner state of fear becomes associated with the unknown, and the fear drives us away from anything unfamiliar. We run amok precisely to the extent we forget the interconnectedness of all. A million psychology texts have been written to partially explore this terrain, but seldom is the cure mentioned: reintegration of the parts with the whole, which is the ground of the Absolute, though called by many names.

The wording that we should merely "endure" the sensory world sounds dismal and is somewhat misleading on that account. When we bump into problematic parts of the work, we should always remind ourself that the purpose of the Gita is to teach us how to be free. If something appears binding or depressing, we simply haven't understood it properly yet. We should ask ourselves, "How will this bring freedom, and from what?"

Titiksha means "to endure or have patience with." Actually, we should enjoy sensory experiences and be engaged with them but just not allow ourselves to be carried away permanently by them. If we are focused on the Absolute ground with a mind poised in neutrality, we can still interact with everything going on, and in fact we become much more alert than someone who craves sensory activities as ends in themselves. Being patient is a way to mitigate the impact of events so they don't dominate us, even as we participate intensely in them.

We could cop out at this point and just allow that Krishna is teaching the rational outlook of the day, the Samkhya system, here in the first half of chapter II. This isn't exactly the Gita's final opinion on the relation of the mind to the senses. But it is such a central question, particularly in the spiritual and religious contexts, that it must be addressed.

Many millions of people down through the centuries have intentionally circumscribed their lives in the belief that it was the spiritual thing to do. Voluntary impoverishment is a vow of monks and renunciates the world over. In rare cases we have to allow that it is spectacularly beneficial. Very often it is not. For the most part we can only imagine what the effect is, since the practitioners avoid the limelight as a matter of course. But there is no doubt that scriptures like this one are often read as exhortations to cease participation in the world and withdraw from it. This contradicts the stated aim of the Gita, repeated in several places, that we should continue to act, albeit from an enlightened perspective. The Gita teaches expertise in action. We have already seen Krishna preventing Arjuna from departing the scene to become a mendicant beggar.

It is easy to comprehend that sensuality per se doesn't bring wisdom. Pleasure yes, but not wisdom. Pleasure and its flip side, pain, are a part of the horizontal polarity of life, while wisdom and blissful merger with the Absolute are vertical. Krishna is instructing us in no uncertain terms not to confuse one for the other, but he is not suggesting we should avoid pleasure and pain, even if we could. They are normal parts of everyday life.

The basic rule of thumb is that whatever has an opposite is not the Absolute. God is not the Absolute if there is something that is not God, and conversely, if God is the Absolute then everything is God. Cold and warmth—which in the Gita are psychological rather than thermal states—are relative and opposite sensations, as are joy and pain. These horizontal polarities produce attraction and repulsion, which are serious impediments to a spiritual directedness. Techniques that try to force us to feel the same about being cold as being hot, for instance, are still focused on the horizontal aspect. The Gita teaches that we turn to the unity that permeates these dualities as the only way to be free of the imperative urges they inflict, and this is the meaning of "do you endure them" here. We cannot defeat them by wrestling with them, or otherwise doing battle with them, which is a prime focus of many religious practices. Verse 59, below, will cover this idea in more depth.

All the same, a sensual life is not necessarily opposed to calm intelligence. In fact, sensory input is essential for the proper functioning of the mind. We learn and grow through so many experiences which come to us through our senses. Denying the senses and living a life of nothing but detached idealism can lead to many types of insanity as the mind becomes unmoored. Overindulgence can have detrimental effects as well, though it doesn't seem to be quite so hard on the psyche, being more likely to produce vapidity than lunacy. The Gita repeatedly comes out in favor of a middle path, and it is especially appropriate around this issue. We should neither totally deny or excessively immerse ourselves in sensory experiences but instead imbibe high quality ones at discrete intervals, separated by periods of reflection or meditation to assimilate their value. Experiences of beauty are tonic to the soul and mind and stimulate more expansive viewpoints. Life is always offering us beauty to contemplate, and that is part of the slight positive impetus symbolized by Krishna's enigmatic smile while he teaches.

As an example, if you attend a music concert you will be benefited on many levels. (The various levels will be covered in verse 23.) It would be absurd to sit there "enduring" it, just biding your time until it ends. You can block the whole event out of your mind, but why? You gain the most by opening yourself up to it as much as possible. On the other hand, if you do nothing but go to music concerts all the time your intellect will become lopsided. And if you stay home, you will secretly envy all your friends who had no qualms about attending. Moderation, everything in modest amounts, is the key.

Few would deny the simple fact that reason stands apart from touch, taste, smell, hearing, and seeing, though the latter two are highly persuasive all the same. To purify reason, the Gita wants us to know how to shake off the convincing but deluding incursions of the steady stream of sense data. We can only think clearly when we aren't merely running errands clandestinely designed to stimulate our pleasure centers. So patience with sense contacts means to take those things for what they're worth, no more and no less, and find ways to take breaks whenever possible. How to do this will be taught in depth in later chapters. What is said in this verse is a perfect example of a basic scientific formula that has been misconstrued over time as religious dogma. The myriad Gita commentaries are full of such misunderstandings, and we'll root them out wherever we can in this study.

THAT HUMAN INDEED OF FIRM
MIND WHO IS UNAFFECTED BY
THESE, EQUAL-MINDED IN JOY AS
WELL AS PAIN—HE IS DESTINED FOR
IMMORTALITY.

Interesting. . . . Can it be true that all that's required to obtain immortality is to withdraw from focus on the senses? That's too easy!

Actually, coming to equal-mindedness is not as simple as it sounds. It is called *samadhi* in Sanskrit and is ever associated with advanced states of absorption in meditation. We could also think of a mathematician engrossed in a complex problem, an artist shrugging off bodily feelings to concentrate on the project at hand, or a writer who is utterly absorbed in the story she is weaving. Scientists, mystics, and artists know that when you give yourself totally to your project, amazing things can and do happen. Inspiration rises up from the depths to reveal new pathways and solve riddles.

The use of immortality here seems somewhat excessive; perhaps it is a bit of hyperbole. Krishna has already asserted in verse 12 that we are all immortal, and he will soon make the point that the eternal unitive state he is describing is not accessible as a product of any particular set of actions or attitudes. Immortality, by the way, doesn't necessarily mean living forever, which is the materialistic interpretation. It indicates the global perspective of higher consciousness, as opposed to the limited, or mortal, outlook of ordinary consciousness. When we are raised up out of our tomb of ego fixations to a universal or absolute vision, we have become immortal in that sense.

This short section at the very beginning of Krishna's teaching, which culminates in the next verse, deals with sorting out the real from the unreal, also known as the lasting from the temporary. A disciple cannot get very far until these two aspects are clearly distinguished. The temporary side of life is comprised of things that die, and the eternal is that which persists. Immortality is thus used here in that sense: it is a natural result of interest being redirected from the things that are born and die to the things that do not.

The most practical way of interpreting these last two verses is that oppressive circumstances are what we should endure, not all circumstances. This is directly related to Arjuna's quandary on the symbolic battlefield (don't try this on an actual battlefield!). All through our life things happen to impede our progress and interfere with our ability to concentrate. Trivial diversions, social obligations and repressions, mundane necessities: I'm not going to list them all, you should be perfectly familiar with most of them yourself. If we thrust them violently away we create a countermovement that takes its direction from the oppressive circumstances themselves. Of course, if we welcome them we won't even have begun our spiritual journey. The yoga of the Gita counsels us to not pursue them or resist them but to endure them with a neutral openness. By not giving them any additional energy we loosen their grip on us more quickly. Then we are left in peace, with clarity of mind, destined for immortality as it were.

WHAT IS UNREAL CANNOT HAVE BEING, AND NON-BEING CANNOT BE REAL; THE CONCLUSION IN REGARD TO BOTH THESE HAS BEEN KNOWN TO PHILOSOPHERS.

Religious neophytes often make a lot of noise over whether other people "believe" or not. You must be a "true believer" to be among the saved. This verse points out a simple truth that such beginners have overlooked. Krishna might be asking: "If a thing exists, does not believing in it make it cease to exist? On the other hand, if something doesn't exist, does believing in it make it come into being?" Certainly there is an operational existence for such false beliefs insofar as they motivate behavior, but the philosopher will not be fooled. In other words, fear of an imaginary God may make a person behave according to an established code of conduct, but it's a pathetic and unsatisfying motivator all the same. Krishna wants us to act as free human beings and would never stoop to such lowbrow pressure tactics.

Either something exists or it doesn't. To an Indian philosopher, for a thing to exist it must persist forever, and if it doesn't persist, that is evidence it doesn't truly exist. Its existence is mere appearance. The search for lasting value in a world of temporal flux is the story of the spiritual quest.

Since the root of virtually all conflict is belief, the implications of this verse are staggering. This simple understanding mitigates aggression and supports peaceful and harmonious interaction with others, regardless of their beliefs.

When people ask if you believe in God, what they're really saying is "Do you believe in a very large angry parent-figure who will punish you eternally if you don't comply with our (my) way of interpreting events?" Because we learned very early in life that we don't have a say, that other people make the important decisions, we've learned to defer our dharma to outside "authorities." Religious and political leaders more or less consciously assume the role of surrogate parents to provide the expected discipline and not coincidentally pocket the fee. Trusting souls follow the well-intentioned training of their childhood and play right into the hands of these betrayers of trust. Few are the leaders, and fewer still their followers, who say, with Krishna, "Follow your intuitive promptings based on all you've learned, and act in accordance with your own best understanding, for this is the true light of the world. Learn to heed your authentic inner voice, because it's the voice of God sounding within you."

This verse is usually "fixed" by commentators to read something like "What is unreal cannot have being, and what is real cannot ever cease being." The translation by Nataraja Guru above is technically correct and equally symmetrical.

Without pounding this to death, it is safe to say that the philosophic notion here is that reality is eternal, while unreality can never be. Keeping these separate is one main thrust of Samkhyan thought.

Verse 16 closes the first natural section of Krishna's teaching. It is related to the previous verses in that much of our oppression comes from unreal difficulties stemming from our confusion or misunderstanding, and if we endure these without feeding them they tend to fade away of their own accord, as long as we're intent on growing away from them. Real problems obviously need to be addressed more directly. Sorting out the real from the unreal is one of the key building blocks of a spiritual way of life. This is where discrimination comes in. It takes a keen intelligence and often requires help from an outsider like a close friend, therapist, or guru, since we are habituated to many false notions to the point we believe them to be true. Constructing a whole new outlook based on false premises should make the seeker shudder. We must be cautious not to build our castles on sand but dig down toward bedrock certainty. And it must be our own certainty. If we are unsure and so adopt the beliefs of someone else because they seem convinced, we are asking for very big trouble, as any former cult member will attest.

The word translated as "philosopher" here means literally "a knower or seer of first principles." We could say apropos of the above that a veritable philosopher is someone who has dug down to their own bedrock certitude.

KNOW THAT TO BE INDESTRUCTIBLE BY WHICH ALL THIS IS PERVADED. NONE CAN BRING ABOUT THE DESTRUCTION OF THIS THAT KNOWS NO DECREASE.

This verse and the next form a matched pair, in which Krishna presents the age old philosophical polarity of the one and the many, also described as the transcendent and the immanent, the general and the specific, and so on. In the present instance we are looking at the Absolute on the one hand and manifestation on the other. The former is eternal while the latter is temporary. The Samkhyan system being enunciated by Krishna calls these purusha (spirit) and prakriti (nature).

A familiar example of this primary duality is the triangle. There is a general triangle existing as a concept or idea that is ever present. When we draw a triangle on paper we have made a specific example of a triangle, and when we shred the paper it is destroyed. The destruction of the specific triangle does not affect the general triangle in the least. Thousands of triangles are discarded every day, as structural members in buildings, chalk on blackboards, mechanical drafts, and even accidental arrangements of random objects, but it is impossible to put an end to the conceptual triangle. It is eternal.

The Absolute, often referred to simply as That, is likewise the general form of life or consciousness from which specific instances are derived. When our life begins or comes to an end, the Absolute is no more affected than the ideal triangle. When the Bible says that man is made in God's image, this is how the phrase can be comfortably accepted by philosophers.

Aristotle argued that there were only specific instances and that no general form exists anywhere. He is the best-known grandfather of those who insist on taking everything in isolation, without reference to a unifying ground. Such isolation divests separate objects from any meaningful connection to the whole of which they are—or may be—a part. Krishna will argue in the following verse that awareness of the intrinsic connection between the part and the whole is precisely what provides meaning and therefore a reason to live. What we do is connected to everything else and therefore affects everything else. Each of us is one of the infinite sources of impact on the world as a whole. Contemplating the sea of interrelated causes and effects provides endless delight and stimulation of deeper understanding.

How often are philosophers of isolated materialism found to be both depressed and depressing? If life and its elements are stripped of meaning, why even bother to go on? But if it's "right" that nothing has meaning, why does all the rest of creation hum along sans depression? It is equally or more right that everything does matter and is neither isolated nor purely material. Realizing this should instantly restore our natural drive and zest for living. We matter, and what we do matters. Our value as an individual may be invisible to everyone else, but we should know it for ourselves.

THESE BODIES (HOWEVER) OF THE EVERLASTING INDESTRUCTIBLE AND UNDEFINABLE EMBODIED ONE ARE SPOKEN OF AS HAVING AN END. THEREFORE GO ON WITH THE BATTLE, O ARJUNA.

Now Krishna presents the "many" side of the dichotomy between the one and the many. He knows that an integral vision of how individuals relate to the totality will lift Arjuna out of his confusion and restore his mental health. As we move away from horizontal dualism toward vertical unity in the course of the Gita, the tragic gulf dividing spirit and matter will be effaced.

Far too many commentators take Krishna's last sentence as an exhortation to literally fight. This is absurd. We are in a psychodrama in the Gita, not an actual war. Krishna is using this phrase to urge Arjuna to return to participation with life. Yes, he is a warrior in a war, but the juxtaposition of a righteous warrior and a righteous war is so limited as to be almost nonexistent. A general meaning is intended here. When we become exhausted by those "slings and arrows of outrageous fortune" our mentor might urge us along the lines of "pick yourself up and get back in there!" We have to pull ourselves together so we can go back in the game. Frank Sinatra sang, in "That's Life" of all things,

Each time I find myself
flat on my face
I pick myself up
and get back in the race.[4]

Is this evidence that the Gita was known in Las Vegas in the 1960s? The last verse of the same song includes the line, "Many times I thought of cuttin' out but my heart won't buy it." It's definitely the same idea in contemporary lingo.

The meaning of the verse is that precisely because things change, having a beginning and an end, we can engage with them and improve them. We have zero impact on the unchanging Absolute, but its temporary expressions invite our involvement.

What is confusing to Arjuna here at the outset isn't confusing to holistic philosophers. After Krishna shows him how to visualize his predicament, he should be able to leap back into the fray. For him this means picking up his bow, but not for you, I warrant. For you it means something more appropriate to who you are. Say you've cut off an old friend because of a disagreement or are furious and not speaking to your spouse. Maybe you've sworn to never listen to anything your boss tells you ever again. The advice is to pull yourself together and reestablish contact. You are sulking because your feelings were hurt. But you are supposed to be equal minded and not lose your balance. Once you see both sides of the issue you can get over the pain. Then it is your duty to reach out to the other person, who is also nursing their own wounds. Continuing to stonewall means the death of many healthy possibilities. Reopening doors means letting the fresh air in once again. A wise person can always make the first move toward reconciliation because they refuse to be hampered by their childish feelings and personal preferences.

Or you are looking for work. You get home after a day of frustrating interviews and curt dismissals, and you are exhausted and depressed. There doesn't seem to be any hope. You could very easily start drinking heavily or veg out in front of the TV, either of which would allow the state of negativity you are in to continue unabated. The Gita's advice is to spend some time regaining your balance, coming back to yourself after relating to dead ends all day. Think of something positive about yourself or do something constructive to counterbalance the day's negative feedback. Once you are harmonized again, you will be ready to make a fresh start in the morning.

This problem vexes nations as much as individuals. In the short run it is easier to fire weapons at your perceived enemy, but in the long run this degenerates into an all-too-familiar disaster. It is infinitely better to "swallow your pride" so you can negotiate with insight into all parties' points of view.

In all these situations, realizing that you and the other side have common interests and can mutually either help or hinder each other provides all the impetus needed for a healthy engagement with whatever is happening.

VERSE 19

HE WHO THINKS OF THIS AS THE
KILLER, AND HE WHO THINKS OF
THIS AS KILLED—BOTH THESE
KNOW NOT. THIS DOES NOT KILL,
IS NOT KILLED.

Having distinguished the indestructible from the destructible, a long series of verses is provided to describe the former. It begins with a negative: what you see is not the Absolute. You see things that affect other things and that are affected themselves. The Absolute is beyond that arena. If you are going to seek it, don't look for it as a surface phenomenon. In particular, don't imagine that you can rearrange the world in a certain way that will magically reveal it. The Absolute is completely independent of temporal existence, while mysteriously supporting it also. Neophytes often imagine that they merely have to redirect their ordinary thinking to become realized, and that does have some value, but full realization requires a quantum leap out of all conceptual frameworks.

This and the next verse are lifted directly from the Katha Upanishad, which has a similar flavor to the Gita throughout, especially Yama's (Death's) instruction to his disciple Nachiketas. This is Katha 2:19.

THIS IS NEITHER BORN NOR DOES THIS DIE, NOR, HAVING ONCE COME INTO BEING, CEASE TO BECOME ANY MORE: UNBORN, PERPETUAL, ETERNAL IS THIS ANCIENT ONE. IT IS NOT KILLED ON THE KILLING OF THE BODY.

This is the same as Katha Upanishad 2:18. The two verses must have been carried over because they fit the discussion so well, are dialectically structured, and beautifully expressed to boot. There isn't much elucidation needed, either. They are perfectly clear.

The mystery of a simultaneously detached and involved Cause permeates philosophical and spiritual contemplation. The ancient Indians posited three rotating principles of creation, sustenance, and destruction, and named them Brahma, Vishnu, and Shiva. Somehow they emerged from the primal unmanifested Absolute to begin the play of existence, and they will continue to create, maintain, and destroy as long as the universe lasts. Things have to go away eventually or we would have a static universe, forever frozen, filled up with stuff. Therefore the proper philosophic attitude is "Oh great, that's over! Now something else will come along." You might cherish the memories for a little while, but don't let mourning impede your embrace of the ever-new flow.

From a human perspective, certainly, these "bodies" that die are very important to us. They are our mothers and fathers, our brothers and sisters, our children and friends, and they are supremely precious. When they go we feel a devastating sense of loss. Krishna does not mean for us to become callous to life's tragedies but only to put them in a larger context that we often lose sight of when we are overcome with grief. Arjuna has become undone by that very fact: his friends and family are about to be hacked to pieces in a stupid war. Yet his regret has led him to turn to a source of greater understanding. Krishna is working to console him so he can begin his discipleship free from upset feelings. This is a preliminary argument to counter Arjuna's exaggerated emotions and lift him to a neutral state of mind where he will be able to learn effectively.

Teachers are well aware that the students who arrive in class distraught by their unhappy home life will not benefit from the instruction. Their mind is elsewhere, and it won't be present until the misery is coaxed into the background or even better eradicated. Once their state of mind has been stabilized, the day's lessons can be registered. This is certainly not a simple problem that disappears with a few words. A lot of work is required to clear up the psyche at the outset, and this verse is merely hinting at what is involved.

This is Krishna's first use of the exalted meter of eleven syllables per line, the equivalent of underlining the verse for special notice. Poetic and profound though it is, the meter may just be due to its being lifted from the earlier Upanishad.

ABOUT HIM WHO KNOWS THIS
AS THE INDESTRUCTIBLE, THE
EVERLASTING, THE UNBORN, NEVER-
DECREASING ONE—OF SUCH A PERSON
HOW COULD THE QUESTIONS ARISE
"WHOSE DEATH HE CAUSES,"
"WHOM HE KILLS," O ARJUNA?

Translated thus these two are the same question. The intent must be "who is the killer?" and "who is killed?"

A rhetorical question artfully presents one of the classic elements of Indian philosophy. As individuals, we come to believe that we are the knower, the enjoyer, and the doer of actions. We are "in charge." These are highly dualistic beliefs. There is "I" and the things I know, "I" and the things I enjoy, and "I" and the things I do, kept separate from all the things I don't know, enjoy, or do. As we examine the mysteries of life more closely, this duality dissolves. We no longer see ourselves as isolated actors, we are integral parts of one harmonious whole. The new awareness is that there is knowledge, enjoyment, and action, all unfolding as the natural creative expression of the universe, in which we are privileged to participate. Our conscious mind weighs in only at the very end of the process, as scientific observation has confirmed. A lot of processing goes on in our unconscious before the final product arrives in our awareness and we imagine we have just thought of something.

Krishna is here showing the way to this unitive realization. We are to come to know the Absolute, and he even provides identifying qualities to guide our search. It is unborn, everlasting, and not subject to decrease. That pretty much rules out everything we perceive with our senses, at the very least.

The "standard interpretation" is that Krishna is urging Arjuna not to pay attention to the impact of his actions, so he can become a mindless killing machine. This is where the literalists give up and go somewhere else. But look more closely: the key is to first know This. On the face of This, beings are continually being born and dying, and we can get severely upset by it when our loved ones leave us. The antidote to despair is to know the ocean from which the wave arises. Then instead of lamenting the death of the wave, we can relish each new event as it rises up, breaks, and sweeps toward the shore.

Once again, we are hearing the standard argument of rationalism in the time the Gita was set down and not necessarily an ultimate assessment. In the final analysis Krishna will extol virtues like non-hurting, compassion, kindness, and thoughtfulness, and rate "disregarding consequences" as a serious fault. However he does echo this verse in XVIII:17, which says, "He who is free from ego-sense, whose intelligence is unaffected, though he kills these people, he neither kills nor is bound."

This is a complex subject that can't be boiled down to a simple truism. We have to wrestle with it in order to find the motivation for our actions and feelings within ourselves rather than being guided by arbitrary rules. For a provisional understanding we might think of a police officer called upon to shoot a deranged killer who is attacking innocent people. His killing is part of a job and is a way of saving lives. So while he may still have to wrestle with the trauma, he is innocent of being a murderer. Arjuna himself is in that very position.

Once again, however, we can generalize this advice to apply to the vast majority of us who are not soldiers or police officers. Pure actions are when we act harmoniously in concert with the requirements of the situation, while selfish actions are out of kilter with the same requirements. The former "accord with the Absolute," the latter do not.

VERSE 22

AS A MAN CASTING OFF HIS WORN-OUT GARMENTS ASSUMES OTHERS THAT ARE NEW, LIKEWISE CASTING OFF BODIES THAT ARE WORN-OUT, THE EMBODIED ONE TAKES TO OTHERS THAT ARE NEW.

This and a number of other verses in the Gita address various notions of reincarnation. Nataraja Guru cautions us not to adopt any puerile (childish) beliefs on the basis of any one of them in isolation. Reincarnation will be examined in some detail later in the Gita. Already here, though, the first image from verse 13 is upgraded to the Absolute being what reincarnates, rather than a personal soul. We have begun our rise out of individuality toward universal wholeness.

The problem with the idea of reincarnation from a spiritual standpoint is that in the hands of the ego it can become yet another excuse to avoid facing up to what we need to deal with. The ultimate procrastination is to imagine "I'll get to it next lifetime." Krishna's exhortations to fight are meant to press us to cope with things *now*. In spiritual life we need to sweep away the multitude of prevarications we are capable of posing and engage with the opportunity that has been flung at our feet.

I would like to suggest another interpretation of this verse more appealing to common sense: it is speaking of stages of the present life and not a series of separate lives.

Our unitive "I" sense persists throughout our entire life as a steady vantage point, intimately familiar, with which we wholly identify. If we think that this spark of awareness comes from the flame of the Absolute, we can call it the embodied One, or Embodied One. It's just a fancy name for consciousness.

All through life this spark of awareness passes through different stages, consisting of discrete definitions of the world, if you will. The child sees things one way, the youth has another cant, and young and old adults have their mindsets as well. There is continuous change but also distinct steps that can be identified. While it may seem to us that we grow and change through our personal mental processes, these stages are also integral to our natural unfoldment and more or less hardwired into the system. We don't let go of one until it no longer suits our understanding, but when we do it's exactly like throwing away the old clothes we used to wear and trying on a new set. And like bubbleheaded consumers on a shopping spree, we often discard the old outfit with a vengeance and rush eagerly to don the new one, which is why recent religious converts and teenagers can be so obnoxious. Others of us will continue wearing our favorite garb even when it no longer fits or is thoroughly worn out.

Moreover, clothes are like attitudes in that they are purely superficial. While dressing up our personas to impress others, they have minimal effect on the core of our psyches. If we grasped this, we would be far less inclined to fight over ideas, any more than we fight over fashion statements. Now we can discern a valuable spiritual lesson in the present verse: Once we realize our ideas are no longer fitting, we should trade them in for a new outfit.

Interestingly, right after writing this idea I heard an excerpt from E. E. Cummings' *A Fairytale* on the radio: "People have different opinions, probably, or neckties. . ." It was a confirmation from the surroundings.

The image of this verse is a lovely way to visualize how we pass through different phases in our life, and it could teach us compassion and tolerance if we take it in this sense. The exalted meter of extra long lines occurs again here, tipping us off that there's more than meets the eye in the content.

WEAPONS DO NOT CUT THIS, FIRE DOES NOT BURN THIS, AND WATER DOES NOT WET THIS; WIND DOES NOT DRY THIS.

This and the next verse form a symmetrical pair. They continue the description of the Absolute as being beyond any possible effects caused by events within creation. Oddly enough, no commentary I have yet encountered has done justice to their symbolism.

The dialectical presentation is again worthy of note. Verse 23 presents intentionality from the side of creation, and verse 24 presents the reciprocal action from the perspective of the Absolute. Weapons don't cut this and it is uncuttable, fire doesn't burn it and it's unburnable, and so on. Interesting, but there must be something more being transmitted to Arjuna here. There is. This is shorthand for an entire cosmology.

The ancients had four or actually five categories of nature—namely, earth, water, fire, air, and space. (These correspond to the modern solid, liquid, energy, gas, and space.) When we think of weapons as being solid like earth and wind being the moving form of air, with fire and water mentioned explicitly, we have the first four presented here. Less well known is that these symbolize aspects of the psyche. Earth symbolizes the physical body; water, the emotions; fire, linear thought, in connection with mental digestion and heating up of the system; and air, the vital *pranas* or energies, associated with intuitive, nonlinear thought.

The fifth, the quintessence, is ether or space, that which makes room for everything to exist. Beyond these are two more realms, consciousness as the sixth and the Absolute itself as the seventh, but these are not brought in here. They are symbolized elsewhere by things like sun and moon, day and night, or light and darkness.

The elements are also related to the bodily chakras, the somatic energy centers. The earth element is based in the *muladhara,* the first chakra, near the place where solid waste leaves the body. The second chakra is the watery *svadhisthana,* near the genitals, where water passes from the body. The genitals and other hormone producers are the source of many of our feelings and emotions, our attractions and repulsions. The third chakra, *manipura,* is of fire and is located near the stomach, at the solar plexus. Like digestion, fire consumes fuel and gives off light and warmth, in a similar fashion to ordinary mentation that absorbs sensory input and makes "sense" out of it. The fourth chakra, *anahata,* is located near the heart, associated with air and the lungs, where vital energy enters the system. Breath is the essence of life. The fifth chakra is the *visuddhi,* located in the throat and associated with speech and words. Communication begins the gradual evolution of transcendence in the individual by reaching out through space to other beings. The sixth, *ajna,* the "third eye," is the seat of consciousness and wisdom; and the seventh, at the fontanels on top of the head, the *sahasrara* or thousand-petaled lotus of light, is the "exit" where the individual and the Absolute conjoin.

Meditating on how all these levels interpenetrate each other promotes an appreciation of the unity of all things. The evolution of the individual generally follows the course of the chakras, beginning with physical development in infancy followed by the exploration of feelings. Next is development of the intellect, followed by the opening up to intuition, to teachings from the unconscious. At this stage the individual is capable of great clarity in communication with fellow beings and the embrace of larger groups. Healthy development culminates in wisdom, which leads to reconnection with the Absolute. Certainly all the levels overlap and complement each other; it's not just one level being developed and then the next. All are present all the time, but there is also a general progression and expansion as well, in which each one in turn has primacy.

This is the barest sketch of a complex and very interesting system of interpreting the world and the psyche. Most important for our modern understanding is that in it creation occurs from the top down: our ground is the Absolute, which arouses consciousness, and then space, air, fire, water, and finally earth are progressively created. The universe is not built up from particles; it emerges from consciousness and precipitates outward and downward. Our return journey is up from the heaviest element to the lightest, as we evolve back toward greater and greater consciousness and unity with the Absolute.

We can presume that Krishna spent several weeks introducing this science to Arjuna, and the reporter on the scene summarized the whole bit with verses 23 and 24. In those days this was familiar territory, hardly needing to be spelled out. And this is preliminary stuff after all: the Gita is rushing toward even more subtle and important matters in the upcoming chapters.

VERSE 24

INDEED IT IS UNCLEAVABLE; IT
IS NON-INFLAMMABLE; IT IS
UNWETTABLE AND NON-DRYABLE
ALSO—EVERLASTING,
ALL-PERVADING, STABLE, IMMOBILE;
IT IS ETERNAL.

The same system is hereby presented from the opposite side, that of purusha instead of prakriti, maintaining the symmetry.

We slip into bondage because we're actively suppressing our inner nature, our dharma. Very central to this suppression is our role in society. We don the mask of our persona to protect ourselves from the hostile forces outside us, never realizing that the winds of adverse criticism cannot upset our real self, the fire of hostility and anger cannot burn it, and so on. Identification with the Absolute makes us fearless, because who we really are cannot be destroyed. Krishna makes this point explicitly in the next verse.

This doesn't just mean we have to be some superhero that bullets bounce off of, or some saint thoroughly detached from the surroundings. When we become grounded in our essential self, life is appreciated and enjoyed to the utmost, but its ups and downs don't determine our state of mind. We are already in a great place, and it's not a fool's paradise that can be wiped out by circumstances. It's real, well established on every level.

Our core ground is perfectly stable, and this is what Arjuna is being asked to connect himself with. Physical damage does not have to hurt the psyche, even if it injures the body. Insults to our intelligence or our ego burn like fire, but we have to shrug them off, after gleaning whatever kernel of truth they convey. If we are primarily identified with the Absolute and not our ego, whatever people say about us is perfectly all right. Emotional shocks are like being doused with a bucket of ice water, but we can bounce back quickly from them if we are not overly attached to the feelings (or their objects) involved. And the adverse winds of fate or public opinion, daunting as they are, have to be seen as pertaining to our lower nature only. Our higher nature transcends all of these misfortunes. From this very practical angle, affiliation with the Absolute is our best defense against life's periodic insults.

For those of you who cannot or will not imagine an immaterial spirit at your core, you can picture the world in its microcosmic aspect, as an essentially eternal cloud of atomic and subatomic particles. It is easy to visualize that a knife passes through the cloud without causing the least damage, the wetness of water is not even perceptible at this level, and so on. A few atoms might swirl around when things happen, but they remain the same in toto. The discovery of the invisible microcosm by science is probably the closest analogue we have to what the ancients were getting at.

IT IS UNDEFINED, UNTHINKABLE IS IT, AS NON-SUBJECT TO CHANGE IS IT SPOKEN OF: THEREFORE, KNOWING IT AS SUCH, THERE IS NO REASON FOR YOU TO FEEL SORRY FOR IT.

We enter a section devoted to addressing Arjuna exactly at the level of his stated confusion. Krishna isn't presenting the highest teachings, he is only parrying the commonplace notions that are confusing to his disciple. This is the second stage of instruction, where the guru takes an opposing position to everything the disciple brings up in order to tame the ego and instigate fresh thinking. While perhaps philosophically less rigorous than usual for the Gita, it is very beautiful to see the artful way these subtleties are dealt with.

Why should you feel sorry for something that cannot be affected by anything, that cannot change? Quite the reverse, one should be rapturous in its presence. The only reason we aren't is that we are thinking of it, speaking of it, and defining it in limiting ways, all of which are something other than it. If they were it, we would be overwhelmed, so we can tell by our cold-blooded interpretations that we are off the mark.

This awareness is much more important than it sounds. Neophytes particularly tend to imagine they are in possession of realized knowledge when it is nothing more than a set of interesting and persuasive secondhand ideas. They badger others to try to bring them on board their sinking ship and become angry when their targets appear to prefer some other set of secondhand ideas. The Absolute doesn't care what anybody thinks—or even what anybody does. Creation has a reflexive symmetry which metes out exactly what each person puts into it, albeit subtly and invisibly. It is virtually impossible to trace the sympathetic reactions of the plenum—what Jung called the Pleroma—since they overlap with unbelievable complexity, but humans try to do it all the time. Since there is no obvious tit for tat, all attempts to draw connections are misleading. Krishna will soon be directing Arjuna to the highest conception, which is capable of transcending the dual reciprocity inherent in the universe. Without bringing that kind of yogic rigor to bear, we should be extremely circumspect about asserting that X caused Y. Usually our pronouncements are nothing more than evidence of our prejudices.

Appending the phrase "is It spoken of" averts a logical conundrum of Krishna defining something undefinable and causing Arjuna to think of something unthinkable. Wriggling out of the overarching paradoxical situation requires a slight concession to duality so that wisdom transmission can take place.

OR AGAIN IF YOU SHOULD HOLD THIS TO BE CONSTANTLY EVER-BORN OR AS CONSTANTLY EVER-DYING, EVEN THEN YOU HAVE NO REASON TO REGRET IT.

Whichever way we look at life, it should thrill us, not upset us as it has Arjuna. Here we have the flip side of the notion of the eternal Absolute: the belief that everything is just a temporary accident occurring in a meaningless void. When you come right down to it, that's about as astounding and improbable as a coherently informed universe. Either way, the fact that we have come to exist is a mind-blowing miracle.

So even if you are a staunch materialist and absolutely refuse to accept the idea of the Absolute, there is no reason to be sad. Everything comes to an end, and with people the end is usually unexpected. An intelligent person should expect such things to happen. The overall wheel of life rolls on and is just as breathtaking from any perspective. Clinging to what has passed away only truncates your own life. The regret stems from feeling you have lost something, but if you are not dependent then you really haven't lost anything.

Our life is supremely wonderful and very short. To waste any time at all moping about in sadness is a great tragedy. We should be making every minute count, appreciating everything and regretting nothing.

VERSE 27

IN RESPECT OF ANYONE BORN,
DEATH IS CERTAIN, AND
CERTAIN IS BIRTH FOR ANYONE
DEAD; THEREFORE, REGARDING
SOMETHING INEVITABLE, YOU HAVE
NO REASON TO FEEL ANY REGRET.

Krishna is elaborating the previous two verses and combining their different ideas. A materialist believes the first half, and a holistic thinker believes both halves. Krishna isn't saying that one or the other is right, he is just asserting that there is no reason to be unhappy no matter how you look at things.

One implication of the last part is that if something *is* avoidable, then we are justified in taking action to deal with it. The Gita's message is not about remaining passive or closed down while events happen to you but about how to become a fully awakened participant. It sounds simple enough, but it takes a major, determined effort to bring it about.

BEINGS HAVE AN UNMANIFESTED ORIGIN AND MANIFESTED MIDDLE STATES, AND AGAIN UNMANIFESTED TERMINATIONS. WHERE IS ROOM FOR PLAINT HEREIN?

A seeker of truth needs to reduce complex appearances to their essence, to make them more comprehensible. Here the guru offers an unfiltered overview of the broad sweep of life to a disciple who hasn't yet been able to see the forest for the trees.

Our plight, if you will, is very simple. We are in a manifested state in the present, and any states before our birth and after our death are unknown to us. We can speculate until we are blue in the face—and many people do, even pretending to certitude about such matters—but they will forever remain unknown pending our arrival. Therefore they are a distraction from right living in the present. We may act a certain way because we imagine it will get us something in an afterlife, not necessarily because it is meaningful now. This can only vitiate our engagement in this life, which is the only thing we can begin to know for certain.

Religious tales of heavenly afterlives cause people to tolerate subhuman conditions and perform all sorts of unnatural acts, as they imagine all will be magically set right in the distant future. This is the opiate of the people Karl Marx spoke of, promoting acceptance of suffering in place of taking corrective action. The Gita, by contrast, teaches unitive action, which attends to present problems as they arise and resolves or improves them. This is far healthier in both the short and long run and gives us plenty to do so we will never be bored.

It is well known that the threat of hell is used as a motivational device to force the faithful to meekly follow draconian rules and financially support a priestly caste. This is also discountenanced by Krishna.

This seemingly simple verse presents another basic building block of a spiritual edifice. All hypothetical beliefs are to be cast in the fire of wisdom and burned to ashes, to reveal the hidden core of what is really real, which is that which does not turn to ashes when put to the torch. Speculation about future heavens and hells may be amusing, but it is certainly nonproductive in the wisdom context. In the words of author Philip K. Dick, "Reality is that which, when you stop believing in it, doesn't go away."

When people are insistent about the afterlife, or unable to stop dwelling on it, it indicates disassociation with the present life. They are placed in unhappy circumstances that need to be addressed, and they would rather not. In other words, it is escapism, pure and simple. Any guru worth their salt will redirect the disciple's attention to the here and now, which is the proper place to begin.

As Robert Frost says in his poem "Birches," "Earth's the right place for love / I don't know where it's likely to go better."

A CERTAIN PERSON SEES THIS AS
A WONDER, LIKEWISE ANOTHER
SPEAKS ABOUT THIS AS A WONDER.
ANOTHER HEARS OF IT EVEN AS A
WONDER, BUT EVEN HEARING NO
ONE UNDERSTANDS THIS AT ALL.

The Absolute is not only beyond nature, it is beyond our understanding. That's what defines a mystery, described at this stage as a wonder. Later in the Gita (IX:4–5), Krishna further elaborates this ultimate mystery with some baffling, mutually contradictory assertions.

The state of wonder is conducive to contemplation, while the attitude that you already know everything pretty much slams the door on further investigations. Science seeks certitude, as it should, but it can never arrive, because the mystery is unattainable. Every static picture is limited, and the Absolute is unlimited. Even within creation itself there is always something more to learn. This is a healthy attitude with which to open up the mind.

The Gita is filled with graded series, and this is a less obvious one. Seeing is our most beguiling sense (this chapter's verse 69 claims that what we see is "night"), yet vision reveals only surfaces. Speech comes from thought and thus is much deeper than sight, while hearing can carry things like wisdom discourse and music into the mind. It is the deepest sense of all, but senses, no matter how refined, do not attain the Absolute.

Seeing has been equated with knowing since the dawn of history, and since the Absolute is invisible that is certainly the sense meant here: that we can never see it. Some people know it is a mystery, but that doesn't bring them an experience of anything. Lots of people talk about it, but again, it's just hot air passing over vocal cords. No experience of the Absolute will come from saying words. And plenty of people hear about it from other people or read about it in books. Christianity especially makes a lot of noise around "Have you heard the news?" But news is always secondhand information. It might get you to join a group, but it will not provide a direct experience of the Absolute, whether it's called God or anything else.

Religious bans against idolatry or even saying the name of God stem from the same realization as this verse expresses. When you say "God" you are referring to a set of concepts, and the reality of God is anything but a set of concepts. Idols substitute images as the idea of God. Sets of concepts or images become outmoded over time, but That which sustains the whole universe can never go out of date, or the whole shebang would give up the ghost.

Like the Absolute, music is intangible and ineffable, a wonder. If we take it for granted and believe we know it, it's like explaining music scientifically in terms of vibrational frequencies striking the ear drum, which translates them into nerve impulses that register in the brain. MRI studies demonstrate that many different areas of the brain are excited by music. All very interesting, but it doesn't convey what music is in the least. And plenty of us talk about music, and have lots of nuanced opinions about it, but again that is something other than music. Actually hearing music is a very immediate and transformative experience, but we still cannot say we understand it. To do so would be highly presumptuous as well as deadening. The most we can say is that we have experienced a handful of instances of it, but there is obviously much more where that came from. The possibilities of musical expression are infinite.

Thus it would even be possible for Krishna to have said, "Even experiencing no one understands it at all." The direct experience of *anything* is so overwhelming as to defy description and consequent understanding. Direct experience is extremely rare for human beings, who mitigate their experiences with all sorts of concepts and analogies. Conceptualizing isn't all bad, except that we tend to lose contact with experience and have nothing left but the concepts, and this makes for a hollow life, devoid of meaningful content. Direct experience is the content that a spiritual search attempts to restore. Arjuna is heading for one of his own in chapter XI and then will spend the rest of the work struggling to understand it.

All this being said, the Gita is an attempt to transcend the limitations of words and induce a unitive experience in the listener. It offers the technique of intelligently equalizing opposites, known as yoga, to achieve what linear thinking never could. It easily ranks as one of the best attempts in the history of the human race, and we can leave it at that.

Not surprisingly, this stirringly beautiful verse is expressed in the exalted meter.

THIS EMBODIED ONE WITHIN THE BODIES OF ALL IS EVER IMMUNE TO KILLING, ARJUNA. THEREFORE IN RESPECT OF ANY BEING YOU HAVE NO REASON FOR REGRETTING.

Verse 30 ends the section that began with verse 17, exploring the duality of spirit and matter. This is still very preliminary material. It establishes a sound mental framework based on common sense, by which to set Arjuna on a path for the highest realization. Over the course of the Gita, duality will be first resolved in unity and then reappear steeped in that unity, purified and justified, to reenter the world of give and take.

In this study we should be on our guard to not visualize the Absolute as something external. It is our very self, our inmost truth. While we may fear death, something in us is unmoved by it. We call that eternally steady place in our core the Absolute, for lack of a better term.

Krishna is basically saying that good and bad things happen to everyone, so while we should aim to minimize the pain we cause, we don't need to immobilize ourselves with guilt. Humans have the chance to learn from everything that happens to them, so long as they don't get stuck in mental black holes.

The disciple must be free of regrets in order to make the most of what is being offered by the teacher. Regrets are a way of clinging to the past, and the seeker of truth needs to be firmly grounded in the present. This transition was traditionally symbolized for a spiritual aspirant by the guru burning his clothes and hair, disposing of his effects, and handing him a simple cloth and a begging bowl to indicate his dependence on happenstance from moment to moment.

Modern seekers can achieve the same state by realizing that they don't have to tote their mental baggage around all the time. Once it has impelled any necessary changes in behavior, regret is an unnecessary weight that no longer serves any purpose. It comes from the ego trying to assert its importance in an unhealthy way. There are a large number of mental aberrations that could loosely be classed as forms of regret or clinging, and they must all be corrected at the very outset. This is no small task for most of us, because we can't just ignore them or they continue to fester. They have to be actively rooted out. Once regrets are laid to rest, direct engagement with events as they occur is so exciting as to utterly absorb one's interest. In fact excited engagement kicks in early on to assist the spiritualizing process once the ball gets rolling.

FURTHER, HAVING REGARD ALSO
FOR THE PATTERN OF BEHAVIOR
NATURAL TO YOU THERE IS NO
REASON FOR VACILLATION, FOR
THERE COULD BE NOTHING MORE
MERITORIOUS THAN A WAR THAT IS
RIGHT FOR A TRUE FIGHTER.

Verses 31–38 make up a subsection where Krishna is saying, "Look, even if you reject all the myths that have been inculcated in you by society about who and what you are, you should still be a full participant in the game of life. Don't permit the failings of others to become your downfall. You should fulfill your dharma, not abandon it." Arjuna has lost faith in those social myths and has consequently lost his sense of direction, so his teacher will describe for him the logical conclusions a thinking person should draw. That's also why Krishna mentions merit here: because it's still part of the ordinary attitudes Arjuna is struggling with. Recall Arjuna's direct request at the beginning of the chapter: "I ask you: that which is definitely more meritorious do indicate to me."

In chapter II we are still very close to the actual world, where subjects and objects appear distinct. The Gita is kind enough to begin at the level of ordinary comprehension and build its argument from there.

In keeping with the dualism of this early stage, the second half of the chapter will be a contrasting exposition of yoga. The generally physical and transactional orientation of this first half will be offset by the more mental and intuitive aspects of the second part.

This is a part of the work where orthodox thinkers are filled with delight to find their religious beliefs supported. There is lots of delicious talk of duty and sin, not withstanding the Gita's wholehearted refutation of these binding beliefs. Later on those commentators will have to mangle the Gita's absolutist stand to fit it into the inadequate bed of their dualistic thinking.

In this section especially we have to remember that Krishna is currently presenting the philosophy of rationalism, Samkhya, which we can also call "the ordinary state of mind." The Gita's finalized position is totally free from exhortations to follow prescribed patterns of behavior and is stated in XVIII:63: "Critically scrutinizing all, omitting nothing, do as you like." As early as III:17, we begin to hear the Gita's true absolutism: "But for him who happens to be attached to the Self alone . . . there is nothing that he should do." None of this present section is the Gita's final opinion; it is an exposition of the prevailing attitudes of the day, which are still largely in force in the twenty-first century.

So when Krishna says "there could be nothing more meritorious than a war that is right for a true fighter," don't forget to read between the lines! This isn't just about a warrior in a war situation, even though Arjuna is one. All of us have our unique conflicts to attend to in the way most suited to our interests and talents. The generic version of this idea is that we learn and grow through resolving conflicts, though that doesn't mean we should seek them out arbitrarily, either. The ones that come to us in the natural course of events, brought by the Tao so to speak, are where our work lies. Humans are always mucking about, following someone else's path, looking for instructions on how to be. The Gita would like us to realize that our path is always stretching out from our feet; in other words, the problems we need to deal with are the ones staring us right in the face.

This is not a matter of mystical faith in some divine program. Each of us selects, mostly unconsciously, a tiny segment of the total vibrational world around us to interact with. There are many good reasons for this. I'm sure you're familiar with Aldous Huxley's theory of the brain as a reducing valve, whose job it is to limit the welter of stimuli around us to a small enough piece that we can deal with it coherently. That's definitely one thing our brain does, and it's no small feat. Unsolicited, it provides us a logical starting place for our investigations by weeding out less relevant information.

It's well nigh impossible to discover our unique values or abilities if we are merely trying to be an imitation of someone else's idea of what we should be. A huge amount of struggle is expended in forcing ourselves to fit the prescribed mold, which in the flux of life is outdated almost as soon as it's cast. Redirecting that intensity to spiritual goals that free us is one of the most exciting endeavors one can imagine.

This is the first place that Krishna mentions a term central to Vedanta, dharma. Orthodox Hindus think of dharma as meaning "religion" or "duty," which the Gita considers to be prime examples of bondage. In a spiritual context the word refers to "one's true inner nature," a state that emerges when all the poisons and perversions from external forces are neutralized.

Sri Aurobindo has defined dharma very well in his *Essays on the Gita:*

> Dharma in the Indian conception is not merely the good, the right, morality and justice, ethics; it is the whole government of all the relations of man with other beings, with Nature, with God, considered from the point of view of a divine principle working itself out in forms and laws of action, forms of the inner and outer life, orderings of relations of every kind in the world. Dharma (the word means "holding" from the root *dhri,* "to hold") is both that which we hold to and that which holds together our inner and outer activities. In its primary sense it means a fundamental law of our nature

which secretly conditions all our activities, and in this sense each
being, type, species, individual, group has its own dharma. Secondly,
there is the divine nature which has to develop and manifest in us,
and in this sense dharma is the law of the inner workings by which
that grows in our being. Thirdly, there is the law by which we gov-
ern our outgoing thought and action and our relations with each
other so as to help best both our own growth and that of the human
race towards the divine ideal.

Dharma is generally spoken of as something eternal and unchanging, and so it is in the fundamental principle, in the ideal, but in its
forms it is continually changing and evolving, because man does not
already possess the ideal or live it, but aspires more or less perfectly
towards it, is growing towards its knowledge and practice.[5]

Most commentators think Arjuna's duty is to get back into the battle
as a fighting warrior. What is often overlooked is that the most important
thing is that Arjuna turns to a guru—a principle of enlightenment—for
instruction. This is where all dharmas are leading. When we get to the
point of wisdom instruction we are fulfilling the highest calling in life.
After he instructs him, Krishna no longer tells Arjuna to fight in the
war, he tells him to look carefully at everything and do what he decides
is best. That's the general message for all of us. So the emphasis on fulfilling the duties of a warrior is seriously misguided for the nonwarriors
among us. The point is to turn to truth, not to fulfill society's expectations. These are quite at odds most of the time.

Arjuna is, however, a warrior in a righteous war. A contemporary
analogy for his situation would be the police sharpshooter called to
shoot a mass murderer that we have already mentioned. It would be
utterly absurd and tragic for the officer to shrink from the allotted task.
Any mental reservations to performing what is required must be dealt
with in advance. This does not mean that everyone should be ready to
shoot people, because society only needs a few of that type. The rest of
us have other fish to fry.

We can't do better than quote Guru Nitya Chaitanya Yati on dharma, from a class for Australian psychologists titled *Therapy and Realization in the Bhagavad Gita:*

> In the Gita, Krishna wants Arjuna to know what his dharma is and how he should perform it. Implied in this is a revaluation of the value system to which man should conform, and of the proper functioning of those values in our life. For that, Krishna, as a teacher, is also doing what the psychologist is doing to his patient. The psychologist is not there to provide a plank for the patient to lean on which will always be held up by the therapist. Rather he should help him to stand on his own feet. That is possible only when the patient obtains an insight into his own problems, his own being. When he knows what he is and how he should function, he will be able to function by himself. The very basic attempt of a psychologist is to make the patient realize himself.
>
> If self-realization is the motive of the psychologist, why do we stop half way? Why don't we push it all the way until the patient is no longer a patient but a student, and further, not a seeker but a seer? Krishna functions here not merely as a therapist, he offers much more than therapy. He educates his patient. His patient becomes illuminated. He is no longer simply a patient in relation to a psychologist—the seeker has become the seer.[6]

Verse 32

TRUE WARRIORS HAVE REASON
TO BE HAPPY, ARJUNA, TO HAVE
THE CHANCE OF SUCH A WAR
PRESENTING ITSELF UNSOUGHT
BEFORE THEM AS AN OPEN
DOOR TO HEAVEN.

Be sure to read "seekers" in place of "warriors" here—not to minimize the heroic nature of unitive contemplation. Arjuna is a warrior, but this is also about us. Most of the significant events of our lives arrive unexpectedly on our doorstep. Whether we accept or reject them determines the course of our life in no small measure. We usually imagine we are in control, but there is a tidal current in life that determines the overall context for the tiny amount we are actually able to influence. On reflection we can see that the current is flowing toward evolving, toward greater consciousness and ability, greater opportunities for expression. Knowing this, we should welcome the "accidents" that come our way as being invitations to learn and grow.

It is cause for celebration when we have refocused on our life enough so that meaningful problems are delivered to our laps. When we engage these situations it's like walking through an open door to heaven. Becoming centered in the life we're blessed to be living is blissful in the extreme. Here we are, in heaven. Heaven and hell exist only in the here and now.

How often people think, "I wish I could get out of this mess I'm in so I could have a chance to be *really* spiritual." Or worse: "Life really sucks, but someday I'll get to heaven and everything will be all right." We want to walk away from our spouse who we're fighting with, or our crummy job or whatever. So many fantasies to keep us immobilized! We give ourselves a cheap excuse to avoid working on what's needed by hiding it behind the confusing bustle of the present, out of reach. The Gita is saying here that whatever comes to you is where to work. There is no "spiritual" ground somewhere else you need to travel to. There is nobody more spiritual than you are now. These are just ego tricks to derail your progress.

Or perhaps the thought is "If only I had more time to practice, I could become spiritual." Spirituality means at the minimum being actively engaged in your life. Not some particular kind of remote life, in a cave or an ashram, but yours right now. And while those practices might well have a spiritual component, that type of fantasy is a mental version of what Arjuna was doing at first on the battlefield, that is, giving up.

It is amazing how much resistance this idea engenders. We insist that circumstances prevent us from being happy! But why? Is it because we are afraid to be ourselves, or is it a learned attitude? We really need to look into it. Happiness will be found in everything around us when we give up the longing to escape.

One of the ways we lose touch with our dharma is by assuming that the important events in the world are happening elsewhere, that we don't really matter but others do. What a bad joke! One of the many unfortunate byproducts of this idea is that we don't bother to come to grips with the world around us, because ours is just some second-rate life in an obscure neighborhood. Who cares? Pfft! WRONG! It's the most important life you'll ever have, and it won't ever go away. But it won't be much fun, either, until you participate more seamlessly in it.

So let other people worry about their bit. You're busy wrestling with your own.

We need to unburden ourselves of another whole panoply of wrong notions in order to reap the merit of fighting a "war" that is right for us, otherwise known as living our life. So few get to this point of fighting our own battles—the Gita calls it one in a thousand—because we're so busy daydreaming about other people's problems. We're experts about what other people should do! Too bad they never take our advice. . . . The secret is, we have to take it first.

IF, ON THE OTHER HAND, YOU WILL
NOT TAKE TO THIS BATTLE WHICH
CONFORMS TO THE REQUIREMENTS
OF RIGHTEOUSNESS, THEN
THWARTING WHAT IS CONSISTENT
WITH YOUR OWN NATURE AND
YOUR GOOD REPUTE YOU WILL
BECOME INVOLVED IN EVIL.

The righteous battle is, as always, staying awake and alive to the requirements of the present moment, so we can meet them with expertise. This
should almost never involve killing, or indeed, rendering any kind of
harm, though in rare instances it might.

Here's how to thwart your nature: watch screens, get drunk, get
distracted, get busy. And so on, ad infinitum. We have become masters at thwarting our dharma and blending in to the social environment
instead. Only when our internal dissociation becomes uncomfortable
enough do we turn to a spiritual outlook to liberate ourselves.

As hinted at previously, when we get distracted by other people's
problems and hypothetical mind games we stifle our natural propen-
sity to unfold and grow. We thwart our potential. Engaging in our own

nature is eminently enjoyable, but it requires bravery, because it can be very much in conflict with external demands.

The Gita is not peddling any program other than the divine adventure we naturally embody. Arjuna, like all of us, has lost touch with who he is and needs to be brought back on track.

You can almost hear the religious-minded slavering over the mention of good and evil in this verse, but the horizontalized good and evil of religion is not countenanced by the Gita. There is no latter Day of Judgment. The evil is only of not allowing our life to unfold. It's like damming a stream and continuing to build the dam higher to prevent the water from ever escaping. Sooner or later something's gotta give!

Neglecting your spouse or dear friend as being an immovable source of oppression is an example of the evil spoken of. Almost everything can be worked out, but it takes effort, intelligence, and above all an ability to transcend your personal point of view. If you retreat into sulkiness and resentment, your relationship suffers (you lose your "good reputation") and the situation becomes a prison of misery for both. Again, evil is not something later on and far away. It is the measure of unhappiness—both kinetic and potential—inherent in the present moment.

Another example: Americans defer a vast amount of energy to their presidential elections. Instead of addressing their problems directly, they become immobilized by the hope that the next guy, the replacement for the current loathsome creature, will solve everything. Meanwhile civic problems become ever more desperate, because everybody is waiting for someone else to take care of them. By postponing useful action, hope can itself be an evil as powerful in its way as confusion or hatred.

Rather than attending to things ourselves, we long for someone else to handle them the way mommy and daddy used to in the good old days before we grew up. Presidents and monarchs play into this foible, as do messianic religions. This is a much greater evil than one would at first imagine. We defer to exploiters and then wonder why we are exploited. Losing control of our lives may at first be relaxing, but later on it is scorching.

The immediate pleasure of letting someone else manage our life is enervating in the long run. By not finding our own calling, not taking care of our own business, we lose energy. Depression thrives where life interests are not being addressed. But when we are engaged, the natural, ebullient energy that we are made of comes back to us, enabling us to deal with everything with joie de vivre. So being our own master is not as daunting as it seems. In fact, it's a tremendously enriching activity on all levels.

A real evil—if the term is to be used at all—in negative withdrawal is that miscreants will not be shown the error of their ways. Whatever twisted attitude energized their position will appear to be confirmed by the withdrawal of the very person who could introduce justice into the situation. Thus their rapaciousness continues unchecked. This is exactly the situation on the battlefield of Kurukshetra. The Kauravas have been taking more and more of what rightfully belongs to Arjuna's side of the family, and they don't intend to stop. If Arjuna has any duty at all it is to stand up for fairness in the battle of life. Maintaining his "honor" with the enemy is valuable to the extent it furthers this.

Have you ever been in an argument where you know you're right but the other side is so persistently aggressive that you decide to just give up and concede? At some point this may be the only option, at least temporarily. The false victor doesn't just walk away smug and satisfied, he invariable derides and mocks you in a display of pure ego. Such venting can go on and on, even building in intensity as the "victor" senses a hapless victim. It is highly dubious that this will serve any therapeutic purpose. It is more likely to confirm the egotist's conceits. So the Gita's recommendation is to shrug off personal feelings of pain and dishonor and stand up to the bully. This is a dialectic key to nonviolent action to combat oppression.

LIVING BEINGS WILL ALSO PRONOUNCE A NEVER-ENDING VERDICT OF CALUMNY ON YOU, AND TO ONE USED TO HONOR, DISHONOR IS WORSE THAN DEATH.

Krishna touches some purely transactional matters in this section, to demonstrate to Arjuna that denying his dharma and withdrawing from the conflict will result in a very poor outcome. When we fill our legitimate place in space with our wholehearted beingness, events go as well as can be, and when we abandon the field they go haywire.

Bringing this up to date, when you don't hold up your end of things your boss will get on your case, or your mother or your spouse will. Nowadays we call "never-ending calumny" hassling or nagging or persecution, and it can most certainly feel like a fate worse than death. No one should have to berate you to get you to do what you should be doing, and protesting that you're busy meditating doesn't usually get you off the hook!

Doing things only because we are being harassed about them is certainly a poor program of action. It is typical of teenagers who are confused or preoccupied about trivial matters, but most everyone has days like that. It would be far better to take care of our commitments swiftly, leaving us free to do what we want afterward. Fewer commitments means more free time, but almost no one can get along completely without them and have all free time. Too bad!

The insistence on honor is actually very odd, though few commentators seem to notice it. Later on (for instance, VI:7, XII:18, and XIV:25) the Gita will speak of equalizing honor and dishonor and not letting them affect you. Take a look at XVII:18: "That discipline which is practiced for gaining respect, honor, reverence, and for the sake of show, is named rajasic, changeful, and insecure."

The essence of unitive action is to let it arise from the depths of the self, authentic to our deepest dedication. By contrast, honor implies we should base what we do on how it will be perceived by others and how they will judge it. In other words, by seeking honor, dharma is converted from acting in tune with our true nature to behaving as we are supposed to by society. The Gita's teaching is all about getting out from under that kind of pressure. It's curious that so many commentators automatically stand up and salute honor, when it is tangential to the teaching at best and extremely hostile at worst.

Nataraja Guru believes that Krishna is trying to whip Arjuna out of his negative despondency with some heavy-handed exhortation here.[7] He is still testing him to see if temporal rewards are enough to satisfy him.

I sense this section contains more of the sly teasing with which Krishna began in verse 2. Why not try simple peer pressure and see if that will satisfy Arjuna? But to his credit, Arjuna refuses to be lured off course. He still insists on knowing everything he can from Krishna about how the world and his psyche work. When he asked for instruction, he very eloquently demonstrated that he was not in the least interested in superficial matters such as honor or heaven.

In verse 39, Krishna reveals that he is merely offering the Samkhya or rationalist take on Arjuna's position at the moment. The first half of chapter II basically lays the groundwork for the more penetrating science of yoga in the second half and beyond, which is the Gita's revaluation of ordinary thinking.

THE GREAT CAR-GENERALS WILL LOOK UPON YOU AS QUITTING THE BATTLE FROM FEAR, AND HAVING BEEN HONORABLY LOOKED UPON BY THEM YOU WILL BE HELD IN DERISION.

Car means "chariot" here. Nowadays we might use terms like "hot-shots" or "top dogs" in place of "car-generals." In the transactional realm, those in charge are unlikely to understand your confusion and unwillingness to do the simple tasks assigned to you. They will think of you as an inferior employee. Not too many people question the basic rules of social life, and those that do usually receive short shrift from those who cling to order and obedience as if they are divinely ordained rules of life. Then again, if you're hired to do something, and after you sign on you refuse to do it, that's another matter.

Dishonor may not sound too painful, but it is surprisingly powerful. Alain de Botton has written an entire book called *Status Anxiety,* which explores how deeply dependent we are on other people's opinions of us. Working our way to the state the Gita will eventually recommend, of equal-mindedness in honor and dishonor, is a tremendous, long-term accomplishment.

What's really being said here is the opposite of how it's usually taken, because this is about a spiritual orientation above and beyond transactional concerns. Arjuna as a disciple must be prepared to act independently of outside opinion, and Krishna is testing him with the kinds of negative pressures he will encounter as a spiritually dedicated person. He is asking, "Can you hold to truth when those around you despise you for it? Are you free from making psychological adjustments to coddle your friends and associates and get them off your case?" Once again, only those hooked on orthodoxy could imagine that caving in to social pressure is the Gita's final recommendation. We need to learn to stand up to mediocre opinions, to have enough faith in our own decisions to stick to those instead.

The deepest spiritual instruction here is that you should give up the need to defend yourself against false accusations, of which there will be many in the life of any seeker of truth. Only the ego wants to defend itself: the spirit is at ease and content with itself. When people hurl calumny on you, you can examine your hurt feelings and your urges to respond in kind, realize that they are merely the ego's game, and discard them. Accepting criticism without being humiliated and getting defensive is another excellent achievement of the truth seeker.

VERSE 36

THOSE AGAINST YOU WILL SPEAK OF YOU IN UNSPEAKABLE TERMS, SCORNING YOUR ABILITY; WHAT PAIN COULD THERE BE KEENER THAN THIS?

As nearly always in the Gita, the least important element in a series is given last, and here it is. If we withdraw from the conflict, others will not understand our position and will heap scorn on us. From our ego's point of view, at least, this is unquestionably acutely painful.

Interestingly, in verse 38 one of the Gita's most important recommendations is reiterated: treat pleasure and pain equally and stand above them. You have to admit that the importance of pain is seriously undermined by that statement. Elsewhere dishonor is to be treated together with honor. Clearly, such opinions of others should have no effect on us. Only when we're stuck in our personal ego can these things matter.

Krishna is administering an early test of Arjuna's understanding. The correct answer to his rhetorical question, "What pain could there be worse than being scorned by important people?" is, "The pain of losing contact with my true self." That is the pain that trumps all others and that prompts us to move mountains to reestablish our authenticity.

In his autobiography, my guru Nitya describes an incident where his guru, Nataraja Guru, emulated Krishna in this verse and went so far as to provide the insults himself. It occasioned an explosive argument, and Nitya was storming off down the road, intending to leave and never come back:

Then Guru caught up with me and tenderly held my hand. "If you really are going, I can't let you go scot-free. I should punish you." I agreed, and held out my cheek like a martyr. He slapped me lightly twice. Like an ideal Christian I turned the other cheek, and he slapped me again. Then, in a prayerful voice full of benediction he said, "I am beating you so that the world will not beat you."

I was still determined to leave him, and I started to turn away. He held my hand with the utmost tenderness and said, "Wherever you go, always remember Narayana Guru's words *alapamatram akhilam* (it's all a meaningless sound in the air). After all, what we hear from others is only the air vibrating. It can sound like praise or blame, but that is only our interpretation. True spirituality is to cancel out all pairs of opposites and maintain one's equanimity." My feet faltered. My anger was gone. Peace and a sense of great blessing came.[8]

VERSE 37

DYING YOU WILL ATTAIN HEAVEN
OR WINNING YOU WILL HAVE
THE ENJOYMENT OF THE EARTH.
THEREFORE ARISE, O ARJUNA,
MAKING UP YOUR MIND TO FIGHT.

Literal-minded readers look at this verse and say "Aha! You see, the Gita supports fighting and war." Well, yes and no. Literally, Arjuna the warrior should almost certainly fight, as his present situation requires, though not necessarily in mortal combat. Figuratively, we are being coaxed with him out of our state of indecision to live our life with determination and valor, in whatever path we choose.

Don't forget that Krishna is winding down his presentation of the next-best philosophy of Samkhya rationalism, as well as testing Arjuna's resolve; however, a very clever thing is happening at the moment. With his precisely chosen words Krishna is counteracting Arjuna's equally carefully expressed negativity from II:8. Compare Arjuna's complaint with Krishna's response here: "I cannot visualize what could rid me of this distress . . . even should (it transpire that) I obtain unrivalled dominion of the earth's plenty or overlordship of the gods in heaven too." In Arjuna's state of mind, losing and winning both have unacceptable consequences, while here, with an upgraded psychological orientation, the results of either case would be excellent. The guru is employing a secret dialectic with his disciple, while quite definitely not recommending either outcome. In a sense he agrees with Arjuna that literal fighting is not the goal, as if he's saying, "Either way you'll get what you don't want." Both guru and disciple are interested in liberation through wisdom, and specific behavior is of secondary import at most.

The Gita's way is to unite opposites in dynamic tension and is not about favoring one side over the other. Both heaven and the enjoyment of material objects are treated as beside the point or even hostile to the point in numerous places. It's Arjuna's *engagement* that matters, not the fruits he anticipates enjoying at harvest time. Krishna is teaching him to enter a state of clarity free of desires for expected outcomes so he can decide for himself what to do.

Part of the guru technique demonstrated here is the way Krishna counterbalances every attitude of Arjuna. It is a rare privilege to work with someone who can sense your state of mind and offer its exact opposite as an antidote. If you trust them enough, it helps you to let go of your fixations. Of course, if it's someone you perceive as an enemy, it only heightens the polarity. Although it's veiled, the Gita is portraying an incredibly dynamic aspect of the guru-disciple relationship here.

We can't restate too often that the battle that is being fought is our ordinary involvement with life and all its challenges. The teaching is meant to refer to everyone, everywhere, not just to a special case of a warrior in a war zone. If you try your best and fail, you still have your personal satisfaction in holding to your principles. If you succeed there will be plenty of benefits and accolades, but these are not what we should seek, as Krishna adds in the very next verse. All we are asked to do is try our best and see where it leads us.

EQUALIZING BOTH PLEASURE AND
PAIN, BOTH GAIN AND LOSS, BOTH
VICTORY AND DEFEAT, ENTER
WHOLLY INTO BATTLE. THUS YOU
WILL AVOID SIN.

Verse 38 closes the final section of this preliminary material, where Krishna is presenting an introductory teaching related to Arjuna's unenlightened mental state. Equalization of opposites is the secret of yoga, and when this is practiced in the thick of the action of life we optimize our effectiveness. As most of the popular understanding of yoga is off the mark, dynamic equalization will be discussed throughout the work.

Sin, as far as it is admitted by the Gita, consists of not measuring up to your potential. It does not preclude accomplishments in the future, or disqualify you for any merit-based position. No gods will be offended, and there is nothing like damnation possible. Giving every situation your best shot is all that is being asked of you. Even if you screw up, at least you tried. Above all, sin is rectifiable by a change of mind. Our attitudes are malleable, if we permit them to be.

It is important to realize that Krishna mentions sin at the conclusion of his opening salvo because that was the notion that Arjuna was obsessed with at the outset. A guru must connect precisely with the state of mind of the disciple and bring both of their minds into alignment, before the teaching can begin in earnest.

Because of this, it will be worthwhile to have a brief survey of Krishna's instruction so far, because we are being treated to a masterful depiction of a topnotch guru in action. He began by downplaying Arjuna's fears, noting that the Absolute is eternal and unchanging in any number of ways, so Arjuna's worries are unjustified. On the other hand, life itself is temporary and ever-changing, so he shouldn't be nervous from that perspective either. Change, both for better and for worse, is inevitable.

Arjuna feels like he is out of place on the battlefield, but according to Krishna he is exactly where he belongs, so he shouldn't try to escape from the events around him. This implies that when spiritual insights are being allowed into consciousness, we may feel like we are supposed to be somewhere else either physically or mentally, but that's a misreading of the impulse. Something is bothering us, but we aren't sure quite what. Instead of imagining the answer is to be found in some exotic locale, we should open up to our feelings and listen to their message, because what we need to know is right here within us.

Arjuna was afraid that war would cause all sorts of evil consequences, while in II:33 Krishna tells him by *not* fighting he will bring about evil consequences. In the subsequent verses he spells out some of those negative possibilities in detail. Again, the idea is not to uphold the one over the other but to neutralize Arjuna's insistence on making a choice based on inferior criteria.

The bottom line is that equalization of both the positive and negative aspects of every situation allows us to wholeheartedly participate in our life; holding to one or the other either paralyses us or throws us off kilter. Arjuna opened the dialogue by wondering which of the two options, fighting or fleeing, he should choose. Krishna concludes here by telling him to treat them together as one, to see them as polar aspects of the situation and not as an either/or problem. This, as we will repeatedly revisit, is the essence of the Gita's yoga.

WHAT HAS JUST BEEN TAUGHT IS
REASONING ACCORDING TO
SAMKHYA, BUT HEAR NOW OF THE
SAME ACCORDING TO YOGA,
ATTAINING TO THE UNITY OF
WHICH REASONING YOU WILL BE
ABLE TO THROW OFF THE BONDAGE
OF WORKS.

Now we're beginning to get somewhere! Krishna has just clearly presented the rational world view of his day, not unlike our own, and begins to present a revised orientation that will lead Arjuna to a more value-oriented vision. From this point the Gita offers more of its own radical perspective; heretofore it was only setting the stage with an overview of popular and philosophical attitudes, though with its own unique twist. Those attitudes are by no means entirely rejected, but by themselves they do not lead to liberation. They are related to excellence within normal parameters, but Arjuna and seekers like him are aiming to burst those bonds.

The following information is somewhat challenging, so anyone not wishing to mine every last nugget from the work can skip ahead to verse 40.

My lineage, the Narayana Gurukula, defines the three aspects of the Absolute, *saccidananda* (*sat-chit-ananda*), as "existence-subsistence-value (or meaning)," which is different than other systems, especially the *ananda* part, which is usually translated as "bliss" or "joy." Relating what we have studied so far to saccidananda per Nataraja Guru, chapter I was observational, pertaining to *sat* on the lowest level of the vertical axis. The Samkhya section we have just concluded deals with *chit,* the induction and deduction of linear thought. The next section on yoga brings in dialectic thinking useful in matters of ananda or value, at the top of the vertical axis. All these can and should be treated integrally and not sequentially, but it is very important to distinguish the different types of ideation and their proper fields. Nataraja Guru cautions us that "Dialectics is conducive to unitive understanding only, and spoils the case when applied to ordinary situations in life where usual ratiocinative methods or logic would be the proper instrument to employ."[9] He elaborates on this structural scheme in his *Unitive Philosophy:*

> Between a posteriori inferences from experimental data, we pass thus into the domain of such propositions as the famous Cartesian dictum, *cogito ergo sum,* and build rational or theoretical speculations upwards till we touch a region in pure higher reasoning which employs dialectics, called by Plato the highest instrument of reasoning, independent of all visible or sensible facts.
>
> This kind of reasoning, the dialectical, which takes us to the threshold of higher idealistic values in life is the third and the last step in philosophical methodology taken as a whole. The laws of nature refer to the world of existence. Rules of thought, whether axiomatic or based on postulates, refer to the world of subsistence. The third step of reasoning lives and has its being in the pure domain of human values, those referring to the True, the Good or the Beautiful, which are values in life and thus belong to the domain of axiology.
>
> The visible, the intelligible and the value worlds which we can

mark out on a vertical line represent levels of higher and higher reasonings culminating in the dialectical. It is like soaring, or resorting to ascending dialectics as spoken of in certain circles. This level has, just inferior to it, the world of formal or syllogistic reasonings admitting of the limits of contradictions at its lower limit and of tautology at its higher limit, where logistic and propositional calculi are employed.

At the lowest level in this vertical axis, where empirical or at least ontological factors prevail, referring to existent aspects of the physical world actually, perceptually or even conceptually understood, we have a region where certitudes naturally take the form of laws such as that of gravitation, or the conservation of matter and energy. Electromagnetic and thermodynamic laws belong to the Einsteinian physical world, whether treated epistemologically as real or ideal.

Thus existential, subsistential and value aspects of the Absolute have three different methodological approaches, one proper to and compatible with each.

A normal methodology applicable to integrated knowledge whether philosophical or scientific has to accommodate within its scope these three kinds of approaches to certitude, each in its proper domain. The experimental method suits existential aspects of the Absolute, the logical suits the subsistential and the dialectical suits the value aspects of the Absolute. Interest in the physical world gives place in the second stage of ascent to logical psychology or phenomenology, where ratiocination plays its part. Finally we ascend higher into the third aspect of the Absolute where value relations hold good and the instrument or methodology used is that of dialectics.[10]

Clever Nataraja Guru also points out in his Gita commentary that the "bondage of works" mentioned in this verse is a partial revaluation of "sin," made one degree milder thanks to the reasoning applied.

HERE THERE IS NO FORFEITURE OF ANY MERIT, NOR IS THERE INVOLVED ANY DEMERIT BY TRANSGRESSION. EVEN A LITTLE OF SUCH A WAY OF LIFE SAVES ONE FROM GREAT APPREHENSION.

As spiritual growth depends only upon a continuing unfoldment into the Absolute, there is nothing that "causes" it, exactly, though it is abetted by a willingness to direct one's attention into the void or the empyrean, since that's the realm our "life wave" is emanating from. The Gita maintains that realization is wholly independent of horizontal factors, and so there is no piling up of merit through good actions that can make it happen. This is so important it is mentioned first in this section on yoga. Many religions trumpet such a merit-based program, and for a lot of people those ideas are especially appealing because they are in line with their training and understanding. After all, when all you see is the horizontal, in which cause and effect are always operative, it's natural to think of good actions causing good results like going to heaven or some other kind of future reward. Nataraja Guru's quote in the previous verse shows how this comes from a confusion of contexts that "spoils the case."

What is popularly called *karma,* that we reap what we sow, actually implies a kind of merit. Karma is action in general, in all contexts. It's an egotistical conceit that our good karma reserves us a seat in heaven or leads us to enlightenment, or even simply that it is baldly reciprocated in the way we expect. Again, that's an unwarranted mixing up of horizontal and vertical elements. Actions and reactions, with their innumerable factors, are extremely complicated to calculate even in the most mundane cases. We only see the bottom line when nature produces it for us as a fait accompli. Our life is a kind of summary of all the many tangled threads of karma piled up inside us. While we reap some of what we sow, we also reap plenty of stuff we never sowed and certainly never wanted to harvest. We have to deal directly with all that lands in our lap, no matter who sowed it.

In the cosmic perspective, we reap much more than we deserve and never what we expect. Seeing how that operates in our life wipes away the anxiety of trying to "get it right." Nataraja Guru's threefold division of types of events is very helpful. In mundane matters, karma and merit are simple and straightforward: you cook the food and you can eat it. You pick up the brick, put it in the right place, and it becomes part of your house. Put it in the wrong place and the house falls down. Or the food is improperly cooked and inedible.

The world of concepts about the material world is based on logical reasoning, where ideas have more or less merit (utility) depending on their direct relationship to what they profess to represent. This is as far as ordinary thinking goes.

The ananda or value aspect is what we generally call spiritual, the domain of meaning. Here there is no hard and fast rule of absolute correspondence; the game is far more subtle. Value is revealed by yogic reasoning, which is a dialectical assessment of the whole picture. Its most important feature is that it leads us to grow and make forays into the unknown. Recognizing and manipulating the material world is static, a zero sum game. But when Buddha speaks his four noble truths, Hypatia reveals the suppressed genius of women, or Beethoven transmits his ninth symphony of universal joy and amity, value pours into humanity's collective soul. Seeking and finding that source of creative inspiration is the motive for a value orientation, or what we glibly call spiritual life.

Here's how religions start: To begin with, someone becomes realized, in other words, remembers they are the Absolute in essence. They fortuitously stumble onto their inner source of creativity. As karma is extremely complex, this is an utterly mysterious event, independent of predictable influences. If realized souls are outwardly directed, interested in sharing what they've discovered, they soon attract followers who wish to become realized as well. Realization is inexplicable, but what can a teacher do but try? He or she will draw on the events that surrounded the instant of connection, yet these are merely tangential to it, not causative, what we might call window dressing. The followers try out the same program and draw some benefit from the community spirit involved, so they codify those accidents into a suggested spiritual regimen. There is always the hope that it will pay off. Over time the program becomes sacrosanct, worshipped by well-meaning folks who have heard that it worked once and hope that if they follow it, it will work for them. Because it should work and doesn't, the votaries become guarded and defensive about it. They imagine all kinds of benefits they are getting and make it beautiful and attractive to clothe its emptiness. The longer the program goes without doing anything, the more the community is willing to compete with and even fight against other communities to prove their way is superior. Before long another religion is born, and as has been said, "the sect is the mausoleum of the guru." Codified rituals suppress the spirit, but they are easy to see and define.

So how does nonritualistic yoga save us from "great apprehension"? Fear is the prime impetus for action. Most societies, including our own, employ fear as the most important motivator for the protection of life. Fear-based action tends to enclose isolated individuals (as well as whole nations) in defensive barriers, thereby limiting their freedom and consequently their happiness. Fear of pain is a powerful stimulus toward avoidance activities, but the fear of death, of ceasing to exist, is the nuclear blast-force that drives the psyche to continually seek to cling to existence, no matter how imaginary and disjoined from reality the clinging may be. The great apprehension mentioned here is the fear of ceasing to exist. Krishna began his discourse by asserting that that which exists will never cease to exist. It's one thing to believe this theoretically and another to know it in your bones. The Gita is claiming in this verse that the practice of yoga—the uniting of opposites—quells this deep-seated anxiety. By getting to know the reality of our Self, we attain a certitude that dispels all fears.

In the verse, the word *path* is usually added for clarity, as in "Here on this path." Most commentators speak of a path, including Nataraja Guru, but the word *iha* only means "here" or "in this." There is no mention of a path in the original. A path implies causes leading to effects, and the Gita wants us to go beyond that kind of thinking. I have therefore taken the liberty of changing the Guru's opening "In such (a path) there is no . . ." to "Here there is no. . . ." The subject in question is yoga: dialectically balanced reasoning, the dynamic equalization of all aspects of the situation. The idea is that our fears are ameliorated by this kind of intelligence. It's an attitude and way of life in the present rather than a path leading somewhere else. The importance of this minor detail cannot be overstated.

I must also tip my hat to Nataraja Guru for being the only translator I found to use the term *merit,* which is definitely implied in this verse. The idea here is that in yoga no effort goes to waste and there is no backsliding. If you are following a merit-based program, being good at following complex moral instructions codified in a scriptural text for instance, there is always the fear that you will make a mistake that will nullify the accumulated gold stars. Arjuna himself will ask about this later in the Gita (VI:37–38). Hellfire lurks at the edges of such belief systems. But in the Gita's perspective there is nothing to lose, because you already *are* the Absolute. In plain words, if you really know something, it never goes away. If you can get out from under the oppression of guarding your merits and realize you are who you are at every moment, you can relax and enjoy the trip.

HERE, O ARJUNA, THE WELL-FOUNDED REASONING IS UNITIVE, BUT MANY BRANCHED AND ENDLESS ARE THE REASONINGS OF THEM IN WHOM REASON IS ILL-FOUNDED.

The difference between well- and ill-founded reasoning is how closely they are in tune with their subject. The best reasoning is completely familiar with what it purports to describe, while the worst is utterly disjunct from it and tries to compensate for the discrepancy by introducing all sorts of spurious arguments. Most of us have felt the frustration of trying to hold a discussion with someone who keeps veering into tangents and accusations that are beside the point, passing off baseless opinions as unassailable facts. A close look at many religions and belief systems reveals a similarly shaky foundation. Shockingly enough, a sincere examination of our own mental edifice may yield the same result.

Oneness with the Absolute is what is meant by "unitive." In fact, the Absolute is simply the widely accepted neutral term for the oneness or singularity out of which the universe and its consciousness are generated. Well-founded reasoning is based on realization or at least appreciation of the Absolute, which can only legitimately occur in a unitive state of mind. Reasoning by itself does not produce the unitive state, but the unitive state gives rise to unitive reasoning, which is self-ratifying and does not need to be propped up by verbal arguments. It is often referred to as intuitive.

When you think dualistically you can't be in a unitive state, since describing oneness takes you out of it. Each enunciated idea can treat only a part of the whole and therefore needs to be supplemented by another part, and then another, endlessly.

Anyone who knows how to do something and has to explain it to someone else is familiar with this problem. It's very hard to describe things that may be quite simple to grasp, like the directions in the box for how to assemble a tool or electronic device. Often it's easier to demonstrate than explain. Nataraja Guru called the pictorial, hands-on approach *protolanguage* and the wordy, descriptive explanation *metalanguage*. Henri Bergson similarly spoke of knowing a thing from the inside compared with viewing it from outside from any number of different angles. His favorite analogy was the experience of being in Notre Dame cathedral: no matter how many letters and picture postcards of it you sent to a friend, they could never adequately reproduce the elevating sensation of being in it.

The normal human adult has become trapped in a morass of metalanguage, where we are disconnected from the soul-stirring reality of our life and struggle to recapture it using abstract descriptions (or intoxicating substances). Krishna wants to teach us how to revivify our protolanguage, our direct experience of our world, naturally. A picture may be worth a thousand words, but a unitive insight is worth a million pictures. Poetry at its best is a series of unitive insights. Krishna is going to help us learn how to become true poets in our daily life.

While widely applicable, this verse is most germane in matters of religion, and Krishna is about to resolutely disabuse Arjuna of his unexamined beliefs. A realized person may be aware of being realized and may utter meaningful words about the state as well. But their followers, while they might have an idea of what is going on, are stuck with trying to imagine the state and are busy describing it in their minds. Different descriptions lead to arguments, miffed feelings, and eventually disagreements, building to different schools of thought or even into whole new religions. By contrast, the Gita is trying to indicate a state that is all-inclusive and loving, free of superficial conflicts. It calls us to slough off the divisive tendency and look for what unites all the factions.

A unitive state cannot be divided, which means that anyone who says "I am realized" is demonstrating that they aren't realized. In realization the ego sense is subsumed in the totality, so there is no separate "I" to realize anything. "I am realized" is a secondary description of a unitive experience, and pinpointing who it refers to is another "many-branched and endless" project.

Of course there will always be different interpretations of events for different types of people, but it is essential to remember that their goal is the same: oneness or unity with the Absolute, or the true meaning of the event. Knowing this, we can help each other to understand instead of striving to prove ours is the better way, or worse yet, the sole right way. Narayana Guru famously said, "Ours is to know and let know, not to argue and win." When you know, there is no need to argue. You only want to share.

While we may well have an intuitive idea of what we mean when we say "God" or "the Absolute," trying to communicate our awareness to someone else would take billions of years and still fall short. We have to settle for partial communication. Our friends presume the best, and so they agree with us even when we actually have very different images in mind, while our enemies disagree no matter how closely we actually agree. When a relationship goes bad it's very hard to shrug off those very real gaps and get back in accord, because it requires a presumption of innocence.

Each of us knows our own "I" from the inside, and our life is a symbolic, many-branched and endless explanation of that "I" to our fellow beings and also to our own ego. We can never explain it well enough to avoid at least a measure of misunderstanding. Lots of people even give up trying (which is how God must feel, sometimes!). It helps to know in advance that, short of an all-too-rare intuitive connection, only a semblance of communication is possible. Then we're happy to have our friends add their parts to our parts, thereby improving our approximation, instead of arguing over whose approximation is the "right" one. In the long run we are better off by simply being ourselves rather than always trying to explain who we are.

Because of our training we are ready to argue vehemently, even go to war, over who's right and who's wrong. This is one aspect of the great fear that goes away quickly with no more than a smidgen of yogic insight, per verse 40. We should be ecstatic to be alive in such an incredible universe of infinite delight. What do we need to prove? Only insecure egos are compelled to justify their existence by crediting their ideas to a putative god and insisting we agree with them. The minute we begin to realize we are the Absolute in essence, such insecurity is banished forever.

One more area where this verse is relevant is regarding honesty. In a relative world, perfect truthfulness is inadvisable and even impossible, but if you are intentionally truthful to yourself at least, your life takes on an easy confidence. Once you begin to lie and manipulate other people, you have to forge new constructs all the time to keep the game going. Supporting lies with more lies is another endless process. When scriptures advise us to be truthful—and all those I am aware of do—they are attempting to steer us clear of such perverse entanglements. Then the quest for truth leads us into the heart of the Absolute.

SUCH FLOWERY SPEECH AS UTTERED
BY THE FOOLISH, ADHERING TO THE
DOCTRINE OF THE VEDA, NEGATING
ANY OTHER (TRANSCENDENTAL)
VERITY,

THE SELF OF WHICH IS NOTHING
BUT DESIRE-MADE, HOLDING
HEAVEN TO BE THE HIGHEST GOAL,
OFFERING ONLY BIRTH AS THE
RESULT OF WORKS ABOUNDING
IN MANY SPECIAL OBSERVANCES,
WHICH AIM AT ENJOYMENT AND
DOMINATION; IN THE CASE OF
THOSE

WHOSE MINDS ARE UNDER THE
SWAY OF SUCH TEACHINGS, WHO
ARE ATTACHED TO ENJOYMENT AND

DOMINATION, A WELL-FOUNDED REASON DOES NOT COME UNDER THE SWAY OF THE PEACE OF CONTEMPLATION.

The Gita specifically takes on evangelical religion now, describing it as a con job based on wishful thinking that blocks the attainment of peace. These verses are a scathing indictment of organized religion as not only inadequate on its own terms but destructive and suspicious of all truth and wisdom that might fall outside its limited scope of awareness. Certainly Krishna needs to wean his disciple away from the toxic beliefs he has been marinated in for his whole life. Yet while on the surface it sounds like a blanket condemnation of religion, all these faults should be sought within each person's conscience as well, because they are not just somebody else's problem. We all think like this on a personal level, which is why it is reflected in group behavior as well. Let's look at these verses closely:

Flowery speech as uttered by the foolish. Krishna is referring to the many-branched and endless but tantalizing arguments used to peddle everything from trinkets up to religious affiliation. It is easy to be led astray by persuasive language. A dubious proposition may sound just fine when couched in carefully chosen verbiage. As Eve guilefully put it in the most famous subterfuge of all time, "The serpent beguiled me and I did eat" (Genesis 3:13). No need to admit guilt when you can blame your behavior on someone else!

Psychologists have studied the conscious and unconscious effects of words in detail, and the results are widely used to power commercial advertising and political propaganda. Good orators on the pulpit have ever been able to convince those not securely grounded in self-awareness of almost anything, including the desirability of warfare and of sacrificing their lives for any number of ungodly causes. A yogi should never fall for it.

A survey of modern books on spiritual issues demonstrates that flowery speech uttered by foolish dilettantes is still rampant and quite lucrative. Many are filled with circular logic and unprovable assertions about imaginary subjects, but they must be very convincing to some because they sell well. While titillating the imagination, they are basically distractions from the kind of serious spiritual focus presented by the Gita, which does not rely on coercive tactics.

Adhering to the doctrine of the Veda. The Vedas comprised established religion in the Gita's day, so for us this means simply "adhering to religious doctrine." The flowery speech comes from religious believers, in other words. The sincere ones try to convince you because it helps them overcome their own doubts if you will agree to their fictions. The crafty ones are after your money or your free labor.

Negating any other verity. True believers value only what they believe, and everything else is wrong. Such foolish people divide the world into their side, which has an exclusive connection to truth, and all those poor souls who don't agree with it. Once securely ensconced within this self-imposed barricade, truth is systematically excluded, along with the members of other groups.

Nataraja Guru added *transcendental* in parenthesis in front of *verity* to distinguish that this holds for important truths and is fairly irrelevant regarding everyday matters, which everybody has a different take on anyway. He notes the literal translation of this section would be "those who contend there is no second side to a given argument." Since the Gita extols balance and inclusion, one-sidedness is anathema to it.

Most philosophical arguments about truth center around people's beliefs and propositions in relation to facts about the world—horizontal facts—which are infinite in number. There is endless wrangling because, as has been decisively established by scientific and psychological investigations in the twentieth century, facts are a byproduct of consciousness and not the other way around. The revolutionary notion of the rishis is that there is only one unarguable fact, called by them the Absolute, brahman. It is a transcendental fact because it cannot be pinned down. All thoughts, opinions, and religious and philosophical systems aim to describe this fact in the most perfect possible way, but they inevitably fall short. Clashes come about from the different styles of description chosen, not from any difference in the fact itself.

This absolute fact is not entirely comprehensible to any mind, and so only a partial grasp of it can be had by even the most astute observer. We are left with different descriptions of different aspects of a unitive truth, which produces the babelization responsible for the endless arguments humans are famous for. The badly misnamed absolutism of the Hitlerian stripe refers to those who insist their partial view covers everything. It should be called absolute insistence on partiality. Sadly, such extreme attitudes have tarnished the philosophically sound term *absolute* in many people's minds, but rest assured they are not the same thing.

Because of the problem of babelization, silence is highly regarded by the rishis. But silence can be static and empty, unless it reflects absorption in a dynamic awareness. It has to be a stillness that simultaneously crackles with energy.

Thus truth is only grasped when the interpretive apparatus is completely transcended, to have direct, unmediated contact with reality as such. Relative interpretations are all false to the degree they add or subtract anything at all from the immediate experience. All religions and philosophies necessarily are interpretive and therefore partial and subject to conflicting conceptualizations. What they leave out or add on is the measure of their falsity.

A piecemeal or partial kind of truth lends itself perfectly to self-deception, and since no one can ever know the whole truth about anything, we have to be content with a selected version of it. It's a small step to ignoring unpleasant facts that don't match our preferred perspective, and then we begin to engineer and even manufacture facts to support our position. While early on we may feel like a kid getting away with stealing a cookie, the habit is highly addictive, and we effortlessly move on to become chronic dissemblers. Part of the game is to insist we are in possession of the truth, that we know more than everybody else or are on the inside track. Our home team, whether tribal, political, or religious, is happy to reinforce the belief that we are right and others wrong.

This is the common quicksand on which humans build their castles. The cure is to acknowledge our limitations and cultivate a globally inclusive perspective that considers all sides and is willing to listen to everyone's claims. But beyond that is . . . what? What is the truth of which we all so glibly speak, as though it was a perfectly ordinary and obvious object instead of an infinite intangible mystery? We will be looking into that as we proceed.

The Kurukshetra War of the Gita setting demonstrates precisely this type of conflict. The Kauravas want it all their way, and since they are in power they aren't willing to give up even the slightest bit of their false claims. The Pandavas have compromised with them repeatedly, continually giving ground. This has failed to appease the greedy side, merely whetting their appetite for more. Arjuna's initial impulse is to accede to their demands, which means dropping out of the conflict entirely. But Krishna insists that he stay and face the onslaught, and he is giving him an earful at the moment. Those swaggering assertions of the powerful are delusional and poisonous, so anyone dedicated to truth must not surrender to them. Arjuna can have a qualitatively different involvement, if he can only come to know the big picture.

The self of which is nothing but desire-made. This refers to the flowery speech, which is impelled by desires, in other words wishful thinking in place of any actual knowledge. No one has ever seen the heavens described in various scriptures, which should be considered metaphorical at best. Yet wars are waged over which word-picture is the correct image. Wishful thinking can be devastating when amplified by desperation, and clinging to imaginary goals requires an ever more tenacious grip, lest their emptiness be revealed. The oppression instigated by desire will be confronted throughout the Gita.

The artificial self constructed out of desires is our persona, that strategy we first devised in infancy to interface with our caregivers. Our crucial mistake is to come to believe we are our persona and to forget the much vaster being who wears it like a mask. "Realization" or "union with the Absolute" are names for the return to our greater self from the arid reaches of our contrived personality.

Self-help books are big sellers, because so many of us have fantasies about how we should look, eat, behave, worship, and so on. We are taught to be dissatisfied with how we are, and the ensuing schism between who we are and who we think we should be makes us permanently unhappy. One of the most important early steps in spiritual life is to learn to accept ourselves as we are deep down, to sweep away all the fantasies and posturing. As the eminent Tibetan Buddhist teacher Chogyam Trungpa puts it, we have to befriend ourself first, before we can even begin.

Holding heaven to be the highest goal. Displacing the blissful experience of being alive into a far off and hypothetical future is a frequent target of Krishna's scorn. An imaginary afterlife allows people to quietly accept a life of misery and servility, patiently awaiting a better time instead of making efforts to improve their situation to the best of their ability. This is one of the greatest tragedies of the human race, derailing as it does a vast potential energy to make people's lives better in uncountable ways. Even as to pure spirituality, people often become passive or even negative due to maladjustment with the present, once they accept themselves as chosen for election to heaven.

Writer Kurt Vonnegut, in *God Bless You, Mr. Rosewater,* gently chides the belief in heaven:

Heaven is the bore of bores . . . so most wraiths queue up to be born—and they live and love and fail and die, and they queue up to be reborn again. They take pot luck, as the saying goes. They don't gibber and squeak to be one race or another, one sex or another, one nationality or another, one class or another. What they want and what they get are three dimensions—and comprehensible little packets of time—and enclosures making possible the crucial distinction between inside and outside.

There is no inside here. There is no outside here. To pass through the gates in either direction is to go from nowhere to nowhere and from everywhere to everywhere.[11]

We don't have to think only of religious heaven, either. Secular wishful thinking posits heaven as getting that dream job, attaining the perfect figure, meeting Mr. Right, getting rich—so many distractions to channel our energies into, instead of self-realization. We may do any of these things, but we shouldn't treat them as our salvation. We need to remember we are already "saved" just by being ourselves.

So whether we work assiduously toward heaven or become passive in its shadow, heaven is a highly subversive concept we should be very careful with.

Offering only birth as the result of works abounding in many special observances. This refers to the Vedic belief that you can incrementally improve your lot karmically by good works and righteous behavior, which leads you to be reborn in improved circumstances. By the time of the Gita, the rules for proper behavior had become a mishmash of worship practices and other obligatory rituals. Every detail of life was painstakingly spelled out in the scriptures, with any room for free will obliterated. Later, in IX:21, the Gita will point out that life in heaven is in any case a temporary state and is inevitably followed by rebirth. Likewise, life on Earth is a temporary state inevitably followed by redeath. The Gita envisions a state of unconditioned freedom, both from prescribed actions and even from the repetition of births and deaths. Unitive life is its own fruit, as it unfolds in the present, and it does not rely on any future payoff arising from meritorious activities.

Which aim at enjoyment and domination. The flowery speeches may disguise the fact, but all this relativist religion is a sublimated vision of thwarted egos seeking ways to make themselves top dogs. And for a lucky few, it works! Krishna is putting his finger on the essential point of all the smoke and mirrors, that it's a way for insiders to exploit the rest of us. The baffling part is that humans so readily submit to the deception. We lunge for the carrot on the stick and don't step back to examine the whole apparatus that converts us into an unwitting beast of burden. We are lured on by cheesy attractions and ignore our best capabilities. Krishna well realizes the difficulty in distinguishing between dualistic pleasure and unitive bliss, and this will be a major field of exploration for Arjuna quite early in his discipleship. Pleasure is dependent on costly externals, while bliss is our very nature and is free.

We should not miss that Krishna is now wholeheartedly agreeing with Arjuna's rejection of aims like enjoyment and domination, which caused him to recoil from the battle and seek instruction in higher wisdom. It underlines that his previous exhortations in verses 31–38 were meant to test Arjuna's resolve, rather than force him back into the maelstrom, as is often supposed. As Arjuna didn't capitulate but stood his ground, it proved safe for Krishna to reinforce his absolutist trajectory. Krishna wouldn't dare say it to him, but he is clearly very proud of Arjuna's new direction.

The rest of this section merely states that this relativistic approach does not achieve anything worth having; what *is* worth having is called here the peace of contemplation. Peace with a capital P is one description of the aim of yoga, as is a well-founded reason. A better wording of verse 44 might be, "those whose minds are under the sway of such teachings, who are attached to enjoyment and domination, do not come under the sway of either a well-founded reason or the peace of contemplation." The bottom line is that a yogi must not be gullible and will be given many opportunities to find out why.

THE VEDAS TREAT OF MATTERS RELATED TO THE THREE *GUNAS;* YOU SHOULD BE FREE FROM THESE THREE MODALITIES, ARJUNA, FREE FROM (RELATIVE) PAIRS OF OPPOSITES, ESTABLISHED EVER IN PURE BEING, WITHOUT ALTERNATELY ACQUIRING AND ENJOYING, (UNITIVELY) SELF-POSSESSED.

Krishna abruptly introduces the three nature modalities or *gunas,* one of the Gita's most important additions to Indian philosophy. As they were well-enough known in his day, there was no reason for him to lay any groundwork for them. They are discussed in detail elsewhere in the Gita, especially in chapter XIV. The gunas are essentially three psychological states that affect the mind in rotation with various combinations and permutations. Broadly, they are "clear and focused," "colorful and busy," and "dark and stagnant," respectively named *sattva, rajas,* and *tamas.* The reason for their mention here is that in a religious attitude there is often a striving for the clear state, along with a rejection of darkness and even of the colorful, passionate state. In a balancing philosophy like yoga, however, they are to be treated equally as aspects of the same condition of bondage. When they hold sway over the mind, it is necessarily undergoing varying degrees of limited awareness and is not properly attuned to the Absolute. Hence Krishna's exhortation to become free of them, which is a rejection of the typical religious attitudes that advocate becoming more pure, or "more sattvic." Though soundly refuted by the Upanishadic rishis, the emphasis on relative states like "good, better, best" still persists in many places, as with "mirror-polishing Zen" or "holier than thou" attitudes. Much more on this lies ahead.

The relative pairs of opposites have been discussed at length already. One test of absolute values is whether they have a contrary position: anything with an opposite is not the Absolute, which can only be "pure being," containing all. Ideas like "true believer" or "chosen people" clearly fail the test, because they imply there are false believers and unchosen people. Krishna will several times assure Arjuna that such categories are invalid from his perspective.

There is a subtle distinction being made here. Verse 38 advocates *equalizing* opposites, which is the preliminary way for a yogi to deal with them. Pluses are set off against minuses with the aim of synthesizing a condition of neutrality. The present verse goes much farther, all the way to *transcendence*.

Arjuna was in despair at the outset over questions of gain versus loss, victory versus defeat, and so forth. In each case he had the nagging conviction that neither option was acceptable. His first challenge is to see how they are two sides of a single coin and therefore reciprocal, which allows him to treat them with equanimity. Now Krishna is directing him to break entirely free from their influence. When you are established in the neutral state, relative pairs of opposites no longer have the persuasive force they once did to deflect the thinking process. They are mere ripples on the surface of oceanic beingness.

Arjuna is being taught to go beyond the context of the opposites entirely, to become "unitively self-possessed." Only when he is absorbed in the depths of the Absolute will his decision making be unaffected by them.

The next-to-last phrase, which I have rendered as "without alternately acquiring and enjoying," is translated in numerous ways. *Niryogakshema* means literally "without yoga and enjoyment." It is somewhat problematic that in a treatise on yoga, the guru recommends not performing yoga, and that a book about attaining lasting happiness recommends not seeking well-being or enjoyment. Examining how different translators handle ambiguous passages can be very enlightening. Nataraja Guru has it "without any yoga or well-being," which is a very literal translation. He mentions "discipline" as the meaning of *yoga* in this case. His disciple Nitya Chaitanya Yati says "without any yoga (discipline) or well-being (as dual factors)." Stephen Mitchell has it as "being free from thoughts of wealth and comfort," Radhakrishnan as "not caring for acquisition of the new and preservation of the old." Maharishi Mahesh Yogi says "being independent of possessions." George Thompson has it as "free from both the exertion for wealth and the enjoyment of it." All give us nuances of the main implications.

Yoga is being used uniquely in this verse in the sense of "striving for a goal, of stepwise progress toward enlightenment or more specific attainments." *Kshema* is "resting in the result of the striving," imagined as heaven or some other attainment. The Gita recommends a steady state where everything is already present, subtly poised between these two poles of ordinary action. The point is to be lodged in unity and eschew dual factors, however they may be identified.

Krishna is addressing the way we are obsessively goal oriented. We pick an objective, work to attain it, and then enjoy it for awhile before choosing a new goal. This is the ordinary conception of action, resembling an endless series of births and deaths, and it is about to be contradicted in verse 47 with one of the Gita's primary teachings: that we should not perform actions with any expectations of results. The idea is to go beyond mundane transactional behavior to a new state of being. It's a little tricky to get this exactly right, so there will be extensive discussion of it in relation to the next several verses. For now the reader can ponder all the objections that spring to mind and bring them to bear on the subject as we go along. That's precisely the seeker's task in any case.

It's of more than passing interest that kshema, a place of rest, security, or comfort, comes from the same root as kshetra, the field that opened the Gita and will be the basis of chapter XIII. There it is the field of dharma and the field of action. The root *kshi* means "to abide, stay, dwell, reside (used especially of an undisturbed or secret residence)."[12] The sense of rest in kshema comes from having your own place, your own field. We build our house and then live in it, just as we build our world view and live in it. That means Krishna is counseling us not to get stuck in our mental constructs, which cause us to become fixed and limited, caught in the rat race. The relation of this admonishment with static religious beliefs is also at center stage here. It is the opposite of the venerable "idle hands are the devil's playground," the exhortation to always be doing something. It's more like "busyness is the devil's playground." Yogis want to be free to meet every new occasion on its own terms and so keep their programs as open and unbinding as possible.

VERSE 46

THERE WOULD BE AS MUCH USE FOR ALL THE VEDAS TO A BRAHMIN OF WISDOM AS THERE COULD BE FOR A POOL OF WATER WHEN A FULL FLOOD PREVAILS ALL OVER.

A very ancient antiestablishment story is referred to here. A high caste Brahmin, believing he should never drink water that has been touched by the lower castes, kept his own well surrounded by a fence of thorns, to assure that only he had access to it. One day a flood overran the countryside, but the Brahmin procured a boat and calmly rowed out to the site of his well, where he proceeded to dip his bucket.

The Vedas—or in our terms we might say scriptures in general—are the deep well of wisdom to which the learned priest has exclusive access. Down inside this source is the water of the Absolute, and the priest can portion out small doses of it for the private benefit of his votaries and himself. This is the way of religion. But the realized person sees the Absolute everywhere and in everything, so the concept of it being localized is absurd. Anyone can sip all the water they need sitting on the front step of their domicile. We all draw from the same well, or really the same flood.

Religions are like wells guarding precious holy water, but with a full flood intrinsically available to us all, there is no special point in dipping our buckets in any particular place. Still, we should smile and nod to the partisans of each well, who may not know of the flood and so cling tightly to their favorite source as the only one. They may scorn anyone who drinks the same water of life in another place, but that is their blindness, not ours.

VERSE 47

YOUR CONCERN SHOULD BE WITH
ACTION (AS SUCH) ALONE, NOT
FOR ANY BENEFITS EVER. DO NOT
BECOME BENEFIT MOTIVATED; BE
NOT ATTACHED TO INACTION
EITHER.

Relinquishing the benefit of action is one of the Gita's key contributions to the enlightenment of humanity. It inevitably brings up a lot of resistance when first encountered, because it smacks of an insipid fatalism, but that is far from the intent. That's why Krishna includes the caution against inaction in the same sentence.

This principle brings us much deeper into Krishna's instruction for acting on a unitive, rather than a dualistic basis. Opposites must be subtly canceled against each other and then transcended in order to unify our behavior and unleash our creativity. For a socially-constrained adult this is no simple matter, and Krishna will offer plenty of suggestions for practice. It takes time. Patience and an open mind will gradually help bring the whole picture into focus.

Thinking of an eventual payoff leads us away from acting with expertise, which is exactly what Krishna is imparting to Arjuna. The trick is we have to simultaneously employ an effective technique and discard any wishful thinking about its outcome. The resulting highly concentrated and artistic action is more readily associated in the Western mind with Zen Buddhism, but in actuality there is little or no difference between them.

Most action is prompted by desire. All of us have been trained to visualize a goal and work toward it. Our goals are basically in line with satisfying our wants and needs. This is well and good in the realm of transaction, but the Gita is a compendium of spiritual advice. Arjuna has come up against the limits of transactional behavior, and he wants something else, something more satisfying and profound. Krishna teaches that freedom is not found in transactional give and take, nor in evading transactional life. There is a transcendental neutrality that encompasses and engulfs the transactional world, and it is worthy of exploration. In fact tapping into it is the best way to express our own true nature or dharma.

It may take awhile, but once you are established in neutrality there is no desire to accomplish anything, because the bliss of that position is all-fulfilling. Doing and not doing have the same negligible impact. It may well be that we accomplish *more* from a desireless standpoint, however, because the motivation comes from something more profound than desire, such as altruism or creative inspiration.

It turns out that desires mainly *stifle* effective action, instead of initiating it as we imagine they will. Desires are excellent for initiating ineffective actions, of course. As we get pulled out of our dharma into focusing on a desired outcome, we become attached to the results of our activities, and before we know it we've lost our center. We become enmeshed in busyness, and the bliss evaporates. Like Arjuna in the midst of the dueling armies, we sooner or later realize something essential is missing. To rectify this the Gita recommends dropping the attachment to results and just engaging in pure action as the immediate situation requires. Nothing to it! The catch is we've become totally addicted to external values, to living for a future payoff, so letting go is not so easy. Most religions enshrine a future payoff in their program, via heaven or nirvana or something, and it fits right in with our addiction. That's one reason religious programs are so popular. But by merely returning to the now, we remerge with the Absolute, which is our true nature or dharma, and there is nothing else that needs to be done. Whatever we choose to do will be perfectly in tune.

So here's an example. If a teacher stands before a class and thinks something like "I'm going to teach my students such and such, and they will get this and this and this idea from it, which will help them to be better human beings," several things will go haywire. First of all, the teacher is not really absorbed in the subject but having expectations about the outcome instead. Almost by magic the class will also fail to be absorbed in the subject and begin daydreaming about what time the class is over. On the other hand, if the teacher is entranced by what is being presented, then the class is much more likely to be entranced as well. Having fixed expectations will lead to frustration when the expectations aren't met, and what's worse, whatever the students do pick up on will be undervalued as being only part of the intended lesson. Learning is an almost mystical process, where output and input are surprisingly dissimilar. Part of the fun is hearing later what unanticipated insights came across despite the teacher's intentions.

The best teacher forges ahead with their love affair with the subject in front of the class and is not overly concerned with what is picked up. The listeners will be drawn in by the teacher's enthusiasm and will gain a lot with almost no effort. In addition, a good teacher can sense whether what they're saying is getting through or not, which can be a prod to try another tack or offer another example. Rapport with the student is an important part of the transmission of wisdom and even knowledge. But for an absorbed teacher there are no expectations about how it will turn out, since what stays in anyone's mind will always be unforeseeable and inexplicable. As we know, this ideal is universally sabotaged by a world obsessed with grading and assessing minute details of knowledge assimilation, not to mention prerecorded training programs, but that's another issue. Krishna, as an excellent guru-teacher, is interacting creatively with his pupil and not just presenting a rote program for him to adapt to.

With a little reflection, many examples should come to mind of how we lose the flow by being drawn away into anticipating a specific result of our action. This is a very good exercise for contemplation.

The advice about expectations doesn't just pertain to the way we mentally align ourselves to the world. Expectations are often unconscious, and certainly the most insidious ones are. I have witnessed irrational eruptions from seemingly normal people that upon close examination reveal they must have been the product of unacknowledged expectations. The unwitting carrier of them becomes frustrated that someone else is not responding properly and then grows angry, even explosively angry. They are bearing an unsigned contract that the other has violated without knowing it.

This is a common subtheme of personal relations and is a particularly good reason to perform a critical self-examination. If we become frustrated over something, we should ask ourselves why, what is it we expect, and why isn't the expectation being met. Once rooted out, the secret desire can be either discarded with a laugh, or explicitly explained to the other person, who might fulfill the expectation gladly enough. Getting it out in the open is the best hope for a happy resolution.

It is not unusual for a shy person to be smitten with love for another, and yet that person thinks of them only as a nice friend. The lover doesn't dare come right out and declare their love, and the longer it goes unnoticed the more frustrating the impasse becomes. The frustration can begin to masquerade as a range of weird projections, including putting the beloved down or even hating them. Disadoption of one's formerly admired guru has a lot to do with unfulfilled expectations. From a neutral vantage point this kind of entanglement is fairly easy to spot, but from within it can mask itself behind all sorts of chimeras. The Gita wants us very much to avoid becoming caught up in such kinds of deviations from a straightforward, normative attitude. We can call that spiritual, but basically it is just sensible.

ENGAGE IN ACTIVITY, ARJUNA,
TAKING YOUR STAND ON THE
UNITIVE WAY, DISCARDING
ATTACHMENTS, AND CAPABLE OF
REGARDING BOTH ATTAINMENT
AND NONATTAINMENT AS THE
SAME: IN SAMENESS CONSISTS
THE UNITIVE WAY.

How unfortunate that we pin our self-respect on whether we win or lose, succeed or fail. Those are only momentary stages in the long course of life. Yoga means remaining always in a balanced yet blissful state, only minimally affected by the positive or negative outcomes of actions taken.

Sameness does not mean that we shouldn't feel. We should love every drop of experience, enjoying the good times and ruing the bad, crying over tragedies and laughing about our foibles. But if we are grounded in wisdom these experiences won't either knock us down or encourage us to be arrogant. They will energize our determination to overcome adversity, be more creative, more helpful to our friends and associates, and maybe more amusing than ever. Above all we will not be led into absurdities by our desires for or against anything and will be able to optimize our authentic self-expression instead.

This verse contains an early and important definition: yoga consists of sameness or equanimity. It means residing in a deeper place than the ego, so we are not as shaken by events. It means playing the game of life for the fun of it and not just to compensate for deep-seated feelings of inferiority by pursuing the temporary sense of superiority that comes from beating an opponent. This was the alternative mindset Arjuna was casting about for when he decided he didn't want to fight wars anymore. All you need in order to practice sameness is to know yourself in your very core. No specific performance is required.

In this verse "attainments" is a translation of *siddhi,* which often refers to psychic powers achieved through arcane mystical practices. Siddhis are a goal of striving in the religious sphere, and they are viewed with disfavor by the Gita. It is said that in the process of merger with the Absolute, siddhis come to the practitioner unbidden, meaning certain unusual abilities appear as byproducts of our focus on the Absolute. That's fine. But if we strive directly for those attainments, we give short shrift to the most important aim in our life, which is union with the Absolute. If union is achieved, any psychic powers that come along will be handled wisely; otherwise they will be exploited by the untamed ego, and the result may well backfire or rebound to our detriment. It's like trying to force peace onto a troubled region and unintentionally creating more conflict. The famous story of "The Monkey's Paw," by W. W. Jacobs illustrates this principle with spine-tingling horror, where three seemingly innocent wishes generate a horrific shadow side. An open, unegotistical attitude is essential, as it is a humble admission that we don't know enough to choose well, so we are looking to our inner guidance system, which is far wiser than our ego. Even more importantly, it redirects a selfish attitude to a selfless one, which is healthier both outwardly and inwardly.

A ready example in modern life of how people are led astray by a desire for attainment is the craze for sports records or becoming an

Olympic champion. Motivation is drawn from the desire to accomplish some kind of supreme achievement in physical ability. Lured by such a goal, millions of athletes strive mightily, eyes on the prize, pushing themselves to the limit, often causing themselves serious injuries, and even cheating by taking performance-enhancing drugs. It's all about being number one.

Out of those hopeful millions, a very few reach the pinnacle of success, where they remain for a relatively short time. In a system like that there are a handful of winners and armloads of losers. Wouldn't it be better all around if everyone did what they did simply for the enjoyment of it? It's less spectacular, sure, but who needs a spectacle when you're having fun? The Gita's philosophy has a parallel in the adage "It's not whether you win or lose, but how you play the game."

There is no need to dismantle the business of professional sports or ban the Olympics. This is an individual decision and can be implemented at any time. Just stop striving to be a winner and start concentrating on your present performance, seeking to discover who you are. You may well improve faster with such an outlook, and you surely will enjoy yourself more, no matter what you do. By doing this you will have disaffiliated yourself from the context of suffering, which is the defining achievement of yoga given in VI:23. You are in the midst of the same milieu, possibly performing the same actions, but you have turned your focus inward to your true nature instead of outward in competition with the rest of the world.

Everyone wants to be recognized and appreciated and supposes they have to do something awe-inspiring to be noticed. They are welcome to try whatever they like, but the Gita's advice is to discover our essence as the Absolute, which brings us an abiding satisfaction that is not dependent on either other people's opinions or our rating in respect to them.

VERSE 49

FAR INFERIOR IS THE WAY OF
ACTION TO THE UNITIVE WAY
OF REASON, ARJUNA; RESORT TO
REASON FOR FINAL REFUGE; PITIFUL
INDEED ARE THEY WHO ARE BENEFIT
MOTIVATED.

The Gita has led up to a survey of reason beginning here and lasting to the end of the chapter that will call into question many commonly accepted beliefs. In verse 69 it goes so far as to claim it is the exact opposite of normal awareness. The penetrating analysis it presents reflects contemplation at its best. The reasoning in question is dialectical, rather than the linear reasoning we employ in ordinary thinking.

Dialectical reasoning unites opposite poles in an expansive synthesis. This type of reason is literally equated with yoga, a fact passed over in more religious interpretations of the Gita. As with Socrates, intense concentration on the subject combined with thorough questioning of all assumptions is the technique employed. The Gita will later call it the wisdom sacrifice and accord it the highest position in the hierarchy of methods to attain union with the Absolute.

Wisdom transmission is also a dialectical proposition, differing significantly from the linear transmission of information that ordinary instruction provides. Teacher and taught begin as polar opposites in whom a kind of osmotic interchange takes place, each stimulating and edifying the other, until they become as one in realization. It is a qualitative rather than a quantitative process.

Reason is akin to the state of equal-mindedness being propounded by Krishna here. The Gita isn't espousing some strange and mysterious ability, just simple sanity, an ability to step back and intelligently analyze the scene with self-confidence. Too bad the knack is so rare in the human species.

The Bhagavad Gita is a very down-to-earth exposition of practical psychology, which unfortunately has been given a religious cast by generations of superstitious humans. Because of this, its valuable advice for obtaining and maintaining a well-adjusted psyche has been underappreciated. It remains a secret biding its time in plain sight, awaiting a seeker with the proper determination to know it as it is.

Unitive reason incorporates emotional wisdom along with rational wisdom. Many seekers falsely believe they are supposed to repress their emotions to attain enlightenment. Nothing could be further from the truth! Jonah Lehrer, in *How We Decide,* extensively explores the importance of emotions in intelligence. He writes:

> [Because of extensive studies that have been done] we can now begin to understand the surprising wisdom of our emotions. The activity of our dopamine neurons demonstrates that feelings aren't simply reflections of hard-wired animal instincts. . . . Instead, human emotions are rooted in the predictions of highly flexible brain cells, which are constantly adjusting their connections to reflect reality. Every time you make a mistake or encounter something new, your brain cells are busy changing themselves. Our emotions are deeply empirical.
>
> [Our neurons are] continually incorporating the new information, turning a negative feeling into a teachable moment.[13]

Lehrer's book is replete with examples of how easily our vaunted rationality, when segregated from emotional awareness, can be subverted by the most trivial misinformation. Excellent decision making—the goal of the Gita as well—is a complex ability demanding wide-ranging expertise. There is no simple formula we should memorize, or special technique. Thinking clearly is a grand symphonic achievement, not a ditty to hum or a familiar mantra to endlessly repeat.

Yes, it's shocking but true: we can boil down the Gita's teaching to how to make optimal decisions. Recall at the beginning of the chapter, as he was requesting discipleship, Arjuna asked for Krishna's help in deciding his best course of action, culminating in "with a mind confounded in regard to what is right to do, I ask you: that which is definitely more meritorious do indicate to me." After pouring out the cream of the collective wisdom of ancient India in a format perfectly tailored to his personality, Krishna's final teaching is to pass the torch back to Arjuna, confident that he can now make important decisions intelligently: "critically scrutinizing all, omitting nothing, do as you like."

Nataraja Guru qualifies karma here as pertaining to a "way" of action, meaning a rigid step-by-step program of some sort. Often enough religions are structured like the Boy Scouts, where you perform specific acts to achieve abilities advertised with "merit badges" which you wear on your shirt, and when you have enough merits accumulated you can be admitted to the next level or cash them in for prizes. Krishna isn't interested in any cheesy game like that. But he has no problem with action per se. The Gita is building toward an important conclusion in the next verse that "yoga is reason in action." The highly challenging idea is to replace action bound by innumerable constraints to acting with free choice. The third and fourth chapters of the Gita will present karma yoga, unitive action, or unfettered action guided by intelligence, in detail.

This is the teaching of Krishna's that causes Arjuna some confusion, leading him to ask for clarification at the beginning of the next chapter. Krishna is speaking here of more or less unexamined action and comparing it unfavorably to unitive reasoning as it will be taught. Religious seekers performing prescribed acts to secure future payouts in heaven or here-and-now benefits on Earth are the main targets of this continuing diatribe against religious idolatry.

In the business and political spheres, plotting and planning are taken for granted. You could call them part of the fun. But they should definitely include due consideration of their impact. This teaching is not about not being competitive, if such is your nature. But if your planning is overly specific and doesn't take all other sides fairly into account, it would fall under Krishna's blanket condemnation. Many immediately successful tactics have dire consequences in the long run. Cutthroat behavior degrades everyone, while honest and reasonable programs have wide-ranging benefits. The modern day deification of "The Market" as an excuse for an amoral or even immoral strategy will come in for a righteous blast in chapter XVI.

The last line, "pitiful are they who are motivated by benefits or results," tips us off to the type of action being referred to. If you are doing something not because it is your true nature or dharma but because you believe it will get you something in the future, you are acting under delusion, and it's too bad, because it's highly likely to have an unanticipated and unpleasant outcome, not only for you but for everybody else. This is pitiful because it shrinks the rich beauty of life into a kind of spiritual poverty, by first imagining you don't have what you need and then begging or scheming for it. As the Isa Upanishad says, "Relax and enjoy!"

AFFILIATED TO REASON ONE LEAVES BEHIND HERE BOTH MERITORIOUS AND UNMERITORIOUS DEEDS. THEREFORE AFFILIATE YOURSELF TO THE UNITIVE WAY; YOGA IS REASON IN ACTION.

A handful of definitions are scattered throughout the Gita, and here is one of the most important: yoga is reason in action. The subtleties of conjoining thought and action to produce a harmonious life expression are expounded in depth in chapters III–V. Still, it doesn't hurt to have a motto to sum up the subject occasionally.

The assertion here is that by intelligent reasoning it is possible to realize that a merit-based lifestyle is second rate and disregard its allures. Those who take pride in being screw ups, doing their best to perform unmeritorious deeds, are also considered inferior. In yoga there is nothing that you need to believe as a matter of faith, positively or negatively. Nor does realization come about as the result of popular approval, or any other kind of external conferment. Enlightenment comes from the inside, from allowing consciousness to blossom into its widest possible ambit.

The transition being described is from linear thinking to holistic thinking, or from one-dimensional to a multidimensional vision. In

Therapy and Realization in the Bhagavad Gita, Guru Nitya Chaitanya Yati describes the dialectical reasoning under consideration:

> If you are on a rational plane, you won't be able to get into the fundamentals of it. There is a point where you have to give up your surface mind and be prepared to dive deep and also to soar high. Another kind of reasoning is to be introduced here. This kind of reasoning is mentioned in Plato's Republic, where he speaks of dialectics as a hymn. This is the kind of philosophy that a philosopher king should possess. When a seeker goes on step by step using rationality he eventually comes to a point where reason stops and he can only go beyond through an intuitive flash. There, instead of going from a major premise and a minor premise to a conclusion, you are taking two polarized aspects of reality which are apparently giving you a paradoxical enigma, and transcending that enigma. You transcend the paradox through dialectical reasoning. So this dialectical reasoning is applied in the Bhagavad Gita just as it is applied in the Bible. In India we call it Yoga Mimamsa. Mimamsa indicates a critical enquiry; a critical enquiry which unites two opposite poles to make a total truth.[14]

Nataraja Guru refers to the expertise meant by "reason in action" as savoir faire or know-how. Writer, Sanskritist, and surrealist Rene Daumal, who surely knew the Gita, once wrote, *"Art* is here taken to mean knowledge realized in action."[15]

A friend who has been studying yoga for some time related an opportunity to put "reason in action" into practice. Let's call her Z. Briefly, an old friend pulled her aside one day and accused her of betraying their friendship. She was furious with Z. Like Arjuna, Z's initial impulse was to recoil in horror and prepare to flee. She first assumed she was guilty as charged, and she began to give herself a lecture about what a horrible person she was. Then she thought, "Wait a minute, I don't think I betrayed anyone." She mastered her reaction and stood her ground. First she asked if their friendship could be salvaged. Her friend said she didn't think so. Then Z asked her to explain what was the matter. All the time she was struggling to calm herself down. As she became calmer, she began to be able to respond in helpful ways and to present her side of the story more clearly, not to mention to see her friend's point of view dispassionately. Her friend has some personality quirks that were exaggerating the problem, and Z didn't feel she needed to take responsibility for those. But she did take cognizance of them and worked with and around them. After a difficult half hour, Z was able to restore peace and her friend's trust.

This is exactly how to put the Gita's teaching into daily practice. An uninstructed person might have started a war by hurling back defensive accusations, or else retreated with hurt feelings. The friendship might well have been broken. Z had what she described as a rare opportunity to make peace by uniting their two sides of the story. Right in the midst of "ordinary" life, such an opportunity had unexpectedly appeared. Those who become skilled in yoga will find their talents at resolving problematic situations called upon more and more, and in the bargain they can turn an initially miserable encounter into a beneficial one.

By affiliation to unitive reason
the wise, transcending birth
bondage, renouncing benefit
interest, go onward to a state
beyond all pain.

The idea here is that a well-founded reason is transcendentally important. It's the royal road to liberation. We're not talking about just having
a better idea about mousetraps; this is tremendously liberating, affecting
every aspect of our life. It's being able to see through all the veils of half-
baked beliefs and confused ideologies, which are "the dross of vagueness" of the next verse. It means turning away from the relative to the
absolute foundation of consciousness, moving from chaos to calm. That
the way of wisdom will take us beyond *all* pain sounds like hyperbole,
and perhaps it is. Maybe it should just read *most* pain. But the difference between duality and unity in consciousness is indeed profound,
and all sorts of exotic metaphors could be used to describe it. The relief
of suffering is as good as any.

It is now scientifically established that pain is generated and experienced in the brain. Information about an injury in an extremity is
relayed to the brain, where the signal is converted to an unpleasant sensation. There are plenty of examples of people in intense states of consciousness who are impervious to pain. The ninth-century philosopher

Shankara pointed out that when we are asleep we don't feel pain, so something in us must be able to either shut it off or stop generating it. Certainly, suffering can be minimized, if not eliminated, if we don't reinforce it with a negative attitude. This complex subject is covered in more detail toward the end of the Gita.

Birth bondage refers to our genetic makeup along with the social milieu in which we make our appearance on the stage of life. We have discussed these in detail already. It is *bondage* that is to be transcended, not action or life or involvement. Transcendence, as chapter III will make clear, means freedom within the world, not removal from it.

"Renouncing benefit interest" is the same as discarding expectations of specific fruits of action, which was just covered. The important addition here is that the affiliation to the unitive reasoning described in the previous verse is primary, and it leads its adherents out of the bondage of local strictures and false hopes as a natural consequence. We don't have to perform any act as a specific duty or practice; liberation arrives as a new way of being that is intrinsically effortless.

WHEN YOUR REASON HAS TRANSCENDED THE DROSS OF VAGUENESS, THEN YOU ATTAIN TO THAT NEUTRAL ATTITUDE, BOTH IN RESPECT OF WHAT IS TO BE LEARNT AND WHAT HAS ALREADY BEEN HEARD.

A very important instruction is found in this verse. The beginning student is invariably burdened with a lot of false notions, including a concrete picture of what the spiritual path holds in store. Before true learning can begin, these have to be cast aside. There is no monumental, fixed way, writ in stone anywhere, and great teachers must always chafe that their helpful suggestions wind up parroted ad infinitum and codified into scriptures to be misinterpreted to death. What has been heard in the past has now become memory, not living truth. Where one's steps will lead is purely a subject of fantasy, not living truth. Acting on the basis of memories and fantasies is vague at best; most translations of this verse call it delusion, which it most certainly is. The adjective employed means an impervious, impenetrable thicket or heap, which aptly describes the delusion mounted by our expectations. Apparently religious fanaticism is nothing new, for this verse is a carefully worded caution against it. Fanaticism of every stripe is bred and nurtured by fixed expectations.

The word *nirvedam* is almost invariably translated as "indifference," meaning that ideally we should attain to indifference. Nataraja Guru has it as "a neutral attitude," once again a very significant distinction. After all, verse 47 has just counseled us to not be indifferent. Indifference and vagueness may be imagined to be unwanted bedfellows. We should care very much, just not about irrelevancies. The translation here is perfectly in keeping with the instruction of the Gita on unitive action, which will be extensively elaborated in chapters III and IV. Lest there be any doubt, Nataraja Guru unequivocally states, at II:15, that "equanimity [is] a positive quality and not mere indifference."

There is also a play on words at work here. *Nirvedam* can also mean "beyond or without the Vedas," in keeping with the anti-scriptural advice Krishna is giving in this section. We can also take it in the general sense of "beyond or without religion." Religions are constrained to advertise techniques and specify goals, which can't help but inflame expectations. "What has already been heard" and "What is to be learned," being verbal injunctions regarding the past and the future, naturally fall away when the full presence of the Absolute is encountered here and now.

No matter how *nirvedam* is interpreted, indifference is not to be taken as the correct attitude toward these matters. Krishna is beginning to teach Arjuna a secret technique of mental attunement called yoga, where outer forces and factors are counterbalanced with inner understanding, producing a vigorous and alert neutrality of mind, free of prejudice. Yogis must be active in perceiving the effect of religious and social injunctions on their mental balance, as well as examining all their desires for change and improvement. Poorly understood religious injunctions tend to breed guilt and dissatisfaction accompanied by self-doubt. Social injunctions, while likewise capable of providing some measure of direction and meaning in life, can also be debilitating if they arise from those same negative feelings—as they very often do.

WHEN, DISILLUSIONED RESPECTING
THE (CONTRADICTORY
INJUNCTIONS OF THE) SCRIPTURES,
YOUR REASON STANDS UNSHAKEN
AND STEADY IN *SAMADHI*, THEN
YOU SHALL HAVE REACHED YOGA.

Krishna concludes his initial presentation of yoga masterfully and with a verbal shaking of Arjuna for his heretofore ill-considered acquiescence to popular prejudices. One would expect a seeker of truth to have seen through at least some of that detritus before even setting out, but in an odd way it sometimes leads us to our first step. We don't often begin to question the prevailing beliefs of our surroundings until by some quirk of fate we find ourselves on the outside looking in, or like Arjuna we are threatened with immanent annihilation.

Buddhi, the "reason" or "intellect," being elucidated in this section, is much more than the mind, which in Indian philosophy is merely the coordinator of the senses. Intellection bridges the gap between a mundane registration of the obvious and a profound spiritual vision, raising us out of the former and toward the latter. Most Western ideas of the intellect are quite limited and are similar to the Indian concept of mind.

The exalted stature of buddhi may be grasped through the name of the Buddha, the one whose buddhi is completely awakened. In spiritual development, reason begins by exploring the mind, meaning the ordinary transactional coordinations of sensory experience. Gradually it progresses to more and more subtle fields of inquiry, learning steadiness in the face of the impacts of outrageous fortune. Only when the intellect has matured all the way to sameness, samadhi, has it achieved the yogic state of unitive reason.

Among spiritual seekers there is a widespread disdain for the intellect that is seriously misplaced. The basis for this attitude is that when the intellect is enamored of itself as the most important aspect of the psyche, it becomes ingrown and hubristic. What is at fault is really the ego that has yoked the intellect to its impoverished vision. The intellect should be treated as a vehicle to carry the self to the Self, the ego to the transcendental, and not as a buttress of our self-defense.

The Gita regularly speaks of subduing the mind, but that doesn't mean we should subdue our intellect. Since mind refers to the outgoing attention to sensory stimulation, the advice is to restrain that and explore the rest of what we are via contemplation. Inner examination is the domain of the intellect. Confusing these two aspects of the psyche has caused endless misery due to suppression of one of our most important attributes.

Nataraja Guru adds "contradictory injunctions" to scripture, since ideally scripture should not be problematic. Often enough, though, a scripture will contradict itself, because it is a compendium of writings by various authors over a long period of time. What's more, the injunctions of scripture often contradict our innate wisdom and interrupt the artistic flow we are trying to attune with. Our healthy disillusionment is to see that scripture is manmade and not the "Word of God." Knowing this, we can take it for what it's worth, no more, no less.

Even more important are the contradictory injunctions of the unwritten scriptures known collectively as society. Here are a few examples that cause confusion based on illusions: All men are created equal, but you only have to be fair to the ones who give you something in return. Everyone is created in the image of God, yet only a select few can enter heaven or be saved. Actions are irrelevant to reach God, but you must behave yourself or else. Love your neighbor as yourself, but think nothing of killing him if he lives far enough away, beyond some hypothetical boundary. God insists on your honesty, but if you tell the truth you will lose your friends and your job. Be fair and just, but those who aren't fair or just occupy the choice positions. The disillusion these contradictions instill can be a springboard to turn to a more lasting source of satisfaction, here called samadhi, the all-embracing, energetic sameness that is the state of yogic wisdom.

Yawning gulfs exist between what people say and what they do, and a yogi must rise above them. The thrust here is to turn away from getting your directions from religious or legal books and their purveyors and discover the truth within yourself. Truth is not contradictory; hypocrisy is.

VERSE 54

ARJUNA SAID:
WHAT IS THE WAY OF ONE WHOSE
REASON IS WELL FOUNDED, WHO
IS ESTABLISHED IN SAMADHI,
O KRISHNA? HOW DOES HE
DISCOURSE, WHAT IS HIS STATE OF
BEING, HOW DOES HE MOVE ABOUT?

The disciple's initial task is to come up with probing questions and deeply ponder the answers given. In his first opportunity to fulfill his role, Arjuna shows his keen interest and respectfully prods his guru to expound more on the subject at hand.

There are several good reasons for Arjuna to ask these seemingly banal questions. He is admitting he doesn't yet know enough to spot a wise teacher, and he wants to avoid the enervating and even danger- ous possibility of dedicating himself to a charlatan. Of course, Arjuna already has a guru par excellence. Here he is being used as a foil to inform the rest of us what we need to know at the outset. Distinguishing a true rishi from a clever imitation is no simple matter.

Anyone entering a spiritual path would be wise to presume that most of the teachers they will encounter are pretenders of one sort or another. A true guru in human form is rare indeed. Pretenders often take advantage of trusting followers in many ways, particularly sexual and financial, and their impact is often devastating, even though their codependent sects spend a lot of energy covering up their shortcomings. Caveat emptor, let the buyer beware, is especially true when seeking a qualified "remover of darkness."

I have a friend who has made a lifetime study of Indian philosophy. A while back another friend came to visit from India who had recently been given the robes of a renunciate. At the time he was a real neophyte about Indian wisdom, but he had the clothes and the look. He was tall, dark, and handsome, with an erudite-looking beard and the right cut and color of robes. My American friend is totally incognito. Although he is well versed in Indian spirituality, he wears ordinary clothes and doesn't have a beard. Everywhere the two went, people were immediately drawn to the one who looked like a wise man and paid no attention to the one who could have answered their questions but looked unimpressive. We are so easily deceived by appearances. An equal-minded person would have treated the two the same and quickly discovered who was the more knowledgeable, but everyone with a preconceived image of holiness was invariably drawn to the less informed fellow instead. Appearance easily cloaks substance. Clothes make the man, or at least they promote the charade.

VERSE 55

KRISHNA SAID:
WHEN ONE BANISHES ALL DESIRES
THAT ENTER THE MIND, ARJUNA,
SATISFIED IN THE SELF BY THE SELF
ALONE, THEN HE IS SAID TO BE ONE
OF WELL-FOUNDED REASON.

Arjuna's questions have invited Krishna to elaborate the qualities of a true yogi and knower of the Absolute. He begins with speaking about "banishing desires," another piece of advice that is often taken incorrectly at the beginning. People spend years struggling to master their normal urges, imagining that is their spiritual path. They have heard they can only appear before their God squeaky clean, so they feel guilty about aspects of themselves that are thought of as dirty.

Later on, Krishna will assure us that the Absolute doesn't care in the least about such matters. He suggests directing the attention to the Absolute instead, to the meaning that forms the skeletal structure of the world. Once that all-absorbing vision is attained, irrelevant desires fall away naturally, and those that do come up are easily dealt with. So time spent wrestling with desires is time spent on desires, whereas time spent engaged in contemplation is time spent in the Absolute.

Arjuna has just asked about well-founded reason (*sthita prajna*), and now Krishna will discourse on the subject at length. Guru Nitya Chaitanya Yati offers this on the same theme:

> Verticalization is the first thing taught by the Bhagavad Gita, in the second chapter. The verticalized state of awareness is called *sthita prajna*. *Prajna* is pure consciousness; *sthita* means remaining in the state of. When one becomes established in the supreme truth, the individual manifestations of the state of flux are all seen in relation to it. That stabilizes your mind and gives it a vision from within, so it is not getting swayed by the stimuli that are flowing in through the senses. It may often seem to a beginning reader of the Gita that Krishna is off the mark by speaking of *sthita prajna* to Arjuna. Arjuna is in the middle of the battlefield and he doesn't know whether to shoot or not. Instead of saying anything about that, Krishna is addressing himself to the control of the senses, how to look into yourself, what the supreme nature of the Self is, and so forth. The purpose here is to bring about a verticalization. Jesus did the same thing. Before asking a man to be good to his neighbors, he said, "Love your Father, your God, with all your heart." If you love the Father and know his fatherhood, then you will see the brotherhood. If the rhythm of life is to be appreciated, one should know the music of life, the whole symphony of it. The whole symphony of life is known by knowing the vertical principle.[16]

Withdrawing the senses (and mind) from sense objects means turning away from external stimuli to engage the intellect. It is almost never a full-time activity: it is how we are able to perform concentrated reflection or contemplation. When driving a car or playing a sport, for instance, the mind should most definitely be attuned to what the senses register.

Well-founded reason is thought that isn't prejudiced by appearances, or our likes and dislikes. Detachment means undoing attachments, pulling the hooks and arrows of previous conditioning out of our flesh, allowing a much fuller appreciation of life. It is not the blocking of experience by preventing sensory stimulation from reaching the brain somehow. That would be inaction, discredited by the Gita as unhelpful and also impossible, short of coma.

Here's a concrete example. Imagine you're a trial lawyer, and you've got a guilty defendant, a real skuzzball. At the trial you make sure he shows up in a nice new suit and tie, fresh haircut, glasses, and a copy of *The City of God* by St. Augustine under his arm to peruse during recess. You know perfectly well the judge will have a harder time throwing the book at him if he looks like a harmless fellow, who strayed just this once, than if he has "hardened criminal" written all over him. The jury is also inevitably affected by these strictly cosmetic tricks. They are deceived by their senses, even against their will. But at least a wise judge and jury will strive to leave appearances out of their decision as much as possible. They will try to look at the "facts," and come to a conclusion based solely on the merits of the case. If they can do this, their reason is well founded; if they are prejudiced by some tangential matter then their reason is poorly founded, precisely to the extent that it is diverted from the facts.

Of course, facts become mighty fuzzy the closer you look at them, but what else do we have to work with? The point is to bring your best scientific attitude to bear on the problem and not be conned by your habitual preferences and expectations, no matter how much you admire them.

Speaking of science, how many experiments are warped by the expectations of the experimenters? The answer is all of them. Even with rigorous safeguards, expectations demonstrably skew the results, and a lot of thought goes into programming ways to circumvent their impact. In the current climate it's even worse: so-called scientists are inveigled by vested interests into supporting foregone conclusions and throwing out any results that deviate from the expectations of the underwriters of the experiment. Sadly, we give in to fads all the time, in a million ways we aren't even conscious of.

Here's another example. You see a gorgeous babe of your preferred gender in the distance, and your heart gives a leap. A half billion years of sexual evolution has packed you with plenty of motivation. You start to have fantasies based on the deep-seated urge that has just surfaced. As you walk closer, reality (well-founded reason) starts to kick in. You begin to see flaws, not the perfection you had imagined. You start to consider the inconvenience and complications of having a relationship, and as you get close enough to see the "warts" you recognize this is an ordinary human being, whom you may cherish in an abstract way but who holds little interest for you. The zing! of desire has been dissipated by sensible reasoning and will no longer lead you to make an entangling choice.

This kind of thing is happening all the time, not just with sexuality, though that's maybe the most obvious. Literally millions of psychologists working for the advertising and propaganda industries throughout the twentieth century have studied just how to catch your attention and get you to buy their product or their line of BS. Long before advertising existed, humans were susceptible to outside manipulation, or else Krishna wouldn't have brought it up back in 500 BCE or whenever it was. If we don't consciously counteract those influences we are bound to be led astray.

Finally, Nataraja Guru says this about verse 55:

The first thing that happens to a man who begins to tread the path of the contemplative consists in his disaffiliation from the various desires with which he is attached to different grades of relativistic values in everyday life. Such desires are meant to include all those which are capable of entering into or affecting the mind. . . . A man who purposely or actively searches for objects of desire falls outside the scope of contemplation altogether.[17]

> HE WHOSE MIND IS UNAFFECTED
> BY MISHAPS, WHO ON HAPPY
> OCCASIONS TOO EVINCES
> NO INTEREST, RISING ABOVE
> ATTACHMENT, ANXIETY, OR ANGER—
> SUCH A SAGE-RECLUSE IS SAID TO BE
> OF WELL-FOUNDED REASON.

Here we have one of the most misunderstood concepts of all, detachment. It is often held that you should remain "uninterested" in relation to happy and sad occasions, more commonly called pain and pleasure. This has been taken to an extreme in several forms of Hindu and Buddhist practice, not to mention other religions, including the religion of science, as though even noticing that anything extrarational is going on is somehow unspiritual or unscientific. Animals and people are not supposed to have feelings, or if they do, they are irrelevant. We should take it as a given that the Gita does not intend anything of the sort.

First of all, the translation is a bit extreme, and I'm tempted to change it, yet it does reflect how people think about the subject. Radhakrishnan's version is more instructive: "He whose mind is untroubled in the midst of sorrows and is free from eager desire amid pleasures. . . ."[18] Good on him! The Sanskrit word used definitely gives the sense of craving, of strong lust for pleasure, and does not imply that normal reactions, including enjoyment, are to be ruled out. The point is to pare away all excessive carrying on, both about our troubles and our triumphs. We all know people who aren't happy unless they are complaining about something or whining about their personal problems, and we know others who are boastful about their successes. Arjuna himself was a bit undone at the outset of his present conflict and tempted to lose hope. Fortunately his feelings prompted him to take a great leap forward and consult a guru. If he had ignored them he would have stayed where he was.

What's meant here is that a spiritual aspirant should always separate the kernel of truth from the chaff of padded emotions and beliefs, discarding everything excessive. That should make what's left over even more clear and valuable. So after reacting normally to an event, including tearing our hair and screaming and crying if it's appropriate, we should lay the business to rest and regain our cool. Simple enough? If it really were easy our world would be filled with sage-recluses, but such is not the case. Humans easily get stuck in tangential thoughts and emotions. We repeat our miseries, cravings, and misapprehensions endlessly. There will be more in the next several verses to help hone our understanding of detachment in a spiritual sense.

All our motivation boils down to striving for happiness, though it might well be hidden by rationalizations and excuses, by shoulds and oughts. We adopt many ideas that are opposed to happiness, but this is because someone has convinced us that they will in fact lead to happiness somewhere down the road. An honest spiritual teacher might do this with a beneficial aim in mind, while a charlatan would prefer you to unwittingly strive for their own personal benefit. Each seeker must sort this out independently, by not taking anything for granted, and by searching questioning and intuitive thinking.

The happy occasions that we are directed to ignore are the flip side of mishaps. Note that both are things that happen *to* us, positively and negatively. Their synthesis is well-founded reason, which rises above the immediate impact of events to understand their full meaning. It does not hold on to the one and reject the other but dispassionately assesses their value and acts accordingly.

Happiness as the flip side of sadness is clearly not an eternal or absolute value. Anything with an opposite is not absolute. Happiness as a condition either opposed to or causing someone else's unhappiness is relativistic and therefore superficial. Only by uniting opposites in yoga is the true, unconditioned happiness achieved. In this verse the state of true happiness is equated with well-founded reason.

Physicist Robert Oppenheimer once said that trying to achieve happiness is like trying to invent a machine whose only feature is to run silently. He was speaking of the dualistic happiness, of course, because every action makes noise, and action to erase action is absurd. True happiness, which is a byproduct of reason well centered in the Absolute, makes our clunky and noisy psychosomatic "machine" run at top efficiency. It doesn't shut it off.

The three afflictions mentioned here and elsewhere in the Gita are usually translated along the lines of "desire, fear, and anger," but Nataraja Guru's version, "attachment, anxiety, and anger," offers shades of meaning that pertain more to contemplative life. As he says: "The trio are organically related to the subject inasmuch as they make contemplation impossible of being even initiated." Furthermore, he reminds us, "The attempt here is merely to remove impediments to contemplation and not to teach virtues."[19] Detachment is achieved by removing distractions, while not suppressing valuable stimuli.

HE WHO REMAINS IN ALL CASES
UNATTACHED ON GAINING SUCH
OR SUCH DESIRABLE-UNDESIRABLE
END, WHO NEITHER WELCOMES
ANYTHING NOR REJECTS IN
ANGER—HIS REASON IS WELL
FOUNDED.

There are many subtleties surrounding the concept and practice of
detachment, but for now I'd like to mention the main difference
between Vedanta philosophy as taught by the Gita and how it is typically portrayed in the popular imagination. In order to break the karmic cycle, where actions lead to attachments and attachments lead to
circumscribed actions, endlessly, many Buddhists and Hindus recommend detachment. This is often interpreted to mean erecting a barrier
against emotionally charged experience, since the world is seen as a false
projection, hostile to some unearthly "enlightenment." If you get drawn
into involvement with the world, you remain caught. Perhaps this is
useful in some ways, especially as a beginning step if we are caught up
in a lot of junk, but it can easily produce a state of obliviousness that
is far from spiritual. The Gita's method is to turn to the light rather
than trying to cover up the darkness. It teaches being unguardedly

open to experience, without seeking to abandon ourselves to it.

Being ecstatically alive means at the very least being cognizant of what's going on around you. Training yourself to not react to events engenders psychic numbness and mimics death. Vedanta recognizes that such an attitude can easily be the negative side of positive attraction, and as such equally delusional. The correction for this is to embrace experience as an expression of the Absolute with wholehearted participation but then to avoid holding on to the "afterglow" except perhaps as a useful lesson. You don't dwell on the past but move on. Storing up experiences as memories that feed the ego is deleterious, but expansive memories related to the Big Picture are valuable not only in avoiding future mistakes but in intelligently guiding our steps.

The popular catchword is "live in the now." That's fine, so long as "the now" contains the past and the future. The now taken in isolation, detached from memories, is a kind of living death.

Musicologist Clive Waring has possibly the worst case of amnesia ever recorded and is completely unable to create long-term memories. His condition is utterly disabling and hellish, consisting of days that are an endless series of "waking up for the first time" moments. If you are tempted to fantasize living solely in the present, watch the heartbreaking documentary of Mr. Waring.

What being here now really means is that we should discard regrets about the past and anxiety about the future, which can bog down our consciousness with distracting and unpleasant sidetracks that we can do nothing about. Many people are disabled by a variety of distracting thoughts, and learning to detach from them is therapeutic in many ways. It allows us to be more present and have more intensely positive experiences.

The bottom line is please enjoy life fully, but also understand its projections and delusions, which are legion. Then, after thoroughly experiencing something, let it go. Don't hold on to echoes of experience in your mind. They are preventing you from being present for the next occurrence. In contemplation it's very helpful to review your experience, but not while you're in the thick of things. Be alive to what's happening and ponder it later. Learn to move on from the feelings that catch hold of you in a static way, that induce repetitive compulsions.

It's tragic that the idea has caught on from verses like this one that you should avoid experience, avoid life. Why bother to have a body at all, if you aren't going to have fun in it? How will you feel if you get to the end of your life (which could be at any moment) and you look back and say to yourself that you were able to not do anything? How very "spiritual"! You managed to not love, to not admire the wonders of nature, never heard the great music or visited the museums, never created anything beautiful or useful. That's what Arjuna proposed as a solution to his dilemma back in the first chapter, and Krishna told him, "No way! Get back in the game and play it for everything you're worth."

A young American with Buddhist leanings, whose mother was very ill, once asked me, "If my mother dies, what should I do? How do I keep from being sad?" I told him, "Go ahead and cry. Feel how sad it is. Miss her." It can't be helpful to be stifling your natural, legitimate emotions. It's just crazy. This notion needs to be discarded with all the other false ones. Just open your heart to what's going on. Live the moment. You can philosophize about it later if you wish.

Now get out there and have some fun and in the process make somebody else happy too.

VERSE 58

AGAIN, WHEN, AS A TORTOISE
RETRACTS ITS LIMBS FROM ALL
SIDES, THE SENSES ARE WITHDRAWN
FROM OBJECTS OF SENSE INTEREST—
HIS REASON IS WELL FOUNDED.

Thought is the link that connects the senses at one pole to the coordinating self at the other. The Gita's advice to turn away from sense interests is intended to free the self so it can soar high, being no longer glued onto objects in the environment. Yet the self doesn't stay exclusively in the abstract, either. The idea is to synthesize, not to choose one pole or the other. Someone who is only thinking of perceivable matters is wholly bound to necessity, continually reacting to outside input. But going to the opposite extreme is not the solution; it produces the egg-headed, overly abstracted professor type that is widely lampooned. The healthiest route is an admixture of horizontal and vertical factors, of the transactional and the theoretical, where each feeds and tempers the other. That is truly "reason in action," or yoga.

In order to have an inner vision of connection we naturally restrain the senses and focus on the intellect or the heart or whatever you like to call it. Whenever you think hard or contemplate something, this happens automatically. On the other hand, if your senses are calling for attention, it makes you fidget and get distracted. Substantial effort is required to develop the power of concentration so it becomes steadier and more reliable. This verse is merely describing this necessary aspect of meditation in a poetic way. There is no reason to be alarmed that the Gita is asking us to turn off the senses and leave them off. They are absolutely essential to our life, but they are only the jumping off point for the development of intelligence.

The deceptiveness of the senses is well known. Scientists and philosophers alike have learned to be wary of sense impressions from the earliest antiquity, and yet the convincing nature of what we perceive, especially what we see, is undeniable. In order to be certain of our knowledge, we absolutely must analyze the data flooding into the system from a detached perspective. Only when all significant errors are deleted can our reason be considered "well founded," or even reasonably well founded.

The consensual nature of perceived reality has been called into question in the so-called postmodern era of deconstruction, which in some ways resembles the yogic wisdom discipline of the Gita. To give just one example, here Clive Scott cites Victor Burgin in support of his point that "Realism is something our perceptual culture has educated, or persuaded, us into."

> We do not however see our retinal images: as is well known, although we see the world as right-way-up, the image on our retina is inverted; we have two slightly discrepant retinal images, but see only one image; we make mental allowances for the known relative sizes of objects which override the actual relative sizes of their own images on our retina; we also make allowances for perspectival effects such as foreshortening, the foundation of the erroneous popular judgement that such effects in photography are 'distortions'; our eyes operate in scanning movements, and the body is itself generally in motion, such stable objects as we see are therefore *abstracted* from an ongoing phenomenal flux, moreover, attention to such objects 'out there' in the material world is constantly subverted as wilful concentration dissolves into involuntary association, and so on.[20]

OBJECTIVE INTERESTS REVERT
WITHOUT THE RELISH FOR THEM
ON STARVING THE EMBODIED OF
THEM. EVEN THE RESIDUAL RELISH
REVERTS ON THE ONE BEYOND
BEING SIGHTED.

The One Beyond is a poetic term for the Absolute. The gist here is that we may struggle mightily to break free of our fascination with and entanglement in the world around us, and at best we can only partly solve this dilemma. Once we enter rapport with the Absolute, however, there is no need to strive for any achievement. The bliss of the connection is so absorbing that our mundane attachments rapidly lose their ability to captivate us. Anyone who has had a psychedelic or other transcendental experience knows exactly how this feels.

From a practical standpoint, before enlightenment, yogis counterbalance each of their anomalies by intentionally supplying an opposing concept, and this helps establish neutrality. After enlightenment, the neutral state of samadhi prevails as an unshakable reality, so the same anomalies may arise but they quickly lose substance, dissipating into the neutral ground.

For example, if some characteristic of a person produces a negative gut reaction, the ordinary person believes it is because the other person is despicable and leaves it at that. The yogi knows that such a reaction is an unfair prejudice on their part and offsets it by assuring themselves that the person has all the good qualities of the rest of us, but has perhaps suffered excessively or simply chosen a different path. Maybe they're only shaped differently. In this way the negative reaction is minimized and replaced by understanding. Only then can we treat them as they deserve to be treated. With practice, once a neutral attitude has become the norm, everyone appears just as they are. There is no negativity to counteract. Or positivity, in the converse case of undue attraction.

Glowing pictures of heroic seekers struggling mightily to subdue their corporeal interests make exciting scriptural tales and have caught the public imagination in various eras. Just as often, at the stage when the charm of the struggle wears off and the drudgery of excluding enjoyment in life takes over, many abandon the game. They might even tell themselves that spirituality is stupid, so as to excuse their change of heart. But all they've really done is throw out a false notion, a religious fantasy. The drudgery was a message from their inner guru that they were on the wrong track to begin with.

Krishna is saying that we can starve ourselves of pleasures as a way to get over an obsession with objects, but this is a hard road. Paradoxically, pushing something away can make it grow in importance, become secretly more desirable. The better way is to come to know the Absolute, which is so absorbingly interesting that mere objects no longer convey the thrill they once did. We extinguish the torch we are using once the sun comes up. The bliss of the Absolute puts mere transitory enjoyments to shame; more than that, it infuses every experience with meaning and joy so that they are even more fun.

Recent neuroscientific discoveries show that Krishna's advice in this verse reflects exactly how the brain works. Rewiring is going on all the time, as new interests supplant old ones. But struggling to remove old neural connections actually strengthens the existing wiring. The most effective method to change, then, is to attend to the new and allow the old pathways to wither away on their own.

This concept has very practical implications, which can save us from wasting a lifetime in futilely combating our demons. For example, the persistence of addiction has perennially bedeviled societies. Before it was banned, LSD showed excellent prospects for curing alcohol dependency, and ibogaine has shown similar results with a wide variety of addictive substances. Psychedelics owe their efficacy in lifting obsessive users out of their addictions by imparting a vision of the Absolute, or in other words, restoring them to a sense of being a worthy person. The One Beyond is actually who we are. Once it has been glimpsed, it is so much more attractive than the mediocre palliatives currently being abused that the person immediately turns away from them. Without this inspirational factor to upgrade the object of desire, battling addiction is frequently a lifelong struggle. Many socially acceptable programs invoke a higher power, but exactly what that is remains abstract and theoretical and therefore much less potent than it might be if it were "glimpsed." Psychedelic medicines are convincing enough to make the theory of a higher power seem extraordinarily real.

In a sense we are all addicted to our habitual interpretations of reality, and they can be as draining of our psychic energy and sabotaging of our expertise as actual drugs. To counteract this type of dependency, the ancients used a psychedelic substance called *soma,* which is examined in detail in my commentary on chapter XI of the Gita (see *Krishna in the Sky with Diamonds,* Inner Traditions, 2012). Although he wasn't a drug addict, soma worked for Arjuna by thoroughly convincing him of the validity of Krishna's teachings, helping to free him from his bondage to conventional mental frames.

Another good practical example, and one which has a connection to verse 41, where "well-founded reasoning is unitive, but many branched and endless are the reasonings of them in whom reason is ill-founded," is the nearly universal creed to love everyone equally, friend and foe alike. If you are already established in a state of love, blissfully attuned to the Absolute, then nothing could be simpler than to love everyone and everything around you. But if you are striving to love people only because of religious instruction or personal dedication and don't actually feel it, everyone you meet is a separate challenge for you to rise to the state of love for them. Some will be easy and some nearly impossible, and the latter force you to strain mightily to find even a shred of love in your heart. They will drive you nuts instead! Probably they are the ones who need love the most, but they are bound to receive the least.

For this reason the Gita recommends seeking the One Beyond first, and all else becomes perfectly simple and natural. The Bible teaches the same thing when it advises: "But seek ye first the kingdom of God, and his righteousness; and all these things shall be added unto you."[21]

EVEN WITH A MAN OF WISDOM, ARJUNA, IN SPITE OF HIS EFFORT, EXCITED SENSE INTERESTS CAN FORCIBLY DISTRACT THE MIND.

The modern world is drenched in sensory overload. The visceral stimulation engendered by sensory stimuli is enjoyable in the short term, but if that's all there is, it is like having a diet of only desserts—or only alcohol. Stimuli must be processed into a coherent understanding of life and our place in it. At an early stage of spiritual development, the mind rises above its fascination with stimuli to search for meaning.

Computers have gone even beyond television as a source of sensory excitement, because there can be degrees of participation with other people or at least interaction with intelligent-seeming programs. Many users spend all their free time at the computer in a state similar to drug addiction, dazzled by imaginary existences that appear far more interesting than those offered by their drab surroundings. In a world trained to think of sense input as the be-all and end-all of existence, it is hard to enunciate what is wrong with computer addiction. Only those who lose a loved one to it can tell that something is amiss. It makes them suspect a level of solid reality—something that really matters—must exist amidst the chaos of sensory stimulation.

Kurt Vonnegut's viciously hilarious short story *Harrison Bergeron* depicts a future society where intelligent people have tiny radios implanted in their ear that make distracting noises at frequent intervals to keep them from putting two and two together, thus making everyone equally incompetent. It's a perfect method for controlling the populace. In real life we do this to ourselves and don't require a Handicapper General to enforce it: we have learned to interrupt our trains of thought at the half-developed stage.

Intelligence and wisdom need long stretches of careful thinking to flourish, but rapid-fire sensory distractions can seem like adequate substitutes. This is one more venue where the conditions of verse 69 prevail, where night and day are reversed for seekers of truth and seekers of kicks. Ordinary mentality seeks sensory stimulation as its highest goal, while the wise contemplative takes it in small doses, preferring to be excited by understanding and bipolarity with the Absolute.

RESTRAINING EVERY ONE OF
THEM, HE SHOULD REST UNITIVELY
ESTABLISHED, HAVING ME FOR
HIS SUPREME IDEAL. HE IN WHOM
SENSE INTERESTS ARE SUBDUED—
HIS REASON IS WELL FOUNDED.

As noted earlier, a hasty reading of this section leads many to believe that all sensory stimulation is to be suppressed, to make room for spiritual inspiration. Not so! Moderate amounts of input are essential as food for thought and enjoyment. What are to be restrained are *excited* sense interests, not sense interests per se. The Sanskrit adjective used means "harassing, troubling, or tormenting." We are advised to be alert to when we are losing our mental equilibrium and bring ourselves back into equipoise.

Krishna is teaching Arjuna how to concenter his mind, to achieve one-pointed attention. But this doesn't mean that we must screen out the world all the time. That is an unwarranted conclusion. When we are meditating or pondering we need to detach from sense impulses, but at other times they keep us healthy and normal. Repressing them leads to exaggerations of the psyche. They become ever more powerful obsessions until they break through into overt expression. Better to give them their due, as the rest of the chapter attempts to instruct. We continue to "move amid sense interests" while not allowing them to run away with us.

Recent scientifically rigorous studies of "mindfulness," which basically means paying more attention rather than less, have demonstrated improvements in health and mood. This may be due to release of repressions, along with the salubrious effect of being alert and attuned to the environment. It is by no means contradictory to subdue interest in sensory stimulation in order to become *more* aware of the world—that is exactly the point.

Aggressive people aren't generally spiritually inclined, but many of them pay lip service to some scripture or other as a means of increasing their power and influence over others. Arjuna himself may be said to be an aggressive or at least active type, though hardly manipulative. The advice here is perfectly germane for such people. Instead of simply plunging ahead with the program you have impulsively chosen, you should take time to consider how both you and others will be impacted by your actions, and you should not just consider but really put yourself in their place and see how it looks from various angles. You have to detach yourself from your urge to press ahead in order to be able to do this. It may be that your program is perfectly acceptable, or maybe not; but you have to restrain your immediate impulses in order to be sure.

This also suggests a strategy to those impacted by aggressive behavior. Fighting back on the aggressor's own terms only increases the polarization and makes the problem worse. But if you can find a way to present your humanity to them, to get them to see the wounds they are inflicting, they might learn to restrain themselves. This was the key to success of India's nonviolent resistance to the British in the struggle for independence. Unfortunately, it requires at least a minimum of humanity on the part of the aggressor, and this is not always available. But it must be presumed, lest you fall into the trap of demonizing your enemy to legitimize your own viciousness.

This verse is the first of many times in the Gita that Krishna speaks of "Me." It is crucial to be aware that he is speaking of his nature as the Absolute, not as some particular entity or—heaven forbid—God. This "Me" appears throughout the Gita and is described in the most expansive possible terms. Simple minds down through the ages have identified the unlimited Absolute with various incarnations and characters from scriptures, not realizing that these are merely symbols of the One Beyond. This leads to a pathetic kind of contest between Jesus and Allah and Buddha and Krishna and Jehovah as to who is really the true one, while all others are relegated to the domain of falsehood. The bottom line is that whatever way you conceive of the Absolute limits it to precisely that. As the Absolute is unlimited, partisanship is necessarily false in every case.

The Gita definitely directs the disciple to view the mysterious, transcendent, and unlimited Absolute as the supreme ideal. It is tragic that Krishna has been made out as a god, dragging this superlative scripture down under the influence of parochial concerns.

The second part of the verse flows out of the first. When you are able to see the Absolute in all things, your attention is drawn to a deeper level than sensory awareness, conditioned as it is by the impact of vibrations on different types of skin, such as tongues and eardrums. Intellection is pure when it is independent of sensory distractions. In a world where feelings constantly clamor for attention, it takes some effort to quiet them down and hold fast to clear thinking. Sensory preferences prejudice the mind, leading to the disaster described in the next two verses.

MEDITATING ON OBJECTS OF SENSE-INTEREST THERE IS BORN IN MAN AN ATTACHMENT FOR THEM; FROM ATTACHMENT RISES PASSION; IN THE FACE OF PASSION (FRUSTRATED) ARISES RAGE.

Attachment is a very subtle business that gradually creeps up on us without our being conscious of it. At first we are merely amused or entertained by something, so we repeat the experience. We grow to like it. Before long it becomes a need, then in some cases an addiction or obsession, but we don't particularly notice because it's our preference. We identify with it, especially if it resonates with our genetic propensities and habits (vasanas and samskaras) in the depths of our being.

For a variety of reasons, some amusements are more binding than others. We usually learn about these when we try to stop reinforcing them and find that we have hooks in us that make them much harder to relinquish than they should be. The belief that this means the behavior is therefore good for us is incorrect; we can be hooked by both beneficial and harmful interests. Krishna is now explaining where the deleterious ones lead, and it's up to each of us to observe whether we are sliding down a slippery slope or not. Since we are masters of denial, it doesn't hurt to have a guru or other advisor to alert us to the bad news. It is famously hard medicine to swallow the criticism when someone tells us we are going wrong, and our ego will likely shape shift into a procession of demons to resist it. And, as Freud put it, even the willing patient will instinctively push the dentist away when he approaches their mouth brandishing his pliers.

Here's how the process of attachment works. In the normal course of becoming separate individuals, early on we retain a neutral balance in our nature, but very soon we learn to move toward our likes and away from our dislikes. This is where imbalance becomes possible. We can't always escape what we don't like and we can't always have what we do like. Frustration sets in, followed by manipulation and scheming to get "ours." Even small children can be seen to become violently angry when they don't get their way. Later they adopt "tricks" to coerce their caretakers into granting their requests. Adults retain these coercive attitudes, though they are usually much better disguised by civilized behavior. But just try to get an addict to undergo treatment, for instance, and the civilized part falls away quickly enough.

Becoming enraged is only the beginning.

FROM RAGE IS PRODUCED DISTORTION OF VALUES, FROM DISTORTION OF VALUES MEMORY-LAPSE, FROM MEMORY-LAPSE COMES LOSS OF REASON, AND FROM LOSS OF REASON HE PERISHES.

When we're angry we act solely for our own interests. Granting the other person their due drops out of the picture entirely. We're ready to fight dirty, to cheat, and use any subterfuge to fulfill our desires. For example, if you accidentally bump into someone on the street, you say "excuse me" and they nod and pass on. But if the person is filled with rage, they will take it as a personal, intentional affront. They'll want to fight you, no matter how eloquently you apologize. The Gita calls such overreactions the distortion of values.

Distortion of values means we rate what we think or want as more important than our friends' perspectives no matter how right they are and wrong we are. In chronic cases it permits us to be unfair to others, so we can rationalize taking what isn't our rightful share. Politicians and egotists occupy this territory as a matter of course, but we all go there at times, and once you have gotten to the stage where your anger overwhelms your good sense, you are in big trouble.

Pretty early in the process of pursuing our likes and avoiding our dislikes we lose awareness of the connecting link within the dual back and forth movement. Heads and tails are taken in isolation and are no longer seen as parts of a single coin. As soon as we are no longer conscious of the underlying harmony, we have become "normal." We have forgotten our inner balance and know only the manifested world of separateness. We are "lost" in a sense, though we can never truly be lost. Even when we forget our connection with the ground that connects everything, it doesn't cease to exist, fortunately for us.

Loss of reason is the "perishing" referred to. You don't actually die from stupidity—sometimes we wish somebody would—but your mental balance perishes. Recall that unitive reason is the goal of the yoga that Krishna is presenting at the moment, and now we learn that meditating on items of sense-interest is what kills it. Nataraja Guru adds that it is the contemplative state of mind that perishes, not the man himself. There is nothing to be done but sleep it off and resolve to start over in the morning. It's not necessarily a fatal delirium, if we are resolved to change where we direct our attention.

BUT HE WHOSE SELF IS SUBDUED,
WHOSE ATTACHMENT AND
AVERSION ARE BOTH WITHIN THE
SWAY OF THE SELF, ALTHOUGH HIS
SENSES STILL MOVE AMIDST SENSE-
INTERESTS, HE WENDS TOWARD A
STATE OF SPIRITUAL CLARITY.

Verse 64 is very interesting. The popular belief that spirituality achieves otherworldly states of mind is unequivocally ruled out in the yoga of the Gita. Your senses still move amidst sense interests, yet you are slowly trending toward clarity of mind. You are still playing the game, fully engaged. The detachment that's happening is that you're sorting out the true from the false and discarding the false. You are experiencing life in all its fullness, and it's even fuller because you have thrown out the garbage. But there is no final moment of clarity when you become someone else. It's an open-ended process of returning to yourself.

The world we live in is the magical realm we are seeking, if only we have eyes to see and ears to hear. Divinity is all around us. As Walt Whitman put it in "Song of Myself," "A mouse is miracle enough to stagger sextillions of infidels."

Notice that verses 64 and 65 form an inverse match with 62 and 63.

In the earlier verses, sensory attraction leads via a series of increasingly negative stages to disaster. In the second pair, those same sensory factors are prevented from disrupting the state of contemplation by conscious intervention, thus leading by a series of positive stages to a properly established intelligence.

Central to this clarifying process is the restraint of attractions and repulsions that threaten to carry us away. We can still savor every bite of our food, it's just that we don't gobble it as if we are starving or push it away without tasting it.

A balanced outlook is the initial goal of the disciple at this stage of the instruction. The entire second half of this chapter is dedicated to extricating Arjuna from his unexamined beliefs and getting him to stand on his own two feet with what is called the mental state of well-founded reason. When it is claimed that yoga is reason in action in verse 50, the Gita isn't kidding. Although the second half is titled "Yoga," it is all about becoming clearheaded, meaning escaping from the miasma of murky beliefs that constitute ordinary thinking and attaining what we nowadays would call a scientific or broadly philosophic attitude.

BY SPIRITUAL CLARITY THERE TAKES
PLACE THE EFFACEMENT FOR HIM
OF ALL SUFFERINGS, AND FOR ONE
WHOSE SPIRIT HAS BECOME LUCID,
VERY SOON REASON BECOMES
PROPERLY FOUNDED.

This is a very straightforward verse, so it's a little odd that Nataraja Guru has rendered *cetasah* as spirit, as it refers to awareness or thought. His intent is simply "spirit" in the sense of "consciousness." The idea is that when our thoughts become lucid, very soon reason becomes properly founded. It's almost a redundancy, in that spiritual clarity and well-founded reason are basically the same thing: intelligence grounded in a universal vision.

A lot of yoga practice consists of rooting out the subtle distortions in thinking that lead to erroneous conclusions. This should be tempered by the advice of verse 59, where awareness of the Absolute is seen as the ultimate clarifying factor. Once we have become spiritually clear, all else follows. In fact, in true *advaita,* nondualism, there is no time lapse at all, so what follows isn't even subsequent.

The effacement of suffering spoken of makes it sound like lucidity magically does away with all the problems of life. Hardly. What it means is that contact with the Absolute is to be adhered to in both good times and bad. The degree of suffering we experience is in direct proportion to our illusory sense of separation, and when that vanishes we regain our native state of oneness. This certainly mitigates the pain, removing all exaggeration from it, but that's all. Life still features ups and downs, but once our reason is well founded we can float over the waves instead of being drowned by them.

While it does seem that some sages are guided by an invisible hand of instinct to avoid trouble, most of them are well known to have endured great suffering. Some have even "lost faith" temporarily because of the excruciating pain they were undergoing. So glib clichés about the cessation of all suffering or everlasting serenity are misleading. Troubles last as long as awareness persists, at any rate. This may well be the cause of the lightly veiled death wish found in many belief systems. If you are aware, there is pain, therefore you should seek to do away with awareness. Need it be said how devastating such concepts are?

The flip side of believing that realization banishes suffering is that if someone suffers, it must be because they are unrealized. This leads to a tendency to blame people for their troubles even when they have done nothing whatsoever to deserve them, which is a harsh and callous attitude in the extreme. Curiously, this superstitious belief is faithfully held by materialists almost as firmly as the credulous. Most of what happens to us is both outside our control and beyond our comprehension, though we do have a say in what we make of it. Knowing this naturally prompts us to be compassionate. Believing everyone deserves what they get is a way of blocking out reality, of turning our backs on life's conflicts. We do it because we fear the unknown, not for any excuse we make to rationalize our aversion.

Really, seeking to do away with suffering is off the mark, in that we learn and grow from overcoming obstacles. That means a yogi should no more avoid obstacles than manufacture them. Instead, we should meet life head on, in whatever aspect it presents itself to us. The wording here is that we should aim for spiritual clarity, and that has a side effect of mitigating suffering, not that doing away with suffering is the goal. This is an important distinction, since a life without suffering is likely to be vapid and prosaic. Compassion comes from knowing from personal experience how other people feel, not from smugly pitying them as fools.

Brain studies have revealed that we learn through negative feedback, gradually adjusting our behavior toward more positive states of mind. Without suffering, it turns out, we don't learn. As Jonah Lehrer puts it, "When the mind is denied the emotional sting of losing, it never figures out how to win."[22] He adds:

> The physicist Niels Bohr once defined an expert as "a person who has made all the mistakes that can be made in a very narrow field." From the perspective of the brain, Bohr was absolutely right. Expertise is simply the wisdom that emerges from cellular error. Mistakes aren't things to be discouraged. On the contrary, they should be cultivated and carefully investigated.[23]

The philosophy of the Gita is about feeling and living to the maximum, in concert with our fellows. A well-founded reason would envisage no less.

FOR ONE UNBALANCED THERE
CAN BE NO REASON, NOR IS THERE
ANY CREATIVE INTUITION FOR
THE UNBALANCED, AND FOR ONE
INCAPABLE OF CREATIVE INTUITION
THERE COULD BE NO PEACE, AND
FOR THE UNPEACEFUL WHERE
COULD THERE BE HAPPINESS?

When the mind is in balance, the floodgates of intuition open. Intuition implies "teaching from within," in other words, contemplating the inner source of knowledge, as opposed to the more familiar outer sources. Krishna tells Arjuna here that the creative intuition that comes from the balanced state leads to peace and happiness. It's a little convoluted because of being expressed negatively, but that's the gist.

Modern scientific studies have demonstrated that wrestling with a problem and then putting the mind in neutral via rest or a mental vacation is an often-successful strategy to find solutions. Yogic meditation does the same thing, stilling the mental chatter while engaging with seldom-accessed parts of the mind that can provide intuitive insights. Finding a way to break out of habitual patterns is another key to what is sometimes called the "eureka phenomenon," when long-sought solutions finally emerge into consciousness. While being newly discovered by scientific observation, these are mainstream ideas from the ancient world, spelled out here and elsewhere.

Isaac Asimov, a hardheaded materialist if there ever was one, coined the term *eureka phenomenon* and wrote an enlightening essay about it. Here's an excerpt:

It is my belief . . . that thinking is a double phenomenon like breathing.

You can control breathing by deliberate voluntary action: you can breathe deeply and quickly, or you can hold your breath altogether, regardless of the body's needs at the time. This, however, doesn't work well for very long. Your chest muscles grow tired, your body clamors for more oxygen, or less, and you relax. The automatic involuntary control of breathing takes over, adjusts it to the body's needs, and unless you have some respiratory disorder, you can forget about the whole thing.

Well, you can think by deliberate voluntary action, too, and I don't think it is much more efficient on the whole than voluntary breath control is. You can deliberately force your mind through channels of deductions and associations in search of a solution to some problem and before long you have dug mental furrows for yourself and find yourself circling round and round the same limited pathways. If those pathways yield no solution, no amount of further conscious thought will help.

On the other hand, if you let go, then the thinking process comes under automatic involuntary control and is more apt to take new pathways and make erratic associations you would not think of consciously. The solution will then come while you *think* you are *not* thinking.

It is my feeling that it helps to relax, deliberately, by subjecting your mind to material complicated enough to occupy the voluntary faculty of thought, but superficial enough not to engage the deeper involuntary one. . . . I suspect it is the involuntary faculty of thought that gives rise to what we call "a flash of intuition," something that I imagine must be merely the result of unnoticed thinking. . . .[24]

Sounds a lot like creative intuition, doesn't it? He goes on to suspect that scientists routinely invent a logical train of thought after the fact to explain their intuition, because they don't want to admit the existence of accidental inspiration, so this simple technique remains a secret. Nonscientists do the same thing. Our egos are habituated to handing out plausible explanations for everything, even though we actually have little or no idea what our real motivations are.

Essential to the eureka process is that you have to have some idea of what you are searching for before intuition can open up any new insights. Scientific rigor is a springboard for intuition to dive off of. First "break your brain" wrestling with the problem, but then let it rest and discover new avenues without your intentional guidance. After all, you don't know exactly where you are going, so why should you be the guide? Having faith in the potential for wisdom through intuition helps foster it too.

This is one of those verses where the translation matters very much, tipping us off to the mindset of the translator as much as the Gita's intent. I like to compare versions at places like this, because the high value of Nataraja Guru's makes it stand out. What it lacks in poetry is more than made up for by its accuracy and freedom from dogma.

Removing the negatives, the first part of the verse basically reads "balance permits reason," and "balance is necessary for creative intuition" (*bhavana*).

The word for balance (*yukta*) comes from the same root as yoga and refers to the equalizing or uniting of opposites that is being taught by Krishna. Digging into my pile of Gita commentaries, the emphasis on conscious manipulation of the process stands out. Radhakrishnan calls balance "control," Mitchell and Thompson use "discipline," Annie Besant has it as "harmonized," Mahesh Yogi says one who is "established," and my religious version from the Gita Press, Gorakpur, uses "control of mind and senses." Balancing may well include all these other terms in its purview, but it is more subtle and nuanced than ordinary control measures, which tend to draw the practitioner away from creative intuition. Substituting the terms highlights the orientation of these representative translations. Nataraja Guru says "balancing of opposites is yoga," which to my mind is just perfect. Try "control of opposites" or "discipline of opposites." Besant's "harmonization of opposites" is the only one in the ballpark, though Mahesh Yogi's "established in the Self" might carry the same sense except it doesn't tell us how to get there.

The word Nataraja Guru has translated as "creative intuition," *bhavana*, stems from the root meaning "to become." It's worth borrowing his comments about this: "Peace results only when intuition comes into operation, along lines of creative becoming, which reconciles opposing tendencies of the mind. Real happiness is the result of a global sense of being where currents and counter-currents are stilled in happiness, which can be said to be the goal of contemplation."[25] There is a real sense of gentleness in this, delicately nudging instead of controlling.

Nataraja Guru's "creative becoming" in his comments is an even better translation than "creative intuition." It refers to that happy state when one insight leads to another deeper insight, and then to another and another, as we follow up the implications of each one. Opening ourselves with a balanced mind to the spectacularly fertile insights of our unconscious, we enjoy a contemplative flow that at its best expresses itself as wisdom.

We have already noted that bhavana, creative intuition, comes as a result of the state of balance. In other words, it is the outcome of the very practice Krishna is recommending, of yoga. Creative intuition is what we get from the practice of yoga and is therefore a key part of the whole study. It produces peace and happiness, which are the overarching goal, stemming from the satisfaction of an active mind.

Most commentators translate bhavana as "concentration," Mahesh Yogi has "steady thought," and the religious one uses "belief." Asimov has the right idea, emphasizing letting go after concentrating for a while. He notes that we may be able to prepare the ground for insight by concentrating, while the Gita is more definite that it does prepare us to be available to receive the insights. Concentration by itself has too much of a sense of the individual straining hard to think, like Asimov's voluntary thought, and is more about what you put in than what comes out of your efforts, while balance reflects the gentleness of opening up to a deep, inner pool of wisdom. If we're generously inclined, concentering the mind makes it available to intuition and insight, so long as it isn't centered around false notions. Belief relies on somebody else to have the intuition and tell you about it, which, while sometimes valuable, is definitely not the Gita's main thrust.

STILL MOVING AMID SENSE INTERESTS, THAT ITEM TO WHICH THE MIND SUBMITS DRAWS AWAY THE REASONING AS THE WIND DOES A SHIP ON THE WATERS.

Verse 67 presents the converse of verse 64. There the sense interests were not allowed to capture the attention, permitting progress toward spiritual clarity. Here they do catch the attention, leading to distraction away from clarity. The image of an invisible force pressing the mind before it, with no solid ground to help offer resistance, is quite apt, and developing enough confidence in our mental orientation to resist outside influences is a long-term challenge.

We experience this metaphorical wind whenever we try to concentrate or meditate, as distracting thoughts catch our attention. Yogis make sure to bring themselves back to the project at hand as soon as they realize they have been blown off course, but undisciplined people simply follow the fickle breezes wherever they may lead. They submit to them, whereas yogis do not.

Mindfulness includes paying attention so that when you are drawn off on a tangent, you sooner or later notice it and bring yourself back to the center. As Mojo Sam of ZBS says, "It's not difficult to be mindful—what's difficult is to *remember* to be mindful."[26] Staying exactly in the center is almost impossible, but minimizing the psychological wobbles and regaining equanimity as soon as disturbances are noticed is simple enough and brings gradual clearing of the fog.

As is well known, external influences like listening to a persuasive speaker can take us very far out of ourself, especially if we are convinced the manipulative thoughts agree with our own. But the most persuasive speaker is the voice in our head. Even though it is a composite of ideas gathered from many disparate sources, it sounds absolutely like "us." The practice the Gita is describing is designed to break the hold of this inner chatter on our psyche, so we can be more authentically ourself.

The expression of creativity in our life depends on a level of concentration that can withstand the gales of many types of distraction, including criticism, hostility, misunderstanding, and even positive distractions like encouragement. We are quite vulnerable to compliments and can easily be swayed by them. The steadiness of a well-founded reason does not swerve in either positive or negative puffs of wind, which are the attractions and aversions Krishna speaks of.

So many of our thoughts carry us away from where we need to be! Let me give an example. One of my fellow disciples was deeply in love with our guru, Nitya. Many, many times she would burst into tears and sob, "You are going to die and I'll be left all alone. I don't want you to die!" She was so upset it interfered with her relationship with him: because she was so busy feeling sad she didn't actually listen to him half the time. Her self-generated anxiety prevented her from being present, even though that was what she believed she wanted. This went on with varying intensity for twenty-five years or so. Then Nitya really did die. She was perfectly calm and serene about it. Didn't bother her in the slightest. She knew in her heart that there was no "away" for him to go to. The only problem was that he was no longer available to teach her. If she had changed her attitude at the outset she would have spared herself a lot of needless misery, while being a much better listener.

This woman was an extreme example, but we all carry shades of similar dread of future possibilities with us all the time, and it spoils our engagement with life to a significant degree. Why not try to see things as they are right now and work on opening up to the wonderful world around? Instead, we indulge our twisted attachments and block the light of life behind a mental iron curtain. The distracting winds can blow with hurricane force.

Lawrence Gonzales has written a very enjoyable book, *Everyday Survival,* with dozens of anecdotes about people who were distracted by what they incorrectly believed they were seeing and so failed to take necessary action to protect themselves, as well as many examples of the opposite: those who thought creatively and so survived hazardous circumstances. Key to his thesis is that the brain gets programmed to run "scripts," whole sequences of responses to a familiar stimulus. We receive the stimulus (sense interest) and then perform an entire preprogrammed song and dance (like being carried away by the wind). This is fine when appropriate, but sometimes the script kicks in at the wrong time, when we really need a fresh response. By paying close attention, though, we can turn off our scripts before they divert us off course. Gonzales' thesis is an update of the Gita's wisdom based on modern neuroscience, though he seems unaware of its roots.

THEREFORE, ARJUNA, HE WHOSE
SENSES HAVE BEEN IN EVERY
WAY WITHDRAWN FROM SENSE
INTERESTS—HIS REASON IS WELL
FOUNDED.

Summing up what has now been clearly established, Krishna makes sure that Arjuna gets the point. It never hurts to recapitulate the lesson, in case the student has gotten off the track because of the intensity and unfamiliarity of the material.

WHAT IS NIGHT FOR ALL
CREATURES, THE ONE OF SELF-
CONTROL KEEPS AWAKE THEREIN;
WHEREIN ALL CREATURES ARE
WAKEFUL, THAT IS NIGHT FOR THE
SAGE-RECLUSE WHO SEES.

The simplest interpretation of this classic verse is that most people attend only to what they "see" through their five senses, while the contemplative delights in the invisible realms of ideas, ideals, and ultimately the Absolute itself. If you can't see something it is dark to you. Conversely, the realm of sensory stimuli blankets the invisible firmament of thought, and so the sage-recluse has to screen it out to prevent it from blocking contact with everything beyond the reach of the senses.

Transactions based on sense data are where ordinary beings put their attention, while the interstices within the matrix of manifestation remain invisible and therefore unappetizing. The wise seer takes delight in this invisible aspect of the universe, source of creative intuition and much more, and knows that being bogged down in externals will prevent attending to it. As Wordsworth mused,

The world is too much with us; late and soon,
Getting and spending, we lay waste our powers:
Little we see in Nature that is ours;
We have given our hearts away, a sordid boon![27]

The good poet goes on to lament how our getting and spending prevents us from loving the world in all its glory, making us "forlorn." We're so caught up in our business we don't feel anything anymore, externally or internally.

The search for truth has always appeared inscrutable to most people. They can't understand why anyone would spend time meditating, when they could be partying, watching TV, drinking beer, getting laid, making money, or what have you. But for someone searching for meaning in life, these are mostly a waste of time, diversions from the search. They may enjoy them too, in moderation, but they have a secondary importance to the quest for understanding.

Contemplating the enormity or the incomprehensibility or what have you of the Absolute and how it suffuses the world is just about the most absorbing amusement there is. You can call it meditation if anyone asks, and then you won't have to explain it, since everyone thinks they know what meditation is. But that which is dark resists explanation. If you start to get a handle on the Absolute, you can be sure the handle will very soon be inadequate. Believing they know exactly what God amounts to is a comforting device for the terrified, the simple-minded, or the neophyte. Offer such people your smiling reassurance, then go back to wondering. They will not be joining you in the dark, no matter how brightly it shines.

Accessing this mysterious depth through contemplation, prayer, or some other route is another thing the Gita means by being awake in the night. Prayer sets up a bipolar relationship with the deity being prayed to. It doesn't really matter if it's between you and yourself in your own mind, because you're invoking the wise part of yourself out of the dim part, or the transcendent Unknown from the limited known. It helps to gently minimize the ego also, by acknowledging you don't have all the answers. For the most part, however, the preferred direction is inward, not out to some hypothetical deity. The Gita gives little credence to prayer and ordinary forms of worship, but it does acknowledge that they are suited to certain types of people and have some value. Contemplation and intelligent reasoning, on the other hand, are accorded the highest respect.

Structurally speaking, day and night are equivalent to horizontal and vertical in Nataraja Guru's scheme of correlation, representing such polarities as space and time, activity and stillness, becoming and being, physics and metaphysics, and so on.[28] In yoga, these pairs are all to be taken together. You can't have the vertical without the horizontal any more than you can have day without night.

It's an interesting sidelight that the name *Arjuna,* which literally means "ever wakeful," also means "white or silver" (the color of the day), and *Krishna* means "dark or black." The ignorant one is bright and the knower shrouded in darkness. Day and night are thus symbolic of the inversion brought about by the guru-disciple relationship, and with this teaching Krishna is subtly pressuring Arjuna to change his outlook from the ordinary to the esoteric.

Guru Nitya Chaitanya Yati elaborates on this, in his class on *Therapy and Realization in the Bhagavad Gita:*

We have three representative people in the Bhagavad Gita: Dhritarashtra, Arjuna, and Krishna. Dhritarashtra, in our case, can be thought of as a state of blindness: being morally blind, spiritually blind, and intellectually blind. We become blind in so many ways. Arjuna can be another aspect in us, the seeking mind, the searching mind, and the mind that likes to be disciplined. It is the mind that likes to be related to the source of wisdom. And the third is Krishna, the one light, which is present in all of us, the eternal light of the Supreme, or whatever name you may call it. This is qualified in the Gita Dhyanam as "the light that teaches." That light is attributed to Narayana.

The word *Narayana* is again very significant. *Nara* means "man." *Ayana* means "to dwell in." Narayana is that which is dwelling in every man, the shining principle that animates the individuation of every person. Narayana himself teaches Partha, another name for Arjuna. Partha is "the ever-vigilant one."

If Dhritarashtra is blind, then the nature of Arjuna is just the opposite: to be ever awake so that the light which illuminates him is never far from him, but within himself. Another description given to Arjuna is Nara. Here Nara indicates the representative man. Narayana and Nara: the indwelling spirit of man and the man. Narayana himself teaches Nara. The guru is not outside of you. There is no one without a guru. Everyone's guru is within him or her. The questioning mind is the disciple and the conclusive answer that comes from within is the guru. Narayana is within everyone.[29]

Every Arjuna has a choice to make between the blind world of separation from the Absolute ground, with its divisions and hostilities, or the inner light that leads to union with it. The first is in plain sight, the second, subtle and mysterious. Yet what looks bright is spiritually dark, and that which cannot be directly perceived is lit by the energy of ten thousand suns.

STILL GETTING FILLED, WHILE FIXED
FIRM IN IMMOBILITY, THE OCEAN
REMAINS; SO, TOO, HE IN WHOM ALL
INTERESTS ENTER—HE ATTAINS TO
PEACE, NOT THE CRAVER OF DESIRES.

The end of the second chapter soars high, concluding with a mysterious and poetic description of the realized state, in which all polarities such as day and night are equalized. This is the last occurrence of the exalted meter until chapter VIII.

Paradox is synthetically realized and integrated in the one who attains to peace. Events may pour in through the senses like rivers to the sea and pour out like vaporizing mists, but the contemplative remains steady in an oceanic state of mind that is neither added to or subtracted from in the least by what transpires.

One who craves desires feels that events change who they are, and so their identity rises and falls with the waves of occurrences. There is no lasting peace to be had by clinging to that which passes away.

"All interests enter" reminds us that the seer is not closed off from events through a negative withdrawal but participates wholeheartedly in them. This world in which we live is the true heaven, unimaginably replete and varied. By relinquishing our craving for more elsewhere, we aren't left with nothing but become rich in that which is always with us.

THAT MAN WHO, GIVING UP ALL ATTACHMENTS, MOVES ABOUT DESIRELESSLY, WITHOUT OWNING ANYTHING, AND WITHOUT EGOISM—HE GOES TO PEACE.

By now we should have understood the case for desireless action, but if not the Gita provides plenty more input in its next couple of chapters. Here we should bear in mind the hypothesis that such an attitude leads to peace, which is all that Krishna is telling us at the moment. In due time all our doubts will be resolved, but for now they have their value in prodding us to think more acutely about the subject.

The third line is the same as the third line of XII:13, where the translation of "without owning anything and without egoism" is sublimated to "free from possessiveness and egoism." The word "without egoism" is translated from literally means "no mine-ness." The idea here is not that you don't own things, but the selfish sense of "mine," perfectly exemplified by the two-year-old with a favorite toy, has been discarded. We can easily see how the child has a limited perception bounded by pure want, but the same emotion in adults, clothed in "mature" finery, passes largely unnoticed. Selfishness shrinks the world to a pitiful vestige of its potential, whereas selflessness is endlessly expansive.

Possessiveness or the "sense of mine" is explicitly mentioned at least four more times in the Gita (III:30; IV:21; XII:13; XVIII:53). Unitive action, one of the main teachings of the Gita, depends on an openness to the entire situation in which one finds oneself. Whenever you have the idea "I am the doer," or "I am the actor," or especially "I want this or that," it erects barriers to that openness that are obstacles to peace.

THIS IS THE STATE OF BEING IN THE
ABSOLUTE, ARJUNA, ON REACHING
WHICH ONE SUFFERS FROM
DELUSION NO MORE. ESTABLISHED
IN THIS AT THE VERY LAST
MOMENTS OF LIFE, ONE REACHES
THAT FINAL STATE OF PURE BEING
IN THE ABSOLUTE.

At the outset of any endeavor there is a high value in knowing its goal, at least in a general way. It provides direction, whereas a hit or miss approach might lead to going around in circles. We are aiming at identification with the Absolute, which sweeps away delusion. Here it is called "pure being," *nirvana*.

Krishna reminds us that delusion causes suffering. Arjuna's suffering is definitely due to the faulty beliefs he is struggling to shake off. But many people work very hard to ratify their delusions rather than dispense with them. They imagine that if they shout louder than the next guy, or have better connections, or elbow out the competition, they will get their way, and that's the whole point of life. Krishna's view is that there is a magnificent meaning to life that is trying to find expression in each person's heart, but a welter of false beliefs keeps it out of sight and out of mind. By relinquishing delusions, the ideal impulse of the Absolute is automatically promoted to the center stage of the relinquisher's experience. Delusions create a closed system, while pure being is open and dynamic, leading to final emancipation even at the portals of death.

The wording of the verse reminds us that sighting the Absolute, the One Beyond, clears away our misconceptions. We can struggle with delusions all we want, and it is even healthy to do so, but they won't be gone until we attain full realization. All too often we achieve a small amount of clarity and imagine we've been cured of the whole disease. Instead of persisting in working on ourselves, we then become evangelists for the partial awareness we have attained. We should pretty much count on the fact that this is a lifetime program and that the most dangerous delusion is that we have successfully eluded our shortcomings. A little humility will help keep us away from this abyss.

Although we have barely begun to make our way through the Bhagavad Gita, many of the essential features of its spirituality have already been introduced. There is enough in the first two chapters to have a dramatic impact on our lives if we choose to put it into practice. Krishna has begun to redirect Arjuna's attention from external pressures to discover his own inimitable strength to make intelligent decisions. He has shown Arjuna how his conditioning warps his ability to enjoy life and act with expertise, and he has presented a nontheistic approach to such classic concepts as detachment, duty, and desire. Yoga has been clearly defined as a method to achieve clear thinking, free of anxiety, prejudice, and rancor. Such clarity is the best way to combat the ills of a world mired in hostility and selfishness. The self-evident fact that this is still a rare commodity in the modern world tips us off that the Gita's teachings are not yet out of date.

The path, which is no ordinary path but an oceanic state, now lies open before us. Over the next sixteen chapters of the Gita the guru stays with Arjuna (and us if we pursue the study) to guide us through the process of first dipping our toes in those waters, then totally immersing ourselves, and afterward drying off in the sun of wisdom, preparatory to reinhabiting the unique and intuitively inspired course of our life.

EPILOGUE

"It looks like we're off to good start," Krishna said. "Do you see the value of investigating these matters further? Shall we continue?"

"This is a lot for me to absorb," replied Arjuna. "Let me sit with it for a while. I want to spare you any trouble on account of my ignorance, so I'll be sure to sort out what I can before I ask anything more of you."

Krishna smiled in appreciation, then went on. "Let me sketch out the next step, which will assist you in your preparations. We're going to reassess knowledge and action, and see how they fit together. Ordinarily there is a gulf between them, but yoga is a way to bridge the gap. I call the bridge karma yoga, unitive action.

"Our actions begin deep in the psyche, in what you might call our unconscious intelligence, whereas our knowledge is compiled mainly by our conscious mind, so it lies much closer to the surface. That's why there isn't always a good match between our thoughts and deeds, or you might say our desires and the demands of daily life. The chaotic battle you are caught up in is exactly the kind of thing that happens when knowledge and action are out of joint. When our knowledge and action are in accord, though, they function seamlessly. In fact, that's how knowledge is converted to wisdom, by integrating it with our actions. You need to learn how to get them to work together, how to incorporate the impulses—both divine and demonic—from your unconscious into your awareness of the world around you. They are meant to be in harmony, but look what a disaster it is when they aren't."

"I can certainly see the disaster part," agreed Arjuna, "but why is action such a big deal? I thought I was getting out of it."

Krishna shook his head, chagrined. "Action is pretty much the whole game," he went on. "The universe is all about things happening. That's the fun of it. Even thoughts are a kind of action. Our mental posturing either holds us captive in oppressive conditions or frees us from them. A lot of your thinking is still tying you down. So you might want to investigate it a little further.

"I know we've touched on this already, but I don't think you've understood it as much as you could, so let me reiterate. For most people, action means doing your duty. It's like being in a work crew: you have your assigned job in an enterprise, whether it's building a skyscraper, playing team sports, running a business, raising a family, or what have you, and you do it well or poorly, depending on how successfully your task is completed. For most, that's the essence of spirituality, doing your duty well, what other people expect you to do well. And that's fine as far as it goes, but those are actually the most mundane matters. Part of you, what I call the divine part, is desperate to express some of the more complex abilities you possess, and if you don't bring them out, they make you frustrated and depressed. You really are a miraculously complicated creation of mine, don't you know? I always intended humans to do more than scrabble for food or run swords through each other.

"What I want to teach you is how to access your full inner being, because your real duty is to develop your unique talents, to become what you truly are capable of as an independent entity, instead of always conforming to a template laid down by someone else. Your best features have been driven so far underground you don't even remember them yourself. Reclaiming them is the real spiritual quest, and it's the essence of what I'll be helping you to discover. I assure you, once you are in tune with your true nature, you will fulfill your mundane duties easily, and with pleasure. You will also know how to dance, how to flow through life creatively. That's the best contribution you can make to yourself and the world around you. Sound interesting?"

Arjuna nodded thoughtfully. "When you put it that way, how can I refuse?"

NOTES

INTRODUCTION

1. Nataraja Guru, *Unitive Philosophy,* 79–80.
2. *Encyclopedia of Philosophy,* s.v. "Absolute, The."
3. Nataraja Guru, *An Integrated Science of the Absolute,* 135–36.
4. Calasso, *The Marriage of Cadmus and Harmony,* 102.
5. Eagleman, *Incognito,* 2.

PART TWO.
COMMENTARY ON CHAPTER I:
THE YOGA OF ARJUNA'S DESPONDENCY

1. Nataraja Guru, *The Bhagavad Gita,* 32.
2. Surowiecki, *The Wisdom of Crowds,* xix–xx.
3. Moore, *Care of the Soul,* 20.
4. Kullander, "Men Are From Earth, And So Are Women," 17.
5. Yati, *Living the Science of Harmonious Union,* 176.
6. Jensen, *A Language Older Than Words,* 102–5.
7. Nataraja Guru, *The Bhagavad Gita,* 32–33.
8. Sharpe, *A Universal Gita,* 162.

PART THREE.
COMMENTARY ON CHAPTER II:
UNITIVE REASON AND YOGA

1. Nataraja Guru, *The Bhagavad Gita,* 69.

2. Wilhelm, ed. and trans., *I Ching*, 201.

3. de Botton, *The Consolations of Philosophy*, 90–91.

4. Gordon and Kay, "That's Life." Recorded by Frank Sinatra.

5. Aurobindo, *Essays on the Gita*, 153–54.

6. Yati, *Therapy and Realization in the Bhagavad Gita*, 17.

7. Nataraja Guru, *The Bhagavad Gita*, 698.

8. Yati, *Love and Blessings*, 173.

9. Nataraja Guru, *The Bhagavad Gita*, 112.

10. Nataraja Guru, *Unitive Philosophy*, 377–78.

11. Vonnegut, *God Bless You, Mr. Rosewater*, 96.

12. Monier-Williams, *A Sanskrit-English Dictionary*, 1970 ed., s.v. "kshema."

13. Lehrer, *How We Decide*, 41.

14. Yati, *Therapy and Realization*, 31.

15. Daumal, *Mount Analogue*, 152.

16. Yati, *Therapy and Realization*, 37–38.

17. Nataraja Guru, *The Bhagavad Gita*, 163.

18. Radhakrishnan, *The Bhagavadgita*, 123.

19. Nataraja Guru, *The Bhagavad Gita*, 164.

20. Scott, *The Spoken Image: Photography and Language*, 9.

21. Matt. 6:33, also Luke 12:31 (King James Version).

22. Lehrer, *How We Decide*, 47.

23. Ibid., 51.

24. Asimov, *The Eureka Phenomena*, http://newviewoptions.com/The-Eureka-Phenomenon-by-Isaac-Asimov.pdf.

25. Nataraja Guru, *The Bhagavad Gita*, 170.

26. ZBS Foundation, *Somewhere Next Door to Reality*.

27. Wordsworth, "The World," *The Oxford Book of English Verse, 1250–1918*, 626.

28. For more on this, see especially Nataraja Guru's *Unitive Philosophy*, 158.

29. Yati, *Therapy and Realization*, 4.

BIBLIOGRAPHY

Asimov, Isaac. *The Eureka Phenomena,* 1971. http://newviewoptions.com/The-Eureka-Phenomenon-by-Isaac-Asimov.pdf.

Aurobindo, Sri. *Bhagavad Gita and Its Message.* Twin Lakes, Wis.: Lotus Press, 1995.

———. *Essays on the Gita.* New York: The Sri Aurobindo Library, 1950.

Bhagavad Gita, The. Gorakhpur, India: Gita Press, 19th ed. 1969.

Calasso, Roberto. *The Marriage of Cadmus and Harmony.* New York: Alfred A. Knopf, 1993.

Daumal, Rene. *Mount Analogue.* New York: Pantheon Books, 1960.

de Botton, Alain. *The Consolations of Philosophy.* New York: Pantheon Books, 2000.

———. *Status Anxiety.* New York: Penguin Books, 2004.

de Chardin, Teilhard. *The Phenomenon of Man.* New York: Harper Perennial, 1976.

Doidge, Norman. *The Brain That Changes Itself.* New York: Penguin Books, 2007.

Eagleman, David. *Incognito.* Edinburgh: Canongate Books, 2011.

Easwaran, Eknath. *The End of Sorrow.* Petaluma: Nilgiri Press, 1979.

Encyclopedia of Philosophy, The. London: Macmillan Publishing Co., 1972.

Gambhirananda, Swami, trans. *Bhagavadgita, With the Commentary of Sankaracarya.* Calcutta: Advaita Ashrama, 1984.

Gonzales, Laurence. *Everyday Survival.* New York: Norton, 2008.

Homer. *The Odyssey.* Translated by Robert Fagles. New York: Penguin Books, 1996.

Hume, Robert Ernest. *The Thirteen Principal Upanishads.* 2nd ed. London: Oxford University Press, 1931.

Huxley, Aldous. *The Doors of Perception and Heaven and Hell.* New York: Harper & Row, 1963.

Jensen, Derrick. *The Culture of Make Believe.* New York: Context Books, 2002.

———. *A Language Older Than Words.* New York: Context Books, 2000.

Kalsched, Donald. *The Inner World of Trauma.* New York: Routledge, 1996.

Kullander, James. "Men Are From Earth, And So Are Women." *The Sun.* August 2006.

Laszlo, Ervin. *Science and the Akashic Field.* Rochester, Vt.: Inner Traditions, 2004.

Lehrer, Jonah. *How We Decide.* Boston: Mariner, 2009.

Maharaj, Dnyaneshwar. *Gita Explained.* Translated into English by Manu Subedar. 3rd ed. Bombay: Kodak House, 1945.

Maharishi Mahesh Yogi. *Maharishi Mahesh Yogi On the Bhagavad Gita.* Harmondsworth, England: Penguin Books, 1974.

Merton, Thomas. *Faith and Violence.* Notre Dame: University of Notre Dame Press, 1968.

Miller, Alice. *For Your Own Good: Hidden Cruelty in Child-Rearing and the Roots of Violence.* 3rd edition. New York: Farrar Straus Giroux, 1990.

Miller, Barbara Stoler, trans. *The Bhagavad Gita: Krishna's Counsel in Time of War.* New York: Bantam Books, 1986.

Monier-Williams, Sir Monier. *A Sanskrit-English Dictionary.* 1970 ed. London: Oxford University Press, 1899.

Moore, Thomas. *Care of the Soul.* New York: Harper Perennial, 1992.

Nataraja Guru. *The Bhagavad Gita, A Sublime Hymn of Dialectics.* 2nd ed. New Delhi: D.K. Printworld, 2008.

———. *Dialectics.* 3rd ed. New Delhi: D.K. Printworld, 2010.

———. *An Integrated Science of the Absolute.* New Delhi: D.K. Printworld, 2001.

———. *Unitive Philosophy.* New Delhi: D.K. Printworld, 2005.

Radhakrishnan, S. *The Bhagavadgita.* New York: Harper & Row, 1973.

Saul, John Ralston. *Voltaire's Bastards.* New York: Macmillan Inc., 1992.

Scott, Clive. *The Spoken Image: Photography and Language.* London: Reaktion Books, 1999

Sharpe, Eric J. *A Universal Gita.* La Salle, Ill.: Open Court Pub. Co., 1985.

Surowiecki, James. *The Wisdom of Crowds.* New York: Doubleday, 2004.

Thompson, George, trans. *The Bhagavad Gita, A New Translation.* New York: North Point Press, 2008.

Vonnegut, Kurt, Jr. *God Bless You, Mr. Rosewater.* New York: Holt, Reinhart and Winston, 1995.

Wilhelm, Richard, ed. and trans. *I Ching.* 3rd ed. New York: Bollingen Foundation, 1970.

Williams, George M. *Handbook of Hindu Mythology.* New York: Oxford University Press, 2003.

Wordsworth, William. "The World." *The Oxford Book of English Verse, 1250–1918.* new ed. New York: Oxford University Press, 1942.

Yati, Nitya Chaitanya. *The Bhagavad Gita: A Sublime Hymn of Yoga Composed by the Ancient Seer Vyasa.* 2nd ed. New Delhi: D.K. Printworld, 1993.

———. *Living the Science of Harmonious Union.* New Delhi: D.K. Printworld, 2009.

———. *Love and Blessings: The Autobiography of Guru Nitya Chaitanya Yati.* 1st American ed. Portland: Narayana Gurukula, 2003.

———. *Meditations on the Self.* 2nd ed. Portland: Narayana Gurukula, 2005.

———. *Narayana Guru.* New Delhi: Indian Council of Philosophical Research, 2005.

———. *Therapy and Realization in the Bhagavad Gita.* Unpublished, Sidney, Australia, 1975.

ZBS Foundation. *Somewhere Next Door to Reality.* CD. Fort Edward, NY: 2002.

INDEX